Advance Comments on Deborah Gray's *Attaching in Adoption*

"This positive, but realistic book is an important resource for all adoptive families, at any stage of pre and post-adoption. The information on attachment challenges will allow prospective adoptive parents to understand the possible issues of their new children. Those that have adopted will be able to recognize some behaviors of their children and learn methods of parenting that will help all to achieve success.

As an adoptive parent and adoption professional, I found the vignettes heart warming and at other times, heart wrenching, but realistic and achievable within a hectic family setting. The clear explanations of the phases allows parents to easily measure where they are, where their children are and how they can improve their parenting and health of the entire family.

Attaching in Adoption is also a valuable resource for professionals who work with parents. It will assist them to help parents to maneuver the sometimes-challenging path of adoptive parenting. Deborah's focus on the health of the family helps to normalize the specialized skills and techniques taught."

Yolanda Comparan, MSW, Program Manager, Adoption Resource Center Northwest Region (Seattle) Children's Home Society of Washington

"*Attaching in Adoption: Practical Tools for Today's Parents* is a brilliantly written and sensitive educational journey into the developmental world of attachment. The book is a comprehensive and clear depiction of the importance of attachment, the challenge faced by parents adopting high risk children, and the negative effects of trauma and grief on the development of a secure attachment.

The book reflects Ms. Gray's depth of perception, understanding of child development, empathy, and attunement with the children and families she has served in her therapeutic practice.

Ms. Gray provides practical common sense tools for parents that can support them in developing skills that will enhance healthy relationships and connections with their children. Ms. Gray is realistic and honest as she speaks to parents. She empowers them to take charge in a nurturing way. She respects the importance of the balance of nurture and structure.

The chapters on building emotional intelligence, forming a team of support, and suggestions of when and where to seek professional help provide a hopefulness that there is a way out of the darkness of emotional chaos into the light of safety and trust for children suffering from attachment problems.

Although "Attaching in Adoption" is written primarily for parents, I would encourage my fellow professionals to include this book on their "must read" list. It will assist them in their overall understanding of attachment and in their therapeutic work with adoptive parents and children."

Beverly Cuevas, LCSW, ACSW, Co-founder of Attachment Center Northwest, Founding member and Board member of ATTACh, Founding Board member of ADI (Attachment Disorder Institute)

"This book is a must for adoptive parents, adoption professionals and therapists. It stands out because Deborah writes with tremendous empathy and a profound understanding of challenges faced by children who have experienced trauma, attachment and neglect issues. It is a valuable resource for all types of adoption, including infant adoption.

Adoptive parents will feel understood, supported and encouraged. Professionals will find therapeutic techniques that promote attachment and increase the likelihood of success during the course of therapy. Deborah conveys a positive and hopeful outlook based on her extensive experience in working with hurt children and their families.

Throughout the book, there are a multitude of practical suggestions for managing and strengthening attachments. Her guidance is easily understood, each page offering insight and useful tools for a wide array of situations. She emphasizes the importance of working with skilled therapists and provides guidelines on how to find them. Always respectful of the issues surrounding the adoption experience,

Deborah has produced a gem which should become required reading."

Patricia Martinez Dorner, MA, LPC, LMFT, Adoptive parent, adoption professional, co-author of _Children of Open Adoption_, author of _How To Open An Adoption-A Guide For Parents And Birthparents of Minor Children; Talking To Your Child About Adoption_ and _Search: An Ethical Guide For Professionals_

"In _Attaching in Adoption: Practical Tools for Today's Parents_, Deborah Gray is able to translate into the written word the same caring, compassion, and respect that she shows toward both child and parent in her person-to-person contacts. In this book she returns again and again to the importance of both nurturing and structure in working to form close family relationships; the striking part is how well she is able to provide both for parents in the writing of this book. She emotionally nurtures parents while providing clear structure for them in creating a family environment that will promote attachments.

In identifying ways to promote attachment, she follows a clear developmental approach, recognizing the needs of children of varying ages and helping parents identify how and where their child might be stuck in earlier stages of development. This is a very important aspect of this work; what is necessary at one stage may be inappropriate at another.

My favorite chapters of the book, however, are two of the shorter ones. Both fill gaps in the adoption literature for parents. The chapter on *Trauma and Traumatic Loss* translates the more recent information on the physiologic and psychologic effects of trauma, as reported in the professional literature, into material that parents can understand and use in their day to day parenting.

The second chapter that I particularly like is the one on *Building Emotional Intelligence*. In this section, Deborah again takes material from non-adoption sources and translates it into very practical ideas for adoptive parents to use in helping their child build and maintain healthy friendships. She identifies the gaps that children may have in their skills and provides ideas for remediation. As Deborah points out, "Skill in building and retaining healthy friendships is highly correlated with future happiness in life—much more so than are academic skills."

Although this book is primarily written for parents, most professionals in the area of adoption will find a wealth of practical ideas for helping parents be successful in building attachments with their adopted children."

Vera I. Fahlberg, M.D., author of A Child's Journey through Placement

"Deborah Gray has written an excellent book on parenting adopted children who resist being parented. It is not a cookbook, but rather a comprehensive book on parenting adopted children with attachment problems. That is why it is excellent. Deborah does not take the easy road of simply giving recommendations for various behavior problems. Instead she takes the more arduous route of first trying to help parents understand the meaning of their adopted child's behaviors. After helping parents to understand the reasons for their child's behaviors, she then gives them the tools for developing interventions that are most likely to fit their unique child.

Deborah asks us to go beyond concluding that an adopted child has Reactive Attachment Disorder because they manifest a list of symptoms. She asks us first to also understand the impact of grieving and trauma on a child's functioning. She also asks us to know more about the effects of anxiety, cultural changes, and various other diagnoses, such as ADHD, FAE/FAS, and Learning Disorders. Most importantly, Deborah teaches us about the seven stages of attachment, beginning at birth and extending through adolescence, and she helps us to be aware of various interventions that can facilitate development at each stage. Finally, she tells us about emotional intelligence, its failure to develop following early abuse and neglect, and the importance of understanding ways to facilitate it.

Deborah's contribution to parenting adopted children with attachment problems is substantial. It is based on understanding and having empathy for the meaning behind a child's symptoms, along with effective, sensitive, and well-matched parental interventions. At the same time, she addresses the necessity of parental self-care, if parents are to persistently provide the quality of care that their adopted child requires.

After reading her book, many parents will feel certain that Deborah understands their child and their family. These same parents will also be likely to understand their child more deeply themselves, and at the same time be able to develop the unique practical skills that parenting their child requires."

Dan Hughes, Ph.D. author of *Facilitating Developmental Attachment* and *Building the Bonds of Attachment.*

"Deborah Gray's work captures theory, practicality, and sensitivity toward traumatized children—all in one book. Too many books have only one of these components, and her integration of may important facets of all three, comfortably leads the reader to a clear understanding of how children are hurt and how families can help them heal.

I will be extremely comfortable recommending *Attaching in Adoption* to parents and professionals. I also think that it is suitable for adolescents to read. It would help them understand so many of their issues—particularly around the entire birth family "web" and issues of shame and self-blame. I like this book!"

Gregory C. Keck, Ph.D., Founder, Attachment and Bonding Center of Ohio and co-author of *Adopting the Hurt Child* and *Parenting the Hurt Child*

"*Attaching in Adoption* is a valuable resource for parents not only as they contemplate building their family through adoption, but also as they travel their child's emotionally challenged path towards mental health and happiness. Deborah Gray has described attachment and all of the skills and responses that relate to an individual's attachment style and degree of attachment, and she has done so in a manner easily understood by non-professionals. The chapter on developmental stages is an invaluable tool for parents to assess their child's emotional age and determine what tasks have yet to be mastered. Parents who understand and implement the wisdom and methods described in this book will certainly strengthen their families!"

Nancy Spoolstra, D.V.M., adoptive and foster parent and Executive Director of the Attachment Disorder Network

"This is the most comprehensive work on the subject I have ever enjoyed reading. Deborah's incredible insight from her years of experience with difficult kids shines through in this enlightening book. No stone is left unturned in her effort to give a clear understanding of attachment. This book will be a powerful tool to help families with their children wounded by attachment breaks. My wish would be that every adoptive parent could read this book before beginning the journey to adopt."

Nancy Thomas, founder of Families by Design, parent trainer, presenter, and author of *When Love is Not Enough—A Guide to Parenting Children with RAD.*

Attaching in Adoption

Practical Tools for Today's Parents

Deborah D. Gray

Jessica Kingsley *Publishers*
London and Philadelphia

Front cover image source: Can Stock Photo®. The cover image is for illustrative purposes only, and any person featuring is a model.

Circle of Security diagram on p.20 is reproduced by permission of Cooper, Hoffman and Powell LLC. DSM-IV definitions 313.89 and 309.81 on pp.363–366 are reprinted with permission from the *Diagnostic and Statistical Manual of Mental Disorders, Fourth Edition, Text Revision*. Copyright © 2000 American Psychiatric Association.
Definitions of FAS and ARND on pp.366–369 are reproduced by permission of the National Academy Press.

This edition published in 2012
by Jessica Kingsley Publishers
116 Pentonville Road
London N1 9JB, UK
and
400 Market Street, Suite 400
Philadelphia, PA 19106, USA

www.jkp.com

First published in 2002 by Perspectives Press

Library of Congress Cataloging in Publication Data
Gray, Deborah D., 1951-
  Attaching in adoption : practical tools for today's parents / Deborah D. Gray.
    p. cm.
  Includes bibliographical references and index.
  ISBN 978-1-84905-890-2 (alk. paper)
  1. Adoption. 2. Attachment behavior in children. 3. Attachment disorder in children. 4. Adopted children--Family relationships. I. Title.
  HV875.G69 2012
  649'.145--dc23
                    2011040123

British Library Cataloguing in Publication Data
A CIP catalogue record for this book is available from the British Library

ISBN 978 1 84905 890 2
eISBN 978 0 85700 606 6

Printed and bound in the United States

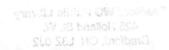

Dedication

This book is dedicated to my family:
Tricia, Joey, Summerlea, and Joseph. Thanks for your
acceptance and encouraging words throughout this project;
And to my much-loved parents, Patricia and Gerald Gray,
who passed the torch.

Acknowledgments

I am blessed to be part of an intentional community of collaborative children's advocates who are working on behalf of families. My mind flashes to the creative Mary-Carter Creech, who works with me using the Nurturing Attachments approach, Brian Andersen (Cascadia Training/Northwest Adoption Resource Exchange), Suzanne Hunsley, Dr. Gwen Lewis, Yolanda Comparan, (Adoption Referral and Information Service), MaryAnn Curran, (WACAP). I have learned and been supported by the clinicians in the Attachment-focused therapy post-graduate certificate program in Seattle (NWARE/Cascadia Training) and the Foster care and Adoption Post-Graduate Certificate Program (Portland State University). Care Therapy post-graduate certificate program participants in Seattle (NWAE/Cascadia Training) and in Oregon (Portland State University). The Center for Adoption Medicine and the Seattle Clinical Consult Groups have been resource rich and generous in support. These relationships show up in the pages of this book, in the pages of my life.

Thank you, honey, to my husband, Joseph MacKenzie, not only for the intangibles of valuing my life's work and this book, but for the practicalities of building and maintaining computers that run well and fast. Tricia MacKenzie helped me with those fast computers. Thanks!

My sincere thanks to the families with whom I work. They have been patient with my restricted hours in order to finish the book. I am also grateful for the many lessons and techniques shared by families as they work with their children. Thank you for teaching me. Thank you for the joy of getting to work with you.

Linda Katz and Norma Spoonamore, leaders in child welfare's permanency planning, took time to mentor my development. Their imprint is on many sections of this book. My thanks to Dr. Elinor Ames, who first encouraged me to write and then took time to critique the writing. Vera Fahlberg, MD, fostered my developmental understanding of children with multiple moves. I am grateful for her templates in understanding children.

Stephen Jones, Senior Editor of Jessica Kingsley Publishers, so impresses me with his knowledge of attachment and child welfare. His kindness and enthusiasm energize me. I am honoured to be published by Jessica Kingsley Publishers. I am also grateful to Perspectives Press, which first published this book.

I have come to acknowledge myself as an attachment-disordered child of a loving God. I am slow to trust and confused between life and God, in spite of evidence of love. I am grateful for this extravagant love, flowing through my life, through my work.

Deborah Gray
Seattle, WA.

Note to the reader:
Facts in the anecdotes and vignettes have been altered to protect the confidentiality of clients.

Table of Contents

Equipping Parents of Children at Risk for Attachment Problems

Parents find themselves in uncharted waters when parenting children who are at high-risk for attachment problems. Their children's challenges are a footnote in most parenting books. This book is a parenting manual written specifically to describe such children and to offer their parents the best possible strategies for parenting. As a therapist who specializes in working with children who have challenges in attachment because of neglect, grief, abuse, and prenatal exposure to substance, I have seen tremendous gains when parents have practical information relevant to their child's situation. This book is written primarily for parents, providing a one-stop source of practical information about why, when, and how to intervene.

This book assists parents in building positive patterns of attachment. Chapter 8 gives specific instructions for attachment techniques for children joining their families. (Parents who need immediate help are invited to turn to this chapter now.) Parents will learn to recognize less positive attachment patterns that children have learned prior to coming to the family—and ways to bridge to more positive patterns.

When parenting challenging children, parents worry about overlooking significant issues that will leave children unprepared and vulnerable later in life. Important issues that need to be addressed for the future well being of children are described for parents. Numerous interventions to improve outcome are suggested as well. Preventative work on behalf of both parents and children is emphasized.

Vignettes that illustrate problems and give solutions are liberally sprinkled throughout the book. The vignettes are drawn from the experiences of other parents and children, who are overcoming similar hurdles.

The book explains extra challenges that must be overcome by both children and parents in order to form a healthy family. It details specific challenges that children must overcome to form healthy personalities.

Parents will learn about the effects of grief and trauma, including their own counter-reactions. Ideas to help children cope with trauma's aftershocks are described so that parents can calm and comfort their children. The book summarizes research describing changes in the brain after exposure to trauma. The information from research informs the use of the best methods to reach a child and best methods to reduce trauma's effects. A chapter covers essential issues in lessening trauma's impact, with stories that describe their practical application. Skills to help parents feel competent with complicated children are taught so that both nurturance and accountability coexist.

The impacts of cultural change, Attention Deficit Disorder, Fetal Alcohol Syndrome, and profound neglect are also explored. Then, the book moves into practical techniques to bring out the best in children in spite of these challenges.

Control and anxiety are common problems for children. While parents understand why their children might be controlling or anxious, they want to know what to do about the behaviors. Many options for behaviorally related issues such as anxiety and control are given, so that parents can choose those techniques that fit best their family and their children.

A child development section is written specifically to describe children who have not been with the same family since birth. Attachment-producing techniques are described, tailored for each developmental stage. Parents can peg their child's emotional developmental stage, see their tasks laid out, and find a to-do list for that stage. Vignettes from families describe the developmental material and parent techniques in a readable story form.

The book considers ways to balance families, giving attention to all family members. Protecting the development of siblings is featured, along with maintaining a family with high self-esteem. The book addresses rebuilding emotional intelligence, so that children learn to read faces and body language of others and to give back appropriate signals. It concludes with ways parents can build family, peer, and professional support for themselves and for their child. A sample interview with a mental health professional is included, with guidance on selecting a mental health provider.

By giving parents early access to specialized attachment techniques, the author and the publisher hope to reduce children's painful attachment problems. Friends of the family and professionals may want to read this book in order to understand and support the methods that the parents are using in the home. This book has been laid out so that chapters address particular topics, making it easy to share sections with a teacher or a grandparent.

I have done my best to make this book down-to-earth as a "how to" and "why to" guide. The work of attachment and healing for both children and parents can seem overwhelming, even with the best of support. The material in the book informs, assists, and focuses the efforts of parents.

The work of forging attachment after loss is some of the most valuable work accomplished in society. Children who learn healthy attachment go on to be healthy attachment figures for their own children. Parents who woo reticent children into fulfilling family relationships have won my respect. Their children have won my heart.

This book has a companion book, Nurturing Adoptions: Creating Resilience after Trauma and Neglect (Jessica Kingsley Publishers, 2012). Readers who are interested in practical home and therapy processes to repair or treat issues of grief, trauma, and neglect are invited to read the companion book.

CHAPTER 1

What Is Attachment and Why Is It Important?

Parent and child attachments are relationships. The quality of parent/child attachments becomes a template for all future relationships and core beliefs. When they nurture and show sensitivity to needs, parents invite children into a good quality relationship. Unless challenges stand in the way, children naturally respond to trustworthy, nurturing, and sensitive parents by forming a trusting and secure relationship. A professional might describe them as having a "secure attachment." Because attachment's effects are so complex, it is important to remember that in its simplest definition, attachment is a relationship. But what a personality-defining relationship it is!

Parents and professionals are impressed by the way that first attachments form the operating beliefs in children's personalities. Infant attachments yield lifelong templates for intimate relationships, emotional awareness, social interactions, and self-acceptance. The templates are later used in adulthood, influencing adult relationships and parenting. Altering first templates based on mistrust takes hard work by parents and children.

Parents and children are building exclusive relationships when they are attaching. They become intimately tuned to each other. Forming such an attachment mutually engages children and their parents in learning patterns of relating to each other. From a child's perspective, attachment requires the development of a set of relational skills and feelings. The signals and responses of this new set of skills lead to the development of a relationship template, predicting for the child whether parents will be trustworthy or not. When humans are forming a secure attachment, there are thousands of successful interactions, plus a small balance of unsuccessful (but not devastating) interactions. From the parent's perspective, attachment requires the use of a set of nurturing relationship skills required for these thousands of interactions. Many of the skills were learned automatically from parent's parents. Other skills were intentionally acquired while poor habits or attitudes were deleted. This book will give descriptions of this parenting skill set as applied to various types of family situations.

Attachment is key to regulating extreme frustration and anxiety. By about 18 months of age, babies with secure attachments and good care believe that parents will come back to them after brief absences, which are measured in hours, not days. Babies learn that their needs are important to their parents, and that parents can be trusted to meet their needs. Babies learn to depend on parents for help. Parents soothe or distract babies when their moods or frustrations are extreme. Babies, using parents' help, build the regulation in the brain for calming down. Babies are rewarded with smiles or nice voice tones when they calm down.

The parent who is forming a secure bond buffers the baby from too much stimulation or frustration. The baby's emotional states, or moods, gradually become more refined. In good relationships, babies and toddlers are learning to stretch out positive moods and signal for help when in pain or frustrated. This ability to calm down gradually becomes hardwired in developing brains. Babies learn that their needs are important and worthy of attention. This opens the door to an essential life skill of being able to identify their feelings as reliable. They also learn to tolerate a typical amount of frustration. Because parental help is at hand, they do not numb themselves to feelings of frustration, loneliness, boredom, or pain. Instead, their lives are a pattern of basic needs getting met and problems getting solved. In a healthy relationship, babies find that parents are fun, loving, and stimulating. They also learn that normal parents take showers, fix dinner, and spend time with others. Babies wait a little or play alone briefly. Babies find that they get a lot of attention when they are being cute, playful, and positive, not just when they have needs.

The terms *bonding* and *attachment* are often used interchangeably. Here, the term *attachment* will be reserved to describe enduring relationships that are formed over time and experience, almost always by members of a family. Losing an attachment figure implies a lengthy and painful grief process. *Bonds*, as we will use the term here, are close relationships which tend to be formed with teachers, friends, and others who have shared experiences and emotions. Children adopted as infants have been shown to enjoy higher than average rates of secure attachment with their parents. Adopted children may also feel a bond with their birthparents, although they may never have formed an attachment with them. Their shared biologic and emotional connection with birthparents creates a bond.

Babies and children do form attachments to abusive or neglectful parents. When they do, attachment skills that children learn from abusive relationships are used in children's subsequent parent-child relationships. Those attachments also form part of children's views of themselves. Helping children to overcome the distorting effects of maltreatment is a focus of this book. (The variations in attachment types learned after neglect and abuse are described more completely in Chapter 3.)

What Is Normal and Healthy Attachment?

Secure attachment helps children learn to believe that they are lovable, that trust in parents is wise, and that others will help them when they have needs. Children learn that parents can help them to get snuggles, explore the world, calm down, solve problems and reduce pain. Without reliable parents, children who are overwhelmed will amplify their distress by raging or shut off their feelings by dissociating.[1] Children with attentive parents learn to signal their needs with a normal

---

[1] Dissociating will be discussed throughout the book. When one dissociates, the integration between an experience and the feelings it evokes are purposefully interrupted by an individual because he cannot endure the feelings associated with the experience. The individual goes into a state in which they feel numb and stop processing the experience.

amount of anger, anxiety, or sadness in order to get help. This signaling of parents is a step in learning the rudiments of problem solving as opposed to raging or denying their own needs.

As mentioned previously, attachments form children's templates for loving relationships. A secure attachment with reliable, sensitive parents helps children to value themselves, trust their parents, trust their own feelings, and care about the feelings of others. It helps children to think that if someone knew them well that they would find them lovable. It helps to insulate children from jealousy (Fahlberg, 1992, p. 20). When discussing secure attachment with me, children say that their hearts or "love tanks" are full. They say that they are not shopping around for new parents to give them love. They are confident in themselves and in the love and acceptance found at home.

Attachment is a two-way street. Both parents and children must begin the dance of attachment. They practice getting to know each other. They learn each other's signals and responses. In normal and healthy attachment, both parents and children believe that they are doing a good job in loving each other most days. They tend to exhibit a smooth reciprocity—a mutual giving and receiving of love—with each other. Children and parents can have such synchronicity that they may look as if they have been choreographed. Parents seem to encourage the right amount of clinging and dependence verses independence and mastery. Young children often show off to an audience consisting solely of their parents.

When children are securely attached to their parents, there is a positivism that glows from them. John Bowlby used the analogy of a thermostat to talk about this phenomenon (1969/1982, p. 372). Children and parents who are close seem warm. When separations are too long, the ensuing chilliness warns them to move closer together. Closeness is comfortable, with both children and parents responding to the right temperature.

Children with healthy attachments have a touchstone upon which to base emotional responses. They learn about their own feelings from looking at the facial and body language of their parents. Their parents serve as mirrors, first reflecting the child's signaled mood, and then supplying to children the facial expression that matches the mood. Parents go on to talk to babies and toddlers about the feelings inside, and what they plan to do to help. The voice tones, words, gestures, and expressions all contribute to learning the meaning of feelings and how to express feelings. Children internalize a sensitive and caring voice when needs are expressed. Later, children use that same voice towards others and towards themselves. Children with healthy attachments have a head start in high emotional intelligence. They have an ability to match up the clues from face, gestures, and words with an understanding of what feelings are being expressed and an appropriate response to those feelings. This is discussed in more depth in Chapter 12: Building Emotional Intelligence.

Children with secure attachments have a head start in developing the positivism, self-control, and mastery skills valued in our society. Such children tend to feel the insulating quality of their parents. Because they feel safe, their brains develop neurology that leads to relationship-building and curiosity. Children without parent figures in their first year of life have been found to have high levels of cortisol, which is produced in response to stress hormones and serves as a measure of stress. Their brains are on high alert. They develop hyper-vigilant capacities at the expense of other learning.

The Attachment Process

Secure attachments normally develop in the first year of life, when parents meet children's needs over and over and over again. The figure on the next page, used by permission by the Circle of Security, describes an attachment pattern of behavior and emotion. The figure shows a positive pattern, or secure attachment pattern, with met needs, emotional support, and positive emotional responses to the little one. These positive patterns of behavior can be developed when children arrive later in childhood as sensitive, emotionally attuned parents meet the needs of their children. Notice that these are patterns of behavior and emotion. Parents are not operating at 100%. Instead the pattern is overwhelmingly positive with some off days and times. The process of developing a secure attachment requires the repetition of this positive pattern of emotion and met needs over and over again.

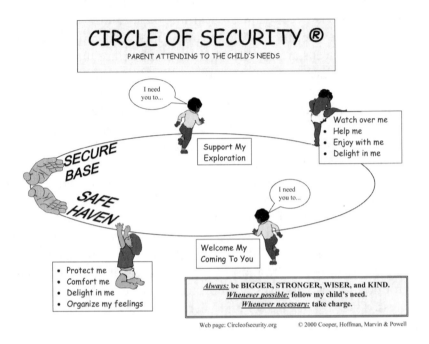

Web page: Circleofsecurity.org   © 2000 Cooper, Hoffman, Marvin & Powell

Parents intervene effectively, alleviating distress. They bring food, physical closeness, dry pants, interesting play, soothing, with gaze. The parents become associated with comfort, with sensitivity, with a feeling of well-being. Through the developing attachment relationship infants (and later, toddlers and preschoolers) literally download the regulated brain patterns of their caregivers. The parent's stable brain patterns help children to settle, to feel better organized or regulated. Over time the parents help children to organize their feelings and, eventually, their thoughts. The parent's brain patterns effect their children's brain patterns, giving children a primitive template for reducing stress.

Throughout the first six months the stage is set for exclusive attachment to caregivers as babies become more attuned to parents. By eight or nine months of age, babies deem the parent as irreplaceable. This is the parent whose presence equals satisfaction and security. The baby's eyes light up for this person, and the baby's world dissolves into wails of distress with the parent's absence.

This attachment process helps babies and children to develop both calming and connection abilities. When children have missed the opportunity for attachment, they can seem to others to be robotic or just plain angry. They have a desperate sadness to them that they rarely express. They no longer expect someone to come—caring, alleviating distress, showing sensitivity. A boy from an orphanage explained, "I feel like I'll get lost in my sad. I think that I am going to die when I get sad." After no opportunities to feel the comfort and welcome parts of the attachment process children try not to feel their despair. But in shutting themselves off from feelings, they may stop opportunities available after placement for parents to comfort them.

What Interrupts Attachment?

Children are vulnerable to a number of situations that put them at high risk for losing or not forming attachment. Some of these are preventable; some are not. Among the common reasons why children lose attachment figures (parent figures) or have attachment issues are these...

1. Separation from parents through foster care moves.
2. Adoption after attachment to another parent figure has occurred.
3. Prenatal exposure to drugs and alcohol.
4. Traumas like sexual abuse, physical abuse, and domestic violence.
5. Major depression, schizophrenia, or manic-depressive illness in the parent figure.
6. Drug or alcohol addiction in the parent figure.
7. Orphanage care.
8. Hospitalization of parent or child, during which children lose access to their parents.
9. Neglect.

Children's inability to respond in the attachment process can result in a counter-reaction in their parents. Parents feel rejected and ineffective when they try to get close to their children. Even in situations that are not extreme, parents can find their emotional resources tapped to the maximum, as in the following vignette about Sherri and Ryan.

Sherri and Ryan had been filled with love as they poured over the picture of Ellie, the toddler daughter whom they were adopting from China. They were expecting a child who would benefit from their parenting skills as much as their three boys had. When Ellie joined their family, Sherri was surprised at how quickly her loving feelings for Ellie turned into feelings of resentment. Ellie batted at her new mother's face, fought for the bottle, and pushed her brothers. She was mute except for a chronic whine that went on for hours, which Sherri interpreted as evidence that she was doing a poor job of mothering. Ellie had been taught not to make eye contact. Sherri, who was highly visual, felt no connection to her daughter. She said, "It was awful! I kept waiting for her mother to come pick her up! I felt immature and guilty that my need for her to accept me was such a big deal! When she finally began responding to me, I did not trust her not to reject me again. I kept my distance. I was yelling at my children constantly, even though I vowed to stop. I yelled at them all, but secretly blamed myself and Ellie."

Sometimes the building of attachment takes much more time than anticipated because children are younger emotionally than their chronological age. When children are adopted at an older age, parents need ample time for bonding activities. A social dilemma already exists about the balance of career versus adequate time for infant attachment. When older children are adopted, there is even less appreciation for the generous amount of time needed for parents and children to form attachments. Before placement, parents may have a misconception that their child has had a sound attachment foundation laid, and that they will be transferring an attachment from a former caregiver to themselves. They expect that their child can begin a normal daycare routine typical for children of their chronological age. As their child becomes distressed with too much time away from their new parents, parents become aware that their child is psychologically very young, with a shaky emotional foundation. Parents encountering difficulty when building an attachment with a child are faced with major questions. Common concerns are

- Does this child really like me?
- Am I the wrong choice to parent this child?
- Is there something wrong with me? Am I going crazy?
- Is this a symptom of a marriage problem?
- Is it possible to feel close with a child adopted after infancy?
- Is this a continuation of my infertility woes?

Some of these questions are etched in despair as parents tell stories like Christy's.

> Christy, the mother of five-year-old Jimmy says, "Everyone tells me how *lucky* I am. Jimmy smiles charmingly at everyone! He'll follow up with a big hug and kiss if we let him. He is always shopping for new parents even though he has been part of our family for two years. He avoids our hugs, prefers sneaking to asking, lies to our faces, and does not miss us when we leave him. We are nobody special to him. Honestly, I do not think it would upset him if we were replaced tomorrow!" Her husband, Joe, a "good dad," sits speechless, his forlorn posture speaking volumes about failed bonding attempts.

Parents are usually the first to know on a gut level that there is something terribly wrong in their child's emotional development. In the vignette above, the parents know that the basic trust that undergirds true independence is missing. Their child's actions announce, "I cannot trust my parents. I am on my own. I am emotionally safer by not caring deeply about my parents."

Parents, as well as children, can enter relationships with issues that will interfere with attachment. Barring maltreatment, parents still may set an emotional tone that prevents a secure attachment. Using Bowlby's metaphor, parents may have "faulty thermostats." Parents who are dismissive of their children's needs for closeness keep the thermostat too cool for comfort for children. They may miss signals of discomfort when their children are lonely, frustrated, or grieving. Parents who are anxious caregivers raise children who feel uncomfortably intense around the parent. Their thermostats are set at "hot." These children may learn to share their parent's mistrust of the world and their safety in it. Parents who have not resolved their own trauma issues may freeze up in the midst of interactions with their children. They have thermostats that malfunction. Children find this distressing, not knowing whether to come close or to stay away. Children move between feeling too hot and too cold, rarely comfortable. Learning emotional modulation from such parents is impossible. In general, when parents are attempting to find emotional security through their children, rather than vice versa, the results are poor for parent and child. In those cases the children become the controllers of the thermostats, providing emotional support for the parent. It is too much pressure for the immature personality of a child.

The rule of thumb is that, when first placed, children will relate to new parents in much the same way that they related to former parents or orphanage workers. Without intervention, often this relationship style persists. Parents who are aware of both their own and their children's challenges in forming trust relationships and emotional modulation are in the best position to develop strategies to strengthen their families and to meet the challenges.

CHAPTER 2

Challenges for Children and Parents

There are unique tasks for both parents and children to master after placement of a more complicated child. The most common challenges are identified for parents in this chapter. These are normal challenges for the more complicated parenting that they are doing, and these challenges are add-ons to typical parenting tasks. Parents must understand that their children are not inferior for having to work through additional tasks during childhood. In comparison to most of their peers, such children will be working harder to enjoy stability and happiness in life. Parents will be working alongside their children toward the same end.

Challenges Facing Children

What is the Meaning of a Family?

By the time young children are hearing stories about the family, they have already formed a working definition of a family's functioning. That definition may be vastly different from the descriptions in the kindergarten books. Children with issues of attachment, grief, and trauma tend to have major differences in their understanding of family functioning. Those differences include their understanding of permanence, power, sharing, and caregiving.

Elizabeth, a twelve-year-old, described the issue of permanence articulately as part of a conference panel

> "The caseworker told me that I would not move again, but I just could not believe that I really would stay in this family. It took me four years to finally believe that I was going to be with my mom for the rest of my life. I was not even moved as much as some kids. I started life in the intensive care unit in the hospital, where I stayed three months because of drug withdrawal, and then was placed into my first adoptive home. I was abused. I had to be re-adopted. But I kept thinking that I would move again.
>
> I thought that I had lost two mothers—my birthmother and first adoptive mother—and would keep losing them. Because I was so hard to handle, I thought that I was the problem. I now know that I was only hard to handle in my first adoptive home because I was being abused. Someone explained to me that my behavior was because of the abuse. Knowing that helped me to believe in myself, and know that I did deserve a family."

Children who have been moved need reassurance about the permanent nature of families. In many cases they have specific worries troubling them. Blanket reassurances do not reassure. In the example above, Elizabeth could accept permanence only after understanding the meaning of her difficult behavior in her placements. Children fearing rejection are reluctant to reveal specific "defects" that they think merit rejection. After all, why draw attention to increase the odds of rejection? In broaching the subject, it helps if parents describe some of their own antics as children, and their own parents' dogged commitment. Parents may find it helpful to branch out into the family tree to find more examples of family cohesion after outrageous behavior. With a wide enough net cast, a child will eventually concede, "At least I didn't do anything as bad as that!" That realization helps him to risk voicing his worries.

Another challenge to permanence is that children worry that their parents will die or go away. This fear is related to earlier loss experiences children have had. Up through five years of age, all children commonly believe that discussing a topic might cause it to occur. It takes some reassurances from parents for them to share their fears. In addressing the fear of a parent's sudden death due to illness, children through high school respond best to a concrete proof. Showing children the medical recommendation on adoption paperwork is an easy proof. Parents can say that the rules of placement are made knowing that it would be too hard for children to have another loss. The judge knows that, so makes sure that parents will not die too early, especially in single-parent homes. Younger children like having the medical recommendation from adoption papers read to them. They are impressed by the formality of the papers.

Sometimes children fear that "bad guys" will kill their parents. The "bad guys" theme responds well to a review of the home's locks or security system. If the family has a dog, the dog's barking can be shown to be a good defense. One imaginative parent managed to convince her son that they had a "guard bird." Prior to placement, this child had had strangers coming into his room at night. Although he had not been harmed, he had a dread of intrusion that extended to his mother's welfare. He slept well after believing that the canary was on watch. Sometimes the "bad guys" theme is the indicator of trauma, and will need exploration in therapy before children truly calm down. Even in those cases, parents' efforts in describing their strength, vigor, and permanence are still helpful.

Power in the family is often a huge issue. Children who have endured domestic violence or abuse naturally equate power with domination and brutality. The concepts of someone being able to be both big and nurturing do not dovetail for them. Regularly children from these violent situations show that they do not know the meaning of their safe families. They do small things during the day to exert power over others. Often, they hurt others in order to dominate.

Rather than spending endless hours correcting the many behaviors related to fear of domination, it makes sense to address the behaviors in an overall context of "learning about your safe family." Children are acquainted with the overall rules for everyone in the family. Common examples are that parents keep the family safe; that parents make sure that there is good food in the house; that parents help children when they are afraid; that neither parents nor guests get drunk and hurt children; that adults get their way not because they are big, but because they are responsible; that children who hurt other children will make restitution; that parents define what is fair. Sometimes families make posters with everyone's roles described in words or pictures. As children learn more, they can add to the list or to the pictures on the poster. The posters serve as good reminders. If a child is falling into an old pattern of taunting the parent to test whether or not the parent will abuse, the child can be asked to go look at the poster for ten minutes. Then the child can talk about how this home is different from his past homes and about what might have triggered his reaction. Or, if the child begins to act afraid of Dad, the child can be asked to remember three safe facts about Dad. This type of discussion promotes a new learning style. Parents work with behaviors but move beyond behaviors, teaching about their family, and learning about their child. There is a continuation of this discussion in Chapters 5 and 11.

Healthy families have a "win-win" emphasis. In other words, they perfect ways in which everyone gets needs met simultaneously. In learning this, children also learn to move over to allow a particular family member to get the limelight when appropriate. Teaching children how to share in families is a basic skill. Children who enter families after missing opportunities for love, attention, or food often respond by wanting everything available. Even after having needs satisfied for years, these kids may continue to believe in a scarcity model of physical and emotional supplies. When others are asking them to "move over," they feel like they are losing. Family members may complain that they feel exploited.

Parents can start dialogues with children about having "enough." After a long snuggle parents can ask children if they have their hearts or "love tanks" full of love. Sometimes children are able to say "Yes." Parents can then go on to say, "Can you hold on to the 'I get enough love feeling?'" Children can practice feeling that feeling. If children do not feel full love tanks after snuggles, they can get more snuggles. If they still have that empty feeling, move on to a discussion about the empty feeling. Sometimes children discover that the empty feeling is not about needing more love and attention, but is about sadness or grief. Children are more receptive to talking about grief after realizing that more parental attention fails to eliminate an empty feeling when they are grieving. Ways to talk to children about grief are discussed in Chapter 4.

The Needing to Win/No-win Spiral

A Child's Fear of Trusting Precipitates Solutions that Lead to a No-win Spiral

Mistrust of parents—or Dependence On Parents leads to

Control of Parents, ensuring that Physical and Emotional Needs are Met. Child does not risk trusting parents or feeling that he is giving in.

Parent Reaction: "I am being treated like an abusive neglectful parent!"

Parent reaction leads to inconsistent parenting:

    a. Increased effort
    b. Outrage
    c. Distance
    d. Depression

Child supplies more control in response to parent's inconsistency.

Reacts with:

    a. Rage. "Why do they keep withdrawing?"
    b. Confusion. "Why are they changing?"
    c. Shame. "Why do parents reject me?"
    d. Grief. "I am alone and unable to keep parents."

Child becomes more controlling as he feels that he is losing.

He exerts:

a. More control on parents,
b. Shows lack of self-control as he gets further in the cycle

Children sometimes want to stuff material possessions or food into their empty hearts. Again, a practical exercise helps in this misconception. One parent approached the discussion this way.

"Jason, I think that you are getting some big lonely feelings. You are asking for more and more stuff so that you feel better. Come get some rocking time with me. Bring your Toy-R-Us ads from the paper."

As Jason rocked and snuggled, he felt his sad feelings. "Sometimes I get so sad when I think of abuse, Mom," he said. He rocked some more, sighing a little and getting comforted. When he felt better, and agreed that he had gotten "enough" loves in his love tank, they looked at the ads together. "Well, I would still like this rocket," he said. "But now I do not have to get it. I do not feel like I need every one of the rockets any more. I think that I have enough."

When children in the family have occasions for exclusive attention, it helps to prepare ahead. For example, Janey and her mother discussed her sister's upcoming birthday party.

Mom said, "How will you feel, Janey, if you take over your sister's friends, or if you blow out your sister's birthday candles before she has her chance?"

"Good," said Janey. "Except I would get in trouble and feel bad later."

Mother said, "Let's figure out a way for you to remember that you got enough attention on your birthday, and that it's good for your sister, Anne, to get her turn."

They took a piece of heavy paper, pocket-sized, and drew on it a picture of Janey, her cake, and her mom, with the caption, "Janey gets enough!" Janey put it in her pocket. She patted her pocket several times during the party, remembering the lesson. After the guests left, she said earnestly, "I hope that you had a nice birthday, Anne." Anne hugged her and invited her to play.

At bedtime, Janey and her mom talked about her great job sharing attention. Mom wrote on Janey's bedroom calendar, "The Big Success!" Janey had learned about "win-win" situations and how good it feels to share in families. Such lessons help develop values of mutual respect. The lesson would have failed if the mother had simply bribed Janey. She would have learned about making a deal based on her own self-interest, rather than on sharing.

Caregiving is a major confounding issue for children who are learning the meaning of a family. There are two ways that children conceptualize caregiving. In one group are children who have, in the past, learned to try to meet some of their caregiver's needs first, so that the caregiver responded, in turn, by meeting children's needs. These children have experienced a classic role reversal. In the second group are children who have learned to put effort into getting their caretakers to become more responsive. They signaled their distress by whining, complaining, and pulling on their unresponsive caregivers, raging and dissociating when conditions got too bad.

Children who reversed roles with their caregivers often go on to idolize those caregivers after a placement. They believe that they just did not do a good enough job in taking care of their former parent, and that if they could just return to the parent, they might do a better job. Of course, they are at the same time furious that they have such a burden. They tend to expend that fury largely on others or on themselves. These children have been their parents' security, instead of vice versa. Sometimes children will go on to try to meet the needs of their new parents. Or, they may behave as if they have no needs for the parents to meet. Yet they argue and bicker over everyday life. A child may offer to make breakfast for her parent. However, the storm clouds gather if the parent asks her to empty the dishwasher. These children have no training in acquiescing to everyday requests placed on them by their parents. Their system of being in charge of themselves precludes obeying their parent. They have the family structure, including who sets the rules, quite confused.

When such a child is coming into a new home, it is better not to tangle with the loyalty issues head on. Rather, it is helpful to explain how and why these parents run their home. Valerie, a foster-adopt parent, talked to Shawna during pre-placement visits in this way,

"I know that you did the best job that you could in taking care of your mother. I respect you for that. Our family works differently, though. I wanted to let you know about that so that you could get used to how things work in this family. In this family I just love to be the one to take care of the kids—including you. I enjoy making your school lunches! What are some of your favorite foods? We can get some of those on the menu. You might think that it feels too easy for me to do this much work! Don't worry, you will have some chores. You have the hard work of learning the family rules, too. That will seem tough for a while."

At this point, her daughter interrupted, "It won't be tough for me!"

Mom laughed and continued, "You'll probably think I'm a bossy mom! But I'm not a mean mom. My bossiness teaches my great kids to have a great life."

This type of interchange is done quickly, with a hug and giggle. The parent can roll eyes over the term, *bossy*. Starting out on a playful note helps to set a tone of playfulness in the home. Yet, the subject gets the attention of children in recognizing different ways that families function. Later, after some adjustment time, parents can mention that it is too hard on kids when kids are in charge of the family. If parents have never had this discussion with their children, and it applies to their situation, there is no time limit to having this talk. The role reversal and appropriate methods for strengthening attachment are discussed in more detail in Chapters 4 and 8.

Children who do not expect consistent and high quality nurture from parents form the second group—children who have misconceptions about caregivers and caregiving. Some children have learned to control the parents due to their mistrust. Others intentionally ignore parents as attachment figures. An example is Stephen.

Stephen was adopted from an orphanage at the age of six. He had been placed in the orphanage at birth. Even at age eleven, after five years in the home, he had no idea what a family meant. To him, this was a particularly well-stocked orphanage that had no shift changes for the adults. (His parents were also leaning towards this definition after five years.) He was social, but continued to see his family as institutional residents. He took little responsibility for school achievement or for preparation for life as an adult. Stephen finally confided that he hoped to marry a woman who would take care of him in much the same way that he currently experienced. His template for living continued to be his orphanage experience. He learned the rules, followed them when others were looking, and formed his closest relationships with other children. He was so uncaring that he failed in the last regard. He missed the concept of his parents as loving caregivers to whom he should form a permanent attachment.

Until he came into therapy, Stephen resisted the challenge of commitment. After he worked at getting close to his parents, he described, "I knew that they wanted to love me. I told myself that only babies needed that. I would do things to make them mad so that they would stop trying and let me alone. Sometimes I ignored my mother and was happy to see her hurt feelings. I'm glad that they didn't give up!"

Children who mistrust their parents' love often require repeated assurances from parents. It is helpful for parents to try to determine when the child is most feeling mistrustful. Doing a piece of detective work with willing kids often gives clues as to why a child might feel a certain way.

Kyle, age four, was a terror in the car. He kicked, yelled, and threw any item within reach of his child seat. He glared angrily at his parents. He had been placed many times. The last three exchanges had been done with no warning to Kyle, after long car rides. He associated car rides with the risk of placement. His dad began to make a pre-trip speech. "Kyle, you are in the family now. We are your parents forever. No more new families for you. Say it after me." He repeated these phrases after his father several times until his father, with his engineer's eye, observed his son and decided that he looked normal. "You look ready," Dad said. Then they started out. They also put a blanket draped loosely over Kyle's head, which soothed him. Soon, his car tantrums were rare. He calmed overall due to his parent's sensible approach to his distress.

Parents make big points as credible and trustworthy parents when they salve their children's emotional hurts. More discussion of techniques that build reliance in the caregivers is found in Chapters 8, 9, and 12.

Parents will notice throughout the book that there is often a limitation recommended for the time that children can spend in daycare. As a group, attachment-challenged children need to be looked at differently. This is a group of children who have experiences and fears of being separated from parent figures. Until they can rebuild some of their emotional security, their time in child-care must be restricted. This is a difficult concept for parents who have work demands. In Chapter 8 there are specific descriptors of emotional development. When children get to older emotional phases, they have completed the emotional work necessary to believe that parents will come back to them. Until that work is accomplished, there must be restrictions on life that parents need to think through seriously. Many parents with whom I have worked have developed creative ways in which to maintain their careers while parenting challenging children. Others have had careers crimped because of their children's needs. While I have no philosophical bias about the need for a stay-at-home parent, the reality is that these children may have an emotional need that requires this for a time.

Asked to Bond to the "Wrong" Parent!

While parents have made the decision to foster or adopt, their child usually has not made a similar decision. Most children are unprepared for the feelings that they will have as a parent makes a bid for parent status. As a boy explained, "I feel like I owe it to my mom not to love this mom too much." At the term, *this mom*, he pointed to the "imposter." Children with unresolved grief and conflicted loyalty like to negotiate a limited commitment to their family. An example is Alocia.

Alocia knew that his mother had died suddenly. In fact, he had gone to the funeral. After adoption he would not get close to his mother. He was a little warmer to his father. Finally he admitted, "I think that she is alive and that she is looking for me." Another conflict for this little boy was his fear that his attachment to his new mother might cause her to die as well.

Parents can get a grasp on these conflicts by thinking of adult attachments. If an adult is married to an abusive spouse, divorce is a sensible solution. Yet, there is normal grief in the decision-making to sever the relationship. Longing for the positive times with the former spouse is balanced against knowing the destructiveness of abuse. Similarly, if a partner callously abandons an adult, grief is normal. Even though the partner may have lacked qualities like loyalty, commitment, or sensitivity, the degree of felt pain is not initially measured by the worthiness of the partner. Only after grieving do people start to realize that their partner's abandonment might be a bit of luck! The legal and emotional ties of children to their birthparents are similar to marriage. Even though their parents may have abandoned, abused, or neglected them, children will not calibrate their love or longing by the worthiness of their lost parents.

Methods that are most successful for grieving children do not emphasize parent replacement, especially in the beginning of placement. Parents who acknowledge that their children are still missing and loving their former parents affirm their children. Parents do not shame their children in any way for their devotion. Instead, parents say that it sounds like the children loved that previous parent the best they could. Sometimes questions give parents a sense of the degree of resolution that a child has about their loss. Examples are, "Did you have a chance to say goodbye? Are you still thinking that you will move back? What might happen so that you could go back?" It helps to ease children into bonding when parents say that they will be giving their children all the love they need, and that children can still care for birthparents or former foster parents. Parents can give matter-of-fact information that all children need someone to love them day-to-day, even if children want to be in another home.

Don't Look at Me! Feeling Unlovable Inside

Great parents give positive comments to children. Children can hear these comments and feel no similarity to their self-perception. They wonder if the parents are either deluded or stupid. Parents who ignore a child's past issues that are shame-producing are ignoring a time bomb. At some point in the child's life, parents will have to find ways to explore why their child feels shame. Otherwise, children will seek out situations over time that seem to match their authentic selves.

Events that cause out-of-home placement often occur during the toddler or preschool years. At that age it is normal for children to believe that they are the cause of life's events. Children's egocentricity, which is a normal part of personality development, results in excessive feelings of responsibility. Children are shamed by the meaning that they derive from maltreatment or loss—that it was something that emanated from them.

> As a technique in therapy, I once looked down a little girl's throat and declared that there was really a good kid inside. I saw that she had a good heart. "Are you sure?" she asked. "Look again!" When I solemnly declared that her heart was sad, but definitely a good heart, she turned incredulously to her parent. Looking hopefully at her mother's face she said, "It's really true what you told me, then? I'm not really that bad!"

Children who will describe themselves as feeling "trashy" inside are reluctant to share the deep shame that they feel. But it stands in the way of bonding and attachment. Children hide their authentic selves, certain that they are to blame for angry and destructive behaviors or feelings. Some parents make a valiant attempt to separate the behaviors from the child. They say things like, "You are not the same as your behaviors. You are wonderful, but your behaviors are what I am having problems with." Children's concrete thinking makes it impossible to follow this abstract logic. Children say that it sounds like, "Blah, Blah, Blah." While the technique of looking down the throat works for small children, older children are too sophisticated to overlook the physiological liberties taken. As they get older, much more detail needs to be put into the explanation of the life history. An integration is necessary between factual explanations for placements and children's shame-based perceptions. The chapters on Grief and Trauma, Chapters 4 and 5, describe the parent's part in this integration process.

Shame is a critical concept in helping children with attachment problems. When children are removed from parents, they tend to feel ashamed that they were not worth the devoted care of their parents. Children are removed from parents with drug and alcohol problems due to their parent's inability to abstain from substance. These children believe that they were worth less than drugs or alcohol to their parent. Children who have suffered deprivation feel that they were not worth the parent's time and energy. Children with multiple placements conclude that they cannot keep the love of a parent. No one considered them worth including in their family.

People in the community who come in contact with children with stressed and emotionally immature behaviors are wont to give warning looks, conveying, "What is wrong with them!" While children might know that their behavior needs to modify, they get a deeper message that they are "too much," or "not right." Shaming fits with the mental template that children are forming. They believe that there is something shameful about them that caused their rejection and losses. They are ashamed.

I found that, among adopted children, over half of the children I asked, "Do you think that an adopted child is entitled to as much love and care as children who are not adopted?" answered, "No," or "Not really." Many shook their heads and looked at me mutely and miserably. While my observations were based on children coming in for therapy, still the number of negative answers was surprising. One goal of parents must be to help their children to rid themselves of unfounded shame. Many children who had been successful in achieving that goal answered my question, "Of course I deserve as much love as anybody else!" I received a look that questioned the species of individual who would think to ask such a question. Those children who responded that they deserved as much love were open to love and attachment.

Small is Humiliating

Children can feel embarrassed by their small size. They equate small size with the humiliation of their helplessness. Their solution tends to be to act bigger and older than they actually are, pretending that they are able to meet their own needs. It is normal to overlook this bravado in children, who routinely take on a persona for a period of time. They may dress and act like a cowboy, act like a dog, or wear a tutu with all ensembles. Parents should notice if their children act as if small and vulnerable creatures in stories, movies, or everyday events should be yelled at when asking for care, or harmed with cold calculation by bigger people. Either in play or reality, children are giving clues when they repeatedly make fun of the needs of small children, preferring to play a large bully. This is not "just play." It is accompanied by disdain for the love and care that small children need. Such children have decided that neediness leads to humiliating dependence. They decide to be independent of needs. An example follows.

Constance woke for breakfast. Her mother greeted her with a smile, a touch, and "I love you." Pushing away, Constance demanded, "Where's my juice?" When Mother tried again to hug, she said in haughty disdain, "I'm not a baby!" At six years old, Constance thought that she was smarter than her too-soft mom. She had been adopted at the age of three from a state-run orphanage. She was underweight and developmentally delayed at placement. Her mother was worried most not about remaining delays, but about Constance's attitude of false independence with contempt for kindness and affection. Her mother formed a strategy to engage the attitude of false independence. Discussions about nurture became commonplace. Constance's rough body language was corrected, often with interpretations like, "It seems that you are not strong in trusting that I will feed you, since you try to be in charge."

Mom insisted that her daughter learn to get and give hugs. They had practices. She counted when she kept hugging. One day she gave a hug that went to the number 50. It was a real hug, too. Her mother told her that she was strong in loving. Constance received a special doll that she and her mother used together. It resembled her. She and her mother played "Baby Constance." Her mother showed her the tender care that she wished that she could have given her. One day, Constance kissed the doll saying, "You are a beautiful and good baby." Although her mother had not mentioned this topic, Constance continued, "I'm sorry that you had to wait so long for your momma." She began to refer to her bravado as "the old way," or "before I knew better."

In describing their feelings during traumatic scenarios, children, as well as adults, express how shamed they felt at their helplessness. While the rescue team, child protective service workers, or medical staff feel compassionate, respectful, and competent, the traumatized person typically feels helpless, small, and humiliated. To compensate, traumatized children are among the biggest advocates of acting older and bolder when their feelings are fear and inadequacy. The long-term use of this defense is notable. Physically and sexually abused children are the most aggressive group in research samples (Mash, Barkley 1998). The connections between trauma, humiliation, and smallness are explored in more depth in Chapter 5, along with techniques to help children.

Re-Abandoned Every Time the Door Closes

After children at least eighteen months old have been in the same home for eighteen months, most come to believe that their parent comes back to them after a separation. They form a mental picture that represents their parent as the parent who returns. But some children do not remember that they even have parents unless parents are right there—physically present. When these children are asked to separate from parents, they experience overwhelming alarm that they are losing their parents again. While this anxiety can be attributed to early abandonment experiences, it is hard to know why some children are more resilient than others after nearly identical experiences. Five-year-old Mung Mung provides an example.

> Mung Mung's anxious attempts to stay close to her mother causes her to utter an insistent "Mom, Mom, Mom, Mom," alerting her mother to come back anytime they are not in the same room. Mung Mung refuses to be on a different level of the home than her mother. She is incessant in demanding attention. She is playful and winsome as long as attention is fully centered on her. When her mother tries to separate, she escalates into hysteria. Conflicted about leaving at bedtime, Mother stays in Mung Mung's room until she falls asleep. It can take two hours for this anxious girl to fall asleep. Her mother, a single parent, is so sleep deprived that she claims that she is fueled by caffeine. She tries to run her computer consulting business at night and with patched-in babysitting. She says, "Adopting her at such a young age, at six

> months old, I never thought that she would have these difficulties. She does not trust that I will be there in the morning for her. She is so anxious! I was told by the adoption counselor to keep her close, and that she would eventually come to trust and feel secure. I'm still waiting."

Children with overwhelming fear are not simply overindulged. They are miserably frightened.

> In therapy with a little boy adopted from Bulgaria, I worked on parent departures. He agreed to try deep breathing while looking at his parents' picture. We discussed that his parents would get up from the couch opposite us, walk out of the door, wait in the waiting room for five minutes, re-enter the office, and hug him. He agreed to the plan with confidence, but panic hit him as the door closed. His pulse jumped from 90 beats per minute to 140 beats per minute. He was terrified, back feeling bereft, in spite of two years of high quality adoptive parenting. By the fifth time that he practiced the exercise, he was beaming. His heart rate increased only to 105. Best of all, he felt some way to be in charge— in charge of his body, rather than of his parents.

Success with this challenge requires pairing techniques with the confident message from parents that children can work on their fear successfully. Children are not inclined to work on building tolerance to fear, unless their control of parents is restricted. Techniques for help with the challenges of control and anxiety are described in Chapter 10.

Controlling Adults—A Logical Solution to Mistrust!

Children are in a bind when they cannot trust adults. In spite of some boasts to the contrary, they know that they cannot take care of themselves. Children exert control when they cannot trust adults to care for them, to stay proximal to them, and to remain safe around them. Children also exert control when they mistrust themselves as being worth care, commitment, or gentleness. Like a player with a bad hand in a high-stakes poker game, they cheat. Instead of building trust, they use control.

Children exert control on parents, rather than developing trust, because it seems less risky. It is hard for children who have not known trust before to risk depending on parents so that confidence can develop. Parents find themselves moving into a counter-reaction of increasing their efforts in order to convince children that they are trustworthy. This effort is not typically met with much change in children's attitudes. Instead children can feel intense pressure to respond to their parents' increased efforts. While some children will respond to this pressure temporarily, the parents' increased effort rarely has a long-term effect on children. Instead, parents become exhausted, desperate, and peeved. Children, who are already shame-based, feel some responsibility for the parent's exhaustion, depression, or distance. They also become worried and angry that their parent is changing emotionally. It feeds back into their emotional mindset, "I can't trust parents!" In response to the parents' changes, children exert even more control. This cycle is in visual form on page 29.

The tricky part of this dilemma is that children are still in charge as long as they are controlling the parent's energy output and emotional well-being. Children actually do much better when parents keep a steady pace with self-care and positivism. This is discussed next in the Parent Challenges section of this chapter.

Ultimately, to promote attachment, a great deal of control has to be taken from children. They are told that they are not ready for the level of responsibility in a particular situation. Ariel's family demonstrates an example of this dialogue between children and adults.

Ariel made it a point to greet visitors at the door. At eight, she had heard thousands of times that the controlling process that she went through was not acceptable. Her routine included monopolizing the guest, correcting her mother's "mistakes" in front of the guest, interrupting attention to her siblings, climbing on the guest, and pouting and arguing when corrected. Her parents told her that they had discovered that verbal instruction was not helping her. They told her that she would have to go to her room when the guest arrived. When she tested by coming out, she was returned to her room. Her mother and father spoke matter-of-factly to the guest during this process.

After abstaining from guest appearances, Ariel finally accepted that she would have to change. Eventually she was able come out of her room when guests came, behaving in a non-controlling manner longer and longer. She revealed that guests to the home made her nervous, due to experiences prior to placement. After this discussion, she problem-solved with her mother and father. She sometimes sat next to her parents when guests came. At times she preferred to read or play in her room. She did eventually become more social, but not controlling. The process took about fifteen months.

Parents who want to work on core issues instead of a succession of behaviors re-define for children their tasks in a family. Children hear that their first job is to stay emotionally close to their parents, letting the parents keep them safe. They also have to practice doing things that their parent asks them to do, so that they can discover the great feeling that it works well. Until children are able to let go of control to some degree, they cannot practice trust of their parents. They tend to be working on one skill set or the other one. Techniques for working with control and trust are contained in Chapters 9 and 10.

Always Angry and Afraid—Maltreatment's Imprint

Children in danger go into a physiological state of fight or flight. They surge with energy that can be used to fight or to run for their lives. Their brains bypass the higher thinking centers, using primitive areas of the brain. Very young children will often freeze in place instead of running or fighting. They try not to move or attract attention to themselves. They may show fear or anger. However, these are two sides of the same coin. The coin's currency is good for survival. It is rare that a child with neglect and abuse is happy or grateful after placement. Instead, they remain preoccupied with the lessons learned from the past, readying themselves for a similar future.

People are sending messages with their anger. The work of Dr. Constance Dalenberg describes some of these:

- "Pay attention to me!" This is a signal for attachment
- "Get out of my way!" This helps in getting to goals.
- "Stop that!" This defends against physical and emotional attacks.
- "How dare you treat me that way!" This restores pride.
- "Serves you right!" This restores a sense of justice.

Dr. Dalenberg goes on to point out that trauma survivors have their anger aroused in more than one area at a time, "as they are physically endangered, shamed, rendered powerless, and subjected to injustice" (2000).

Children who have been through maltreatment send these messages when they dare, or when they can no longer hold back. When children realize that they are in a more accepting situation, they signal their anger more freely. It is hard for parents to determine which of the messages above that their child might be signaling. Many children have told me that they are always angry and always afraid. Some children say that they are angriest around mothers; others say that they are angriest around fathers. This behavior ties to the neglect or abuse by a previous parent figure that was experienced.

Children do not want to feel angry, although some of them are clear that they would much rather be mad than sad. Actually, most children feel that there is something quite wrong with them that they are so angry. Usually, they do not confide this to their parents. Maltreated children can try to "do their mad" on their parents instead of "talking about their mad" to their parents. An example of "doing mad" on a parent is described well by Desiree.

Desiree told me that she was always angry with her mother. In a low voice she told me, "I know that she is not going away, but I still get mad at her like she is going to. Besides, I think that she is probably going to die. She says that she's sick and tired and can't take it. Sometimes I wake up my sisters, hide Mom's medicine, and make faces at my brother. Then, I act nice to Dad, and say I didn't do anything. I don't know why I do this. Sometimes, I wear my mom out, and then she goes to a hotel to get sleep. I'm sorry then, but I don't stop."

This child's anger is signaling "don't leave me." Her mother wonders if her daughter really cares about her. Her daughter is testing whether her mother has staying power.

The high stress from maltreatment causes the body to boost cortisol, which prepares the body for fight or flight. Like war veterans, children who have experienced high stress over time may eventually show a decline in cortisol levels to one lower than average. It appears that for many children, at this stage it takes much less stress to stimulate an alarm response. Their bodies have become over-sensitized to distress.

Maltreated children need the equivalent of a home rehabilitation program. The essential features are

- formation of a safe attachment,
- learning the meaning of a family,
- being buffered from high stress,
- learning to cope with limited stress,
- learning to signal for help appropriately,
- enjoying positive self-control,
- grieving the losses from trauma,
- sorting out differences between past and present,
- and learning to stretch positive experiences.

Therapy is an important part of the process for these children. Techniques for helping these children are found throughout the remaining chapters in the book. A separate chapter on Trauma, Chapter 5, further develops the topic.

Additional Emotional Tasks

After children have a rocky start in life, most adults want to make the next parts of their lives easy. The reality in life is that most such children will have more emotional tasks than do most of their peers. Those tasks include

- grieving losses,
- completing emotional developmental phases later in childhood,
- achieving emotional modulation,
- reconstituting a sense of self-esteem,
- loving after being betrayed,
- coping with traumatic triggers,
- and developing loving family relationships.

Children do best when they are told about the extra work as the following sketch illustrates.

A 16-year old boy came back in to see me. As he sat next to his mother, he philosophized. "Deborah, it's true that I have a pretty good life. But I did the hard work with my parents to get where I am today. Like I have a really good relationship with my mom. She's so cool. And my dad, too, he's cool, even if he is kind of wimpy. I can beat him now in everything. But at the time I did all my therapy it was really hard. Like, I had to talk about things like rape, and I had to learn how to trust my parents. It was really, really, really tough. But, I'm glad I did the work when I was young, because now I have my head on straight. When I got to subjects like drugs and sex abuse in health classes, I wasn't freaking out. I looked at the books. It was all stuff that I knew. I know that I'm a good person. I'm going to have a good life, because I know how to put in the effort to get the outcome I want."

This boy was honest and articulate. His background included prenatal exposure, multiple placements, neglect, sexual acting out, developmental delay, and exposure to violence. Behaviorally, he had been quite difficult. Yet, he worked hard at achieving goals with his parents. He had taken on extra emotional tasks and completed his hard work. He continues to self-monitor and to use relaxation techniques daily. He still uses therapy, although only sporadically.

The enjoyable part of hearing this teen's description of his life was in hearing his mastery and self-acceptance. He did describe, later in our discussion, his parents' exemplary efforts; but he felt that his work had ultimately made the difference. He had his life back.

The extra emotional tasks do not seem overwhelming to children at some stages of resolution. When going through the rough times, however, it can seem as if it is not worth the effort. They are working harder and still seem a little behind peers. It helps kids to know that they are doing some of the emotional work that their peers may be doing later in life. Learning to cope with lack of control over life's events, grief over losing loved ones, betrayal over misplaced loyalties, and shame over feeling inadequate are struggles for everyone over the life cycle. For a percentage of people, trauma will also be their experience. These children may be lagging in some emotional developmental tasks, but be ahead, ultimately, in learning to deal with life.

Learning to Cope , Rather Than to Control or to Dissociate

As mentioned during the discussion of some of the earlier challenges, children control when they feel unsafe. While the control is easy to spot, dissociation is subtle. Dissociation is a way for a person to be physically in the situation, but to leave it emotionally. It is a form of "shut down" that is a last ditch effort that allows a person to survive what they cannot endure.

Children who have been in traumatic situations have described times when they felt so awful that they could not stand it, and then froze, feeling numb. Children from orphanages lacking adequate numbers of caretakers commonly come into their adoptive homes having highly developed abilities to dissociate. While normally some children are more "spacey" than others, dissociation is not an example of a child who is merely enjoying fantasy. Instead, at a sign of threat, children who dissociate return to a response that they learned before to deal with danger or pain. Leila's story is a good description of dissociation.

Leila was describing sexual abuse, "He put me over the desk. The desk was hard and hurt my back. Then, I did not feel myself... or anything anymore. I felt like I was floating up by the ceiling. The next thing that I remember is that I was in my room, and my birthmother was saying, 'Why didn't you answer me when I called you?' And he came up behind her, saying, 'Why didn't you answer her?' I couldn't talk. I just looked at him. His eyes were mean. When I looked at him, I would start to go away again. First I felt scared, and then I felt the nothing feeling."

Parenting Leila was a challenge. When she was afraid, she would not signal for help, but would instead dissociate very quickly. Later, she would rage. She screamed at least an hour per evening. When Leila's mother became aware of the look of dissociation, she was able to stop the process and provide help. "Come back to me," her mother would say. Sometimes she would clap her hands crisply, startling Leila just enough to interrupt the process. Then, they would together determine what had just frightened Leila, and how to cope with it. Over time, Leila dissociated much less. Her coping improved dramatically.

Children from backgrounds with extreme malnourishment and neglect may have dissociated daily for hours in order to live with overwhelming frustration, as well as fear. They may move into dissociation quickly when frustrated. Instead of learning how to cope with frustration, they simply go away. I have seen this type of dissociation when children cannot get their coats off, cannot get their shoes tied, cannot change a topic being discussed, or cannot join their parent in the bathroom. It is important for parents to notice signs of dissociation. The pupils change size, complexion alters, the body pauses, and heart rate may alter. In a confusing twist, some children smile a fixed smile throughout.

Dissociation is not a discipline problem. It is a sign that children need help in finding another way to cope. Providing a drink of water, touching their shoulder, giving a hug, or clapping a couple of times are techniques that may bring children back to the present. Then, they can work on solving the problem.

Parents wonder if dissociation feels negative, since children describe themselves as numb. In fact, the numb feeling of dissociation is among the most common symptoms for which sufferers seek medication. It causes people to feel awful within their own being. It leaves people expressing that they are robotic, without normal feelings for others. While children cannot express the feeling in adult abstracts, children whom I have treated want to be rid of the "nothing feeling." They say that it feels "weird" or "not good." They also notice that they are angry shortly after the "nothing feeling" goes away.

Calming Down and Balancing Moods

Children with attachment gaps seldom demonstrate the modulation of emotion that emerges during the infancy stage, during which children are held to their parents and calmed by the parents' words, slower body rhythms, and comforting actions. They also fail to see the gradations of being a little angry, a little sad, a little frustrated, or a little excited. When they feel an unpleasant emotion, they are subsumed by that emotion.

Helping their children learn to stretch positive emotions is a skill common to parents who are "good with children and babies." In this way children learn to overlook some negatives, in order to enjoy what good event might be next. Parents must be active in facilitating this process in young children who did not learn it in infancy.

Children who are moving homes, especially after a background of neglect or trauma, have bodies on high alert. Their stress mediates against any smooth balance of moods. Moving them into calming rhythms enhances their capacity to calm down. Forming attachment also helps to calm the parts of the brain that are on high alert.

When children have had extensive deprivation with little positive stimulation there is an additional complication. Their neurological ability to regulate incoming information is underdeveloped. They can become wildly overexcited by a trip to the zoo or a birthday party. Sometimes these events end in disaster, with children falling apart before parents even arrive at the zoo or the party. As soon as children arrive in their new families, parents must determine how much stimulation they can handle. Obviously, if children are close to crying, behaving aggressively, or banging into people, the capacity has been exceeded; even if children are asking for more. Especially for those children from international orphanages, parents should start with a calm, simple environment, gradually raising the level of stimulation, keeping pace with their child's growing capacity to tolerate stimulation. Alex, a boy adopted from Russia at age six, illustrates this process.

Alex arrived in his family already in upheaval. By his own description, "I threw up on Momma all day in the car. I was so sick that I didn't even care that she was Momma. I felt no feelings except throwing up. I don't remember the plane home. When I got home, I ran around, playing with all the toys and breaking them. They were probably thinking, 'Oh No! Oh No! We adopted a wild boy!' but I couldn't stop. After a while, they put almost everything up so I wouldn't go crazy! Now I'm all right. I can always go to my quiet space and play there for a while, if I feel wild. Sometimes they have to tell me to go, but usually I can tell when I need to go. They aren't mad at me. I just need a little break."

Techniques for calming down and forming attachment are offered in Chapters 8 and 10. Children who have been traumatized need an additional skill package for calm-down. Their calm-down process must include strategies to help them with unpleasant and intrusive thoughts, night terrors, and in some cases, flashbacks. Techniques for parents whose children have these challenges are described in both Chapters 5 and 9.

Developing Gratifying Relationships

Eight years ago, a woman was talking to me about her daughter, who had joined their family at age four. She was discussing the effects of an overnight trip away from her daughter. I mentioned that she should make certain that she had a fulfilling time on the trip, since her relationship with her daughter was not yet gratifying. At that she started to cry, "That's it. I love her like my heart would break. But she's just not gratifying. She takes everything out of me." When she and her daughter came back in recently for adolescent work, she described, "We have a close relationship."

"Is she gratifying?" I asked.

"Well, yes," She replied, "I would say so. Not every day, but she shows that she cares in lots of ways."

A challenge for children with attachment difficulties is learning ways to demonstrate their love for their parents. Sharing time together, developing common interests, giving expressions of sympathy, grabbing the extra bag of groceries, laughing at mutual jokes, planning fun outings, reading together, hugging each other, and talking are all ways in which children and parents gratify one another.

When children are distressed by grief and fear, they are not gratifying. Many children will not be capable of this true reciprocity until they have been in the home for many months. However, it is necessary for children to learn the skill of reciprocity eventually. They need to be a giving family member, both in their growing up family, and in the family they form later in life.

A man told me that he wanted his daughter to be able to hold his hand. Using the techniques in Chapter 8, he worked on building attachment with his daughter. But like some children from Romanian orphanages, she was still wary of contact with his body, and especially his hands. We used a desensitization strategy. He arrived wearing a shirt and pants with many, many pockets. His daughter was in tow. We filled each pocket with M&Ms. She ignored both of us for long, long, minutes, since she would have to make physical contact to see what we were doing. Cagily, the father took to eating M&Ms, while making "MMMM" sounds like the name of the candy. Finally, the little girl clamored up into his lap for the first time. He put an M&M into his hand, and she reached into his hand, retrieving it. This process continued. When she located full pockets, he emptied its M&Ms into his hand. She reached in his hand, and emptied into her mouth. He insisted on eye contact about half way through. Of course, he was grinning. At the end she fed him some M&Ms as she giggled.

Several months later I received a picture of the two of them on the beach. His head was not in the picture. Her hand, holding her father's hand, was centered in the picture. I am not aware of how many bags of M&Ms this transformation took, but the candy was just the desensitizer. While it was not a necessity to have this child hold her father's hand, it was something that meant a great deal to him. It is important for children to become capable of returning love. Learning to return love in a manner that is gratifying to parents is the icing on the cake.

More discussion of ways to develop this emotional fine-tuning is in Chapter 12: Building Emotional Intelligence.

Challenges Facing Parents

Teaching Children the Meaning of Family

How do children think that families function? Parents who want to help their children to learn about the new family want to find this out. It helps them to make informed interpretations of their children's actions, and to construct focused strategies for the future. It challenges parents' own understanding of the meaning of family when this first step proves difficult. This must be part of the parent preparation offered to adopting families.

The gathering and sharing of background information on children being placed in new families is, unfortunately, not taken seriously by some placement workers. Although such practice is unprofessional, I still hear far too often that information has been withheld. An adoption worker at a recent symposium told me that she did not tell parents the full extent of their child's abuse or prenatal exposure to substance. She said, "I want them to take the child at face value, without preconceived notions. Besides, I don't think that many parents are likely to take children if they know everything." Apparently, this worker was unaware both of ethical issues in the field as well as her legal requirement for full disclosure. Her actions denied the families in her caseload the basics for successful preparation and preventative treatment.

Even with full compliance by highly ethical caseworkers, it can be difficult to obtain accurate information. A parent once showed me records documenting a wonder. Her child had lived at two places simultaneously, with documentation about his adjustment at both of those places. Parents adopting from China and Eastern Europe have reported, on numerous occasions, that records for their children listed several suggested birth dates. Or, that children were, or maybe were not, with their birthmothers for the first year. Parents planning to raise at-risk children are taking the ultimate responsibility for their children, and they need accurate and complete information about their histories.

Parents know that events will have shaped how their child sees them and others. Sometimes details make all the difference in comprehending the "why" of a troubling behavior or attitude. Placement professionals and experienced parents are aware that the issues from the history will surface. Parents want the history in order to handle their responsibilities well.

Certainly there are situations in which the information is simply not available in spite of the best of intentions. There are other instances in which parents are being shown documentation too quickly for them to be able to make notes or to copy information, or they are discouraged from putting caseworkers to so much trouble. But parents must be their children's advocates. When dealing with children who are troubled, parents should to go back to the placing agency, even if several years have passed since placement, and insistently request what they need.

Parents have the challenge of trying to change concepts that were learned during infancy at a nonverbal level. How do they talk with their children about those concepts or demonstrate them? For example, a child who lacked love and attention in infancy may not believe that there is enough love and attention in his adoptive family. Sometimes children change their basic working models naturally; sometimes they do not. It is challenging to find words and techniques that work for children. Chapter 8 is replete with words and techniques for each emotional developmental stage. Still, it is a challenge to intentionally teach children about families, when basic foundation blocks, acquired nonverbally during infancy, are missing or shaky.

Parents often find that they have to verbalize primitive concepts. For example, they may need to say out loud to their children things like, "Mom and Dad are your special people," or "Hugs and kisses are only for Mom and Dad, grandmas, grandpas, and brothers and sisters," or "Mom's job is to make sure that there are food and hugs for you. We go to work to get money to buy your food and toys. We come home again." They often must reassure, "Our poppa does not hurt children—ever," as well as "No one will come in the night to hurt you," and "Big people do not hurt children in this house," or "No one has to leave the family when Momma and Poppa get mad." Parents may need to say, "When you get mad, you can tell Mom or Dad," and "It was not O.K. that you got punched by adults in your old family. When children do not follow rules in this family, we do not punch."

Parents have to wait for children to learn to know and to love them. Children's resistance to love is one of the hardest challenges of parenting these children. Waiting can become discouraging when adults are ready to teach children the loving meaning of a family and children are not ready. Looking for opportunities, using techniques, and remaining patient all help parents.

Parents should be looking for attachment to the caregiver and family within a time frame of two years after arrival. Children who are in placements before the age of four are usually showing the growth of attachment after one year. If there has been trauma, or multiple placements, attachment takes longer. For children who are past four, especially if there is also a cultural change, the time frame stretches longer. If there are not strong gains within two years, however, parents should be concerned.

When children have had severe abuse after early years of neglect, the long time frames are hard to alter. One eight-year-old girl, talking with me about placement, asked for a family who would understand that adjustment would take a while.

"I loved my last mom and dad," she said, "but they gave up on me. I told them that I did love them, but they said that I didn't, or I wouldn't act like I did. I did try, but they didn't know that it took me a long time to get over being mad about leaving the mom and dad before them and my birthmother."

The parents, who disrupted, had decided to put in one year's hard work. They said, "We expected to have her shaped up in a year." Unfortunately for everyone, this time frame was unrealistic from the beginning. After several placements, trauma, and grief, a two-year time frame for attaching to the caretaker and the family would have been a reasonable expectation for the parents. Even though the girl was attaching, it was not fast enough for the expectations of these adults.

Providing Safety and Limits

Parents provide limits for children until children have the ability to limit themselves. Limits keep children safe. They also keep respect and needs balanced in a home. Parents reading this book will usually find that their children are behind their peers in comprehending limits. They may notice that their children do not stay close to them in groups or on outings. Paradoxically, many of the same children can alternate this distancing behavior with excessive clinging. When children do not perceive their parents as a safe base, they do not touch base enough. Vicky, a worn-out adoptive parent, describes this challenge well.

Vicky's daughter, now aged five, had been placed with their family at the age of eleven months, and she had not attached well. At age three she had wandered off at a street fair, and in the twenty minutes that she had wondered, with Vicky following, she had never looked back for her mother. She approached a few complete strangers for hugs. Vicky said, "About that time I thought, 'Go ahead. Any one of these people could be more successful than I have been.' I didn't feel much for her. She didn't think that she was any safer with me than she would be with a total stranger."

Two years later, after using attachment techniques, Vicky said softly, "It's been tough, but it was worth it. Now she knows that I'll keep her safe. She almost always keeps an eye out for me, not just the other way around." In this family, the daughter felt loved and special after accepting her mother's role as one of providing safety.

Parents of attachment-challenged children often find themselves challenged in keeping their traumatized children safe when these children invite dangerous situations.

Julian, age eight, had been sexually assaulted in a previous home. One day he was walking oddly and cried out with pain. He had found and sharpened a splinter from a board, which he hid in his underwear. The splinter had become lodged in his genitals. It had to be removed by the family doctor.

Julian described that he had made this weapon in order to keep his body safe. While on this topic, he revealed that he had sneaked out of the front yard while his father was doing yard work. He had a "spy trail." This included looking in the windows of all of the neighbors to make certain that there were no "bad guys." Julian's parents were uneasy about one of the neighbors. It unnerved them to think of Julian unsupervised looking into any neighbor's window, and especially the neighbor they mistrusted.

Parents like Julian's find that it is unnerving to even think about what their children might imagine. Like all children, their children are trying to master their issues through play. The terrifying difference is that their children try to master traumatic situations themselves. Parents of traumatized children find that they have to keep attuned to the weird or bizarre in order to sleuth out any odd schemes that are in the hatching stage. One parent said, "I am getting really good at this after adopting as many traumatized children as I have. I can smell trauma play that needs to be interrupted. It makes me a little worried about myself!"

Parents find that they must be aware about traumatic issues. This awareness can reduce a person's cheeriness. More on this topic, with help for parents, can be found in Chapter 5.

Parents enforce limits with children because children lack information or inner controls to limit themselves. Teaching about limits is a necessity when children are coming from chaotic homes or institutional care. Sometimes the children are too daring, sometimes too inhibited. Teaching limits includes teaching manners. Manners show respect for others. Some children look like they have limits while in institutional care. Once orphanage structure is removed, parents see whether inner control has really developed.

Children are resentful if parents try to teach limits too quickly. On the other hand, parents have every right to live in a home that feels neither chaotic nor institutional. Parents should protect space for themselves. Limits need to reflect respect for parents.

One parent found that she had no time at home during which she could not be interrupted. She could never prepare for a meeting at home, or read the paper, or enjoy a book. The child's father had the status of a family butler. He, too, was commandeered into constant fetch and carry. This unpleasant family situation devolved over four years before, with the credo, "We're not going to live like this anymore!" the parents decided to set limits. As they worked on enforcing them, they made certain that their child understood the underlying "why." She did tantrum and resist, but also worked on the problems. The family worked sequentially, setting important boundaries one at a time. The first boundary was time alone for Mom. Working towards a goal of thirty minutes, they began at two minutes, extending the time thirty seconds every evening. Their child was rewarded for her compliance through earning special outings with her mother.

The parents supported each other for not rushing in to "save" their child, who would beg, "Please, please, I need my mom. Please Dad, help me to see Mom just for a minute. Please, Please…" Working through a series of issues, they balanced their family again over a year's period of time. Eventually their daughter said, "I am a lot stronger than I used to be. I don't need to be in charge every minute. Dad tells me to wait, and I can."

In the example above, it might seem that individuals would have to be inept to find themselves in such a position. In fact, capable parents have discovered that children, who appropriately need close contact in the beginning of a placement, may not move forward. Parents can find themselves bound into a no-limit infant stage for years. The next section explores this challenge further.

Responding to Highly Anxious Children

When children are highly anxious, parents feel that they should do more. High alarm messages from anxious children translate to parents as "Try harder, try differently, provide more safety, stay closer, and calm me."

After a day with a highly anxious child, most parents feel some of their child's anxiety. Without realizing it, parents start breathing high in their chests, walking with shoulders drawn up, overreacting to noises, and acting disorganized. Parents begin to look a lot like their child. If parents were anxious sorts to begin with, they are more anxious after placement.

Parents do best when they can keep themselves relaxed and maintain themselves as the pacesetters in the home. Taking deep breaths and talking in a reassuring manner to children helps children to gear down, to match their parent's calmer states. Even if children do not calm immediately, because of unresolved trauma or neurological damage, they still feel more secure with a settled parent. Parents also balance their own needs. Telling children that they are safe without visual contact gives parents some minutes to use the bathroom in peace or to get the mail. Within just a few weeks after placement, some of these routines should be established for everyone's benefit.

Parents sometimes want to show anxiety themselves in order to empathize with their children's anxiety. This works poorly over the long run. When parents act like children, there is no safe psychological parent. Instead, a sick exercise develops, with both the child and parent sharing, fearful, and sobbing.

> One parent reported that she would sob out, "I just don't know how to help you!" Then, the duo would cry harder. When the father suggested that he could think of helpful ideas, he was treated like an emotionally stunted oaf.

When parents and children enter shared helplessness, children make no progress. Instead, they experience their parents as helpless peers. Parents who tell children that they are safe, and that ways to continue to help them will be pursued, are beacons of reassurance to children. More techniques for parents are in Chapter 4.

Parents with anxious children will benefit from intentional relaxation every day. They need to re-set their own body rhythms, so that they do not become as unregulated as their children. If parents are home all day, they should take some "coffee breaks," just as if they were working. It also helps if they do something pleasurable during children's nap times, like paint, read, or call a friend. More on self-care is in Chapter 11.

Impact on Parents' Self-Image

When children love their parents in return, it confirms to parents that they are lovable. When children are developing consciences on schedule, parents get feedback that they are doing a good job. When children are behaving sensitively, parents reflect that their home has promoted emotional sensitivity.

Parents with impacted children wonder, "Am I lovable? Am I doing good parenting? Is our home a good place?" And they often answer their own questions, "No," ignoring facts that explain the problems. A sense of failure is normal. Parents are vulnerable to shame. They are sometimes too loyal to share their child's history. On the other hand, parents can feel embarrassed when their child takes a baby's bottle, asks strangers to take her home, or acts like parents are repugnant. People-pleasers can find themselves apologizing for their child.

Parents need to develop a sturdy sense of self-esteem, buoyed by feedback from people who know what the parent and child are facing. Parent support groups or parent mentor programs are a wonderful way to meet this challenge. Therapists who recognize and comment on real accomplishments are another.

One woman came in to see me after a family reunion. Her daughter had melted down twice, for a total of thirty minutes, at the reunion. The mother told me, proudly, how she had handled it. She did not take on shame, go to the hotel, or allow it to ruin her image of competence. Her daughter got back on track much more quickly when she realized that her mother never got off track. For the first time, her daughter got to go to the reunion and participate. Two years before, even one tantrum had lasted sixty to ninety minutes. Taking the whole family, and relying on progress, had been a courageous step. The mother's boosted self-esteem was based on their hard-won progress, not on her daughter's having behaved perfectly at the reunion.

Parents build up self-image with self-talk like this:

- "Not everyone could ignore whining with the dedication that I do."
- "I see the value in my child, and do not need confirmation from her."
- "My child is afraid of the love she wants, not unlovable."
- "I am able to give my child consistent love."
- "I am doing my best job almost every day."
- "I wasn't part of the original problem; I'm part of the problem-solving team."
- "Good parents are parents who give children what they need, not just what they think that they need."
- "Great parents treat themselves well. Self-pity will not get me to the movies—but a babysitter will!"
- "I need to share this success with my friend, so I will make time to call her right now."
- "I can name three things that have changed since the beginning of placement—I am sleeping better, my daughter does not vomit daily, and I have the hot tub working."
- "I can plan an additional good thing today, if today seems too hard."

Over time, most parents end up doing inner work on their own sense of self. They become impervious to casual feedback from the community. They rely on knowledgeable friends, who can understand the magnitude of the work that they are accomplishing with their child. They generate an inner picture of themselves and their efforts that matches their actual situation.

Energy Levels—When Adjustment Turns into a Marathon

Parents may not realize the extent of the needs of their child until several months into the placement. By then, parents often have used all of their energy, and reserves. Parents may have a reality-based perception that the quality of their lives has taken a sharp, downward turn. Parents may have legitimate concerns that they are meeting the needs of one child at the expense of another child in the family.

As parents get increasingly tired, it becomes more difficult to organize and make decisions that will benefit the family for the long haul. Sleep is essential. Regularly, after running sleep deficits of two or three hours per night, parents are nearly emotionally numb, feeling little but frustration. Parents need to get adequate sleep in order to make it for the long haul.

> One family found themselves in a dilemma. Their child was seriously affected from events prior to his adoption. He was unpredictable, suicidal, and, to make matters worse, sleepwalking. After finding him outside on a couple of occasions, and finding him with siblings playing death games, they determined to move to a home with an easy-to-supervise floor plan. First, they set up his bed in their room, moving their bed to block the door. Then, they all caught up on sleep for two weeks. Feeling rested, they located a home and arranged a move. They accepted and solicited help for the move, calling in every favor friends offered.

Respite care is an essential for most families with difficult children. Parents need breaks from the constancy of listening for their child. Parents also need to find wide margins of time in which to do the specialized parenting that their children need. Getting some respite allows parents to start looking forward to their child's return after a day's absence. Many worn out parents are lying in bed in the mornings, dreading the day. One woman dreamed about being alone in her own home. During respite hours for her three daughters, all recent and rambunctious arrivals to this country, she walked around quietly in her own home—relaxing.

Parents sometimes do well to have someone in the home, helping out. Instead of labeling the help as someone to care for a particular family member, the help is best labeled as someone to help the adults. Parents can define the help in the way that supports them most.

> One family had a woman who helped them for three years, fifteen hours per week. Sometimes she watched children while the parents went places together, sometimes she ran errands, and sometimes she cared for the son who had special needs. The support of the whole family was the goal. That, in turn, stabilized all of the children, including the son with special needs. It gave parents time to play board games with the children, go to the park, go work out, or have lunch with a friend. The family started to have fun again.

The important concept for families is to find a pace that they can sustain without needing to pull from reserves. Often, that means relinquishing other commitments that are not feasible any longer. It also means that parents will need to replace reserves through respite or breaks, if day-to-day they are breaking into physical and emotional reserves.

High Nurture and High Structure Parenting

The parenting style that helps most children described in this book is characterized by *high structure* and *high nurture*. Most parents are parenting children who are emotionally younger than their chronological ages. Even when their children arrive at older ages, parents use the amount of structure typically given to a younger child. High nurture means that parents are increasing opportunities for nurturing their children. Meals, bedtimes, walks, and games are tilted to emphasize the nurturance on which children thrive. Recognizing that children have missed dependable nurture, parents are supplying what was missed.

This is specialized parenting at its best, when children are given a ton of love and enough structure to succeed. Since people usually pair high structure with low affection in our society, parents may think that it is loving to reduce structure. Instead, loving parents are providing the structure that helps their emotionally younger or emotionally fragile child have a chance for a good day.

A challenge for parents is enduring the reaction that some people have to structure. Outsiders may believe that if the parents simply relaxed, then their child would not have a problem. This is rarely true. This is wishful thinking. Actually, it is because the parents are aware and responsive to problems that they are structured. Successful parents have seen how much better their child performs with high structure. They work hard to provide that structure. An example of the structure and nurture combination is illustrated in Natalie and John's family.

Natalie and John have lived in their present home for eight months. Birth siblings, they have both experienced multiple placements and have an emotional age of about three and four. In fact, they are six and seven.

As they enter a picnic area for a potluck with their parents and some friends, their parents tell them how happy they are to be with them. The parents get eye contact from Natalie and John, by request, and then repeat the nurturing phrase, since the children were not listening at first. Then they follow up with quick hugs. They hold the children's hands while showing them where the family will be sitting.

Mom says, "First we will eat while you get used to the group. Then Natalie will go with Dad and John will go with me down to the play area. The rules are number one, stay close enough that a parent can touch you; and number two, have a good time with your family. We love you!"

John says, "Why do we have to stay with you? Why can't we play on our own?"

Dad replies, "Great question. When you are good at staying close to us, then you will be ready to play on your own for a while. Today, you are not ready yet. You will be soon. I think that you will do a good job of staying close to us today, buddy. You are a fast learner." John grins. Natalie looks up questioningly. Dad adds, "You, too, Natalie!"

While this seems like a lot of effort, it contrasts positively with a scenario in which the children are migrating to other picnic sites, grazing from strangers' tables, and ignoring their frantic parents. This would be typical behavior for Natalie and John. There would be little nurture showed by fried parents in this alternative scenario. Instead, the children would only get structure after failing.

While parents are using high structure, they want to be mindful that their goal is to develop internal qualities in their children. This cannot occur unless parents are simultaneously pouring in nurturance. High structure, by itself, seems like boot camp. High nurture makes things seem like a family. As children are guided over the years to develop internal control through identification with their family and its values of respect for others, they outgrow the need for parental control. The exception to this process will be in situations in which children have neurological problems like Fetal Alcohol Syndrome, which is discussed in Chapter 7.

Parents naturally choose parenting styles that fit best with their own personalities. For random, relaxed parents, structured parenting is especially challenging. It can feel like a bitter loss, since the style is foreign to their lifestyles and expectations. One parent said, "I was such an easy child. I wanted approval, and just did what I needed to gain approval. My mother, a single parent, used no behavioral consequences that I can remember. Once, I had to sit on my bed and think about something. That was the extent of discipline. I must structure my son's days so carefully! I have to ask my friends what they do for their kids who are my son's emotional age. Why didn't I adopt a little girl, similar to myself as a child?" These discrepancies in style are frustrating realities for parents adjusting to specialized parenting.

Personal Costs of Parenting

In parenting difficult children, parents are surprised to find parts to their personalities that they did not know that they had, especially negative parts. This can require some psychological work at a time when people feel most vulnerable. Many parents feel enough pressure and loss that they require therapy and antidepressants. A side specialty in working with attachment issues in children is treating depression in their primary caregivers.

Sometimes, parents have to ask for help, instead of giving it. This can be disappointing to family and friends, who are used to receiving. Parents, expecting support from family and friends, can be saddened by the neediness of the people on whom they were counting. True friends and faithful family members are fewer than expected. Parents encounter some friends and family who have denial about children's needs. They gloss over the seriousness of the situation that the family faces. For example, a family member thought parents were "making too much of it" when the parents would not leave their newly-placed children to travel for an out-of-state wedding. The children had only been in the country for two weeks and were not even invited to the wedding! More about working with friends and family is found in Chapter 13.

Parents want friends who understand what they are going through. Sometimes these friends are hard to locate. Parents describe their loneliness as one of the hard challenges. Unless parents know that their confidante is reliable, parents often pretend to be doing better than they are. They do not want their difficulties to reflect poorly on their children or themselves. I will have families from the same adoption support groups, who share similar struggles, who state that they are the only ones in the group having troubles. Parents' reluctance to open up is understandable. They feel guilty when they have mixed emotions and wonder if others will relate to them or judge them. After all, parents judge themselves some of the time! In hinting about difficulties to parents without adoption expertise, they risk getting one of two extremes: "Are you sure that you want to continue with the adoption?" or, "You just have a spirited child." When parents do get hooked up with friends who are encountering similar situations, they describe the mutual support as feeling like coming home. As Robert Louis Stevenson said, "A friend is a gift you give yourself."

CHAPTER 3

What Children Have Already Learned about Attachment

Attachment is often discussed as if all types of attachment were the same. Nothing could be further from the truth! As an example, compare attachment relationships in various marriages or between partners. Nurturing, mutually satisfying relationships differ from those marked by disrespect and violence in both their operating beliefs and personal impacts. Children's attachments to their parents vary as dramatically. In hearing about children who have had a rocky start, and whose history reports them as attached, my questions back are, "What was the nature of the attachment? What type of attachment experience will this child transfer to prospective parents?"

In the remainder of the chapter, types of attachment styles are discussed. There are some factors that affect all children when they leave an attachment figure. Using the description in the paragraphs below, parents can identify the operating beliefs that underpin their child's learned style.

Attachment Themes and Styles

Grief as a Theme in Attachment

Grief is one result of losing parents, even if there has been poor attachment between the child and the lost parent. Prior to their sixth birthdays, children are so psychologically merged with their parents that the parent is part of children's selves. Even if they have been abused, children feel that they have lost a piece of themselves after a separation. New parents help to regain important parts of their child's identity when they recognize the positive aspects of their child's attachment to his birthparents or other attachment figures. The following stories provide examples of ways to recognize the positive in an attachment figure.

> During a visit between two biologic sisters who had been placed in different homes, the older sister talked about good memories. Their birthmother, whom they called Ailene, was in end-stage alcoholism. She told her little sister and her adoptive mother about their Easter celebration. "No matter what, Ailene always got us dressed up and got our picture taken. We celebrated it like other people celebrate Christmas! Your eyes were so big when you saw your basket! She did do a great job on Easter for us!"

The adoptive mother was allowing her daughter to reclaim some important positives, not just about her first family, but about herself. Since she was in kindergarten at the time of the move, her identity was enhanced by descriptions of special times.

Another little boy was in a session with his birthfather and his adoptive parents.

> "What time of day was I born," he asked?
> "At dawn," his birthfather said.

> "You were born just as the sun came up on a beautiful day. I was happy and peaceful. I regret not taking proper care of you. But having you, that was one thing I've never regretted."

In neither example were adoptive parents competing with birthparents. Instead, they were recognizing a time in which their children were attached to birthparents. They gleaned good memories on their children's behalf.

Children are so deeply harmed by breaking their attachments that they may not want to attach again. "Julie has bonded before, I know that she can bond again," argued a caseworker persuasively, as she discussed moving a child. I wished that I shared her optimism! The child had become attached to her "short-term" foster parents in the year she had lived there. There is a myth in some child welfare offices that attached children can be moved with the assumption that the future placement will be a reflection of the past. The fact is that every time that attached children are moved, they learn that attachments are ultimately painful. On the other end of the spectrum, some children have never learned to attach. Often the proposed solution for children who are not attaching is to suggest another move, rather than to analyze whether they are willing to attach to anyone.

Secure Attachment—Gratifying for Parents, Rich for Children

Attachment is a learned style of being emotionally intimate. When thinking of attachment, people naturally form an image of a positive, secure attachment, which is just one of the types of attachment. Secure attachment is a relationship involving intimacy, exclusivity, mutual enjoyment, acceptance, and recognition of the other's feelings. It is unusual that I see a child with a secure attachment coming into foster care or adoption. However, I regularly see infants, toddlers, and children who, over a series of months or years, form secure attachments with their adoptive parents.

In infants who have been with the same set of parents continuously, this exclusive attachment has had its preparation period in the first six months of life. By one year, children's attachments to their parent can be measured as secure or insecure. In secure attachments, children have formed what is known as an "internal working model," or template, allowing children to believe that parents will respond to them. When these children signal for attention or care, they are usually successful. Their parents or other caregivers do not stay away long.

Since they can depend on their parents to stay with them, children with secure attachments are free to explore their world and to develop mastery of life skills. If a new situation seems overwhelming, parents provide a context that reassures children. Often children will try the same situation again, this time enjoying it. An example of parents helping children to enjoy a new experience safely is the introduction of a child to a friendly dog. Parents reassure a reticent child. With help he pets the dog and grins. He approaches and pets without help, sharing delighted laughter with parents.

Children with a positive view of life make pleasant companions for parents. They convey the message that their parents are doing a great job. Children glow at the sight of their parents when happy. When children are distressed, parents intervene effectively. This is gratifying for eager parents, who love spending time with a baby or child who enjoys and trusts them. Often parents will refer companionably to their little one, using expressions like, "He's my buddy." They use terms that imply mutual enjoyment.

Research has proven that a parent's sensitivity to her child is an essential attribute in forming secure attachment. Consistency and effectiveness in meeting needs are other critical factors. Some babies are temperamentally difficult. However, research shows that secure attachments are just as probable for irritable babies, as long as the caregiver has resources and social support. Social support for the caregivers (who were mothers in the research project) was the variable that caused a difference in secure or insecure attachment in an irritable child (Cassidy, Shaver, 1999, pp.73-74). When parents are forming attachments with children who are irritable because of trauma and grief, parents will need social support. This support helps them to sustain their efforts in promoting a secure attachment.

As a group, children who are securely attached have the best behavioral control. It is easier for children to maintain self-control when they are feeling well loved and confident in their care. Anxious children have a constant level of distress that works against self-control. When children are separated from their parents in research situations, the securely attached children return most quickly to normal emotional states, with normal heart rates, once their parents returned.

Children with secure attachment histories show good capacity for friendship. In more than one study, children with secure attachment histories were never victims or victimizers. They also scapegoated less often and showed less hostility towards other children. Experts concluded that "being consistently nurtured and responded to empathetically leads not to a spoiled, self-indulged child, but rather to an empathic child…Those whose caregivers are responsive to their tender needs learn that when one person is needy, the other responds; when one person is emotionally overaroused, the other provides comfort or reassurance. All that these children require are the cognitive advances necessary to play the more mature role." (Cassidy, Shaver; 1999, p.78).

Children who have secure attachments can become insecurely attached if separated from their parents too long. Mental illness in the parent, abuse, and trauma can also change children's views of their relationship, evidenced by a change to a different type of attachment.

Insecure Attachment

As opposed to the secure attachment already described, an insecure attachment describes the condition of children who cannot count on their parents as constant, safe bases of nurture and caregiving. These children must deal with the constant possibility of being left vulnerable and alone. Additionally, their needs may be ignored or mocked.

There are a number of subtypes of insecure attachment that are described in research situations. Since adoptive parents are primarily interested in styles that apply to their children, I will limit this discussion to four types of insecure attachment. Insecure attachments are also known as anxious attachments in the literature because children without secure attachments are psychologically anxious children. For clarity, since these children may not *look* anxious, I will use the term *insecure* which is also correct.

Insecure, Avoidant Attachment

In avoidant attachments, children still feel connected to their caregivers, but cannot trust caretakers to meet their needs in a reliable, painfree, or sensitive manner. Children who have an avoidant attachment style do not know whether they will be hugged or hurt when they express needs. They conclude that it would be safer and better if they could be self-reliant. (Sroufe, 1995).

They do seek some attention from the parents. When they want closeness, they tend to back up to parents, offering a shoulder or a back for hugging. They like to initiate any affection. Children with avoidant attachments will prefer to feed themselves and to take care of themselves when in a new home. They are less likely to do their self-care competently, since they do not rely on parents for pertinent information or help. They do not buy into the parent's rules easily, because they are parenting themselves to a large degree and prefer to make their own rules. However, in crises, they will head for their parents.

By the end of their first year with a new caregiver, abused children usually have developed avoidant attachments, or disorganized attachments, which will be discussed later. Avoidant attachments are also seen in families in which caregivers do not abuse, but are insensitive or physically unavailable. Children with avoidant attachments treat strangers similarly to parents, actually becoming more responsive to strangers in some cases. When the parent of such a child comes at the end of a day at day care, avoidant children will turn away angrily from their parent. They ignore or look past the parent. It is as if they are saying, "See, my opinion of you is confirmed. You do not care about me!" In the home, their behavior is often openly angry and non-compliant; and they cry often.

Adam is an example of a child with an avoidant attachment to his mother. He was adopted at the age of three, after having spent the first eighteen months with his birthmother and next eighteen months in foster care. His parents agree that Adam liked them better before he thought of them as his parents. Adam, at age five, still seems like a shadow in the family at times. At family birthday parties, he sits a little outside of the circle. He seems to sulk about his outside position, even though it is his choice. He turns away from hugs from his parents, and rarely returns their smiles. When his sisters get hugs, he is jealous. His nostrils flair, his motions get jerky, and he ignores their welcoming comments to come join them. His sister said openly, "Why is Adam always mad? I don't think that he likes us!" A call to the caseworker resulted in a renewed effort by parents to find ways to show their love to Adam. The effort pays off a little, but Adam seems to have a chip on his shoulder.

"Are all later-placed adoptions like this?" his mother asked. "I can take it if someone will just tell me the truth. I want to be doing everything that I should be doing. Adam is not very happy, but maybe this is as good as it gets."

Parents with avoidantly attached children are confused when the child's internal picture of "mother" and "father" is transferred from their prior caregivers to them. After all, they are the sensitive, empathic, and effective parents who have a track record of secure attachments in their other children or who are capable of forming secure attachments with children. In order to change children's "internal working models," or that internal picture, parents must incorporate ways to challenge the old model and to form a new picture into everyday life. Those techniques are described in the upcoming chapters.

Insecure, Ambivalent Attachment with Anxious, Clingy Presentation

There are two presentations of ambivalent attachment commonly seen by adoptive parents. The first type is an obviously anxious one. Many later-placed adopted children who have not been abused show this type of attachment. They convey that they have finally found someone whom they can trust, within limits. The limit comes at the time that they are expected to believe that their parents can be trusted to return. Their love for and trust in a parent are always in the moment. They seem to believe that the parent will disappear once out of sight. Children tend to show this anxious style after neglect, or after sudden and shocking moves in the first several months of life. It is typical for children to go through a six-month stage of separation anxiety sometimes in the first two years of placement, but the highly anxious child does not go on to learn that parents come back. A parent who shuts the door to the bathroom evokes frantic tears from the anxiously attached child—even one who has been in the home for three years.

Some of the children adopted at young ages from Korea and China have anxious, ambivalent attachments. Their parents are wondering, "When is my child going to trust me?" They know that they do not have the most serious attachment problems—and definitely their child is not avoiding them. Still, everyone in the family seems to be working far too hard, including their child. As the years go on, these anxiously attached children add more control of their parents to their repertoire. At that point, the ambivalence in the child is more apparent. Such a child may show her frustration and anger at parents, who seem so elusive. Parents only wish that they had the ability to be elusive once in a while! Instead, they reassure over and over and over.

Parents of anxiously attached children tend to consider their adoptions successful and fulfilling, albeit exhausting. On a gut level, parents know that they are not having big league problems in the short or long run. They do worry, however, about the excessive demands that their children will place on others in future relationships. They also ponder whether their children will have the emotional strength necessary to master issues of loss and identity inherent in adoption. Parents of these anxious children tend to act a bit anxious themselves, as they describe the fragile emotional balance of their children. It is tempting to think that if parents could calm, their children would be fine. It does help children if parents are even-tempered. However, unless the parent was anxious prior to placement, the child's anxiety is unlikely to be due to parental influence.

Insecure, Ambivalent Attachment

Push me! Pull me! An ambivalent attachment is a style in which children alternately push parents away and cling to parents. Such a child asks for help and then says that the parent is not doing it the right way. Or, he asks for a hug and cries out, "You hurt me!" The parent is enticed to continue to try to find ways to satisfy this child, but he ends up feeling sabotaged much of the time. Parents with children who are ambivalently attached express that they feel like they are on the ropes. The ambivalently attached child can beg the parent not to leave at night and act quite snuggly. As the parent finally leaves the room after a twenty-minute cuddle time, the child might say, quite calmly, "I wish that Uncle Peter were my dad."

Children who have not been traumatized before being adopted from the better Eastern European orphanages are regularly presenting for therapy with ambivalent attachments. In domestic adoption, often children will save this type of attachment for a mother figure either after having been moved without adequate preparation or having been neglected by a previous mother figure. They may form a secure attachment style more readily with a father.

Children with ambivalent attachments still have periods in which they seem reasonably comfortable with their parents. While they control and cajole, they also seem normal a lot of the time. Children with this type of presentation are difficult, but not so far off track that parents worry about their child's future in the criminal justice system. Parents are too busy dreading adolescence. They wonder if their child achieved adolescent angst a decade too soon. In fact, some of the themes are the same: how close and how far should children stay from parents; and do parents really act in children's best interests?

The insecure, ambivalently attached child's internal working model is a mixture of not allowing the parent too close for too long and not allowing the parent too far for too long. However, there is usually no trauma or extreme abuse as part of the history. This child does have an intermittently satisfying relationship with parents.

When parents and friends observe the push-pull that is part of this style, they may comment that the child's "attitude" needs correction. Discipline usually works for some outward behaviors, as do compliments. However, neither resolves the underlying trust questions. As parents apply pressure to get closer and stay closer to their ambivalently attached child, their children's attitude may change, with the child becoming dependent, tearful, and clingy. Parents then wonder if they have gone too far! Then, their child pushes away again. Methods to redress some of the trust issues are described in the rest of this book, specifically in Chapters 8 and 10.

Insecure, Disorganized Attachment

In the styles above, children have developed ways to organize information about, and approaches to, their relationships with their caregivers. They have methods of developing a relationship, even if it reflects dilemmas that are unresolved. They have a template that helps them know how to signal to get their needs met. Children who cannot develop ways to organize information about their caregivers, along with consistent approaches to get needs met, are in the disorganized attachment category. The name references the condition.

Children become fearful, frozen, or disoriented in the midst of signaling some need to their parent. The children show levels of extreme rage. They seem to be either unable to play, or only able to play out violent themes that include separation. When observed with the parents who formed these disorganized attachments, researchers find that when distressed, the children are often more upset than comforted by the arrival of the parent. Parents of children who have disorganized attachments have been frightening or alarming to their children. Often these dysfunctional parents have set the child up for overwhelming situations and then responded in a rejecting, frightening, or abandoning manner. Children with disorganized attachments tend to have a sense of helplessness about their relationship with parents. The parents who raised the child and formed these attachments also report feelings of helplessness about their relationship with their child. (Solomon, George, 1999). Children with disorganized attachments tend to use aggression or dissociation in order to cope. These are children who are having extraordinary problems. They show the push and pull of the ambivalent child, but with increased fear and aggression.

Children who have a disorganized attachment to a parent will relate to new parents with this style after being moved. This style is the only relational skill set that they know. Many techniques in Chapters 8, 9, and 12 are particularly geared for helping these children to change their internal picture of parents and of their world. The goal is for them to develop the attributes of a positive, secure attachment over time.

Both children who were removed from birthparents and then placed in orphanages, and children who have been bounced through foster care placements after traumas tend to present in therapy with disorganized attachment styles. These children are confusing to their new parents. These children try various strategies. Highly controlling, rageful, and dissociative, they are intermittently sweet. When parents attempt to explain the severity of problems, their descriptions may not match the presentation last seen by the caseworker. Because the child does not use the same strategy consistently, professionals become confused. Since the parent is not as confusing as the child, they often decide to "fix" the parent instead of fixing the child. Left too long without help, parents do indeed become candidates for the "fix," or they give up.

The following is a section from a report on a little girl, age four, who had been moved four times in the prior year. She displayed classic signs of trauma and a disorganized attachment style. An inexperienced mental health worker described her as a "normal, energetic child."

> Nadine is a highly anxious child who has had a series of disrupted placements and unsafe living situations. Historically, Nadine has reacted with outrage at simple rules. Since she has begun in therapy, she is able to tolerate some frustration and cooperate with simple expectations placed on her.
>
> Nadine shows a concerning pattern of ambivalence towards her mother. In the office Nadine attempted to destroy something and to pinch her mother. When I prevented this, she began to scream and tantrum. She cried out that she wanted her mother. I assured her that she could go to her, but that she could not hurt her or anything else in the room. She rushed to her mother, avoided her mother's outstretched arms, curled into a fetal position next to but not touching her, and began yelling at her, "Don't touch me!" If her foster-adopt mother did attempt to touch her, she shrieked. The foster mother said that this is normal at home.
>
> Nadine dreams that she is being beaten or choked by her birthmother. At a fundamental level, this child confuses closeness with her mother with danger to herself. Over the last six weeks Nadine has stopped displaying this behavior pattern at home. The foster-adopt mother spends time in focused play in order to build bonding and compliance through fun activities. Mother has been available for Nadine's night terrors.

Nadine could not organize herself to cope in a coherent manner. She froze in place, behaved aggressively, asked for closeness, and resisted closeness. Trying to follow the signals of such a child is extremely confusing for a parent. In Nadine's situation, the caseworker and original therapist did not see some of her problems because they emerged after she was asked to relate to a parent. Nadine became fearful, aggressive, and clingy as she began to form her attachments. Until she was placed in a family able to sustain a consistent and nurturing approach, Nadine could not change her style of attachment in response.

Children with disorganized attachments tend to violate the rights and property of others, getting a diagnosis of Oppositional Defiant Disorder in early years. Without help, their aggression level tends to increase with time, until later diagnoses of Conduct Disorder, Depression, Anxiety Disorders, and Posttraumatic Stress Disorder are common. These are at-risk children who need help from the inside out.

Helping children with disorganized attachments is addressed in Chapters 4, 5, 8, 9 and 10.

Trauma Bonds

A trauma bond is a type of bond best understood as the type of adaptation that a prisoner has to a captive. In the famous case of Patty Hearst, her affiliation with a violent and radical movement lasted only until she was freed from her brutal captors. As a form of survival, a child will take on the values and beliefs of the person who is terrifying to them. By referring to figure of the Attachment Cycle in Chapter 1, readers can see how the trauma bond mimics the attachment cycle—up to a point. When children get needy, helpless, and hopeless, adults come. Rather than bringing comfort, when providing for the child's needs, the caretaker inflicts fear and pain. Closeness is paired with violence and high arousal on the part of parent and child. It does connect the pair, but dysfunctionally.

It is hard to know whether an abused child has a trauma bond or an attachment to a person until a child is moved into a stable home and believes that he is protected in that home. When children feel protected, they can begin to express their fears. Some children will test their new parents, inviting the new parents to form a trauma bond. This is a form of acting-out distress, rather than expressing it in more helpful ways.

Shelby was referred for therapy as "a child who has a lot of grief and loss for relatives." Two relatives were her last placement. She was persistent in inquiring when she would see them. The abuse and degradation that those relatives had meted out were extreme, with criminal charges pending. A visitation schedule was out of the question. As I explained this to Shelby, she wailed, "I'm afraid that they'll die before I can get back at them!" She had detailed plans for hurting these people. I did not assess her as attached to these relatives. She had a trauma bond. Her longing was not for emotional closeness, but for physical proximity, so she could pay them back for humiliating and abusing her.

Shelby's parents noted that she tried to activate trauma bonds with them. They had noticed a bizarre sense about some interactions. She tried to turn interactions into violent re-enactments of her traumas. Her parents acquired skill in sidestepping these instances. In one, her dad said, "Shelby, you have a weird look. You are posed to fistfight, your shirt is open to the waist, and we are only talking about your shower. I am not planning on a fight on the stairs or a wrestling match into the shower as the evening entertainment. In a few minutes, I'll check to see if you are ready for the kind of help that *parents* give in figuring this out. I'll be in my room, reading, until then."

Shelby explained, "Sometimes I get confused. My parents just are not into that kind of stuff, though. They think it's sick. I do, too. I'm doing better this year in stopping myself."

Children can be attracted to the power that the traumatizing person wields. It helps to have an awareness of when children felt most powerless. Often they want to replay the scenario, this time mastering or acting as the abusive person. Families do best with a well-discussed plan for avoiding incidents that promote trauma bonds. Over time, teaching children compassion for themselves during times of vulnerability and empathy for others during times of helplessness, turns the tide on sadistic replays. Security in the family, and compassion from the family, break the power of the trauma bond.

Who Is Unattached?

Few children are unattached. Children with insecure styles as detailed above can be described as having attachment issues that pose difficulties ranging from mild to severe.

While there are exceptional infants who are doing this emotional work younger, in general, infants under the age of seven months are setting the stage for an attachment to a primary caretaker. They are not considered attached, yet they are not "unattached," since they are developmentally on target.

Children who are in new families, and who are going through the process of attaching to their families, are not "unattached." They are becoming attached. Attachment takes time. Checking in at six months post-placement for younger children and at twelve months post-placement for older children gives time to assess whether attachment is progressing.

Children can still be attached to a former parent figure. They are not, however, "unattached." Instead, when children are attached to prior caregivers, it is the adults in the new family who have the problem. Their question is how can this child be helped to grieve the finality of his loss, and begin transferring the attachment to a new parent?

> One child in my colleague's practice has been moved twenty-two times in her seventeen years. She has attachment to no one. She has felt attached, but she lost her attachment figures years ago. She says that she no longer feels a tie to them, even to the memories she has of them. She describes herself as unattached and unable to attach. Her expertise is compelling; her conclusion is correct. This young woman is unattached.

As a group, children from Romanian and other Eastern European orphanages have entered Canada and the United States as unattached.

The majority of these children have never had anyone in the orphanage available with whom to complete a cycle of attachment. They are unattached when coming into their families. After a two-year follow-up on a group of Romanian orphans, researchers found that the majority had attached. While many still had attachment issues, many had also became securely attached. (Chisholm, Carter, Ames, and Morison, 1995).

The child who has severe attachment issues poses concerns in the adoption and foster care community. If a child has been in the new family for two years and still views parents as orphanage workers, the family is in trouble. Whether the child has severe attachment issues or is unattached is not the question. Quibbling about the label simply delays treatment of the problem. It is imperative to obtain a formal diagnosis with a matching treatment plan.

What Is Reactive Attachment Disorder?

Parents often hear the term *Reactive Attachment Disorder* in a context which seems to imply hopelessness. But what does the term really mean? One woman came in for an assessment. "Well," she said. "Do I have a *RAD* kid? On the Internet my group is telling me that my son sounds *RAD*. Does that mean that I just give up on him? Isn't there something that can be done at the age of four?"

Since a good diagnosis leads to appropriate treatment, it is important to be clinically correct when diagnosing attachment issues. The following information is technical. However, parents may wish to read about technical criteria in order to understand terms that are in common usage. This section is not a substitute for diagnosis by a professional, but it can be helpful, when speaking with a professional, to work from the common reference provided by this section.

Reactive Attachment Disorder is the formal diagnostic category for children with the most serious attachment problems. There are two widely accepted diagnostic manuals listing criteria. They are the *Diagnostic and Statistical Manual of Mental Disorders* (DSM-IV), and *International Classification of Diseases* (ICD-10), by the American Psychiatric Association and the World Health Organization, respectively. The DSM-IV diagnostic criteria are reprinted in the Appendix on pages 363-64. Parents who have any suspicions at all that their children have RAD or whose children have actually been labeled this way by an adoption professional or a family therapist should carefully read this formal definition. These manuals agree that the source of the problems in Reactive Attachment Disorder is parental or institutional abuse, neglect, or harsh treatment. They also concur that a disturbance occurs in the child's social relatedness, beginning prior to the age of five, and extending across social situations. ("Social relatedness" includes relating normally to parent figures.) A third point of agreement in these defining manuals is that the disturbance cannot be due to pervasive developmental delay. Finally, there is agreement that there are two types of the disorder seen. One is an inhibited type, with an ambivalent, inhibited, or hyper-vigilant reaction centered on one or more adults, including the parent. The other type is disinhibited. These children approach unfamiliar people for affection, comfort, or social needs. This occurs across a range of social situations.

The diagnostic criteria for Reactive Attachment Disorder are more general than the specifics in the research and treatment literatures. This reflects the evolving nature of attachment theory and research. Efforts to further detail the diagnostic criteria are in process. In the meantime, the DSM-IV definition, which has been in place for over twenty years, is the diagnostic standard for professionals.

Individuals with severe attachment problems have almost always had traumatic events in the early years. Often the abusers were caregivers. Reactive Attachment Disorder is sometimes informally described as Infant Traumatic Stress Disorder, as the following chart describes.

A Summary of Impairments of Children Exposed to Complex Trauma
as Reported by the Complex Trauma Taskforce in 2003
(Cook, Blaustein, Spinnazola, and van der Kolk, 2003, p.2)

Attachment	Boundary problems
	Social Isolation
	Difficulty Trusting Others
	Interpersonal Difficulty
Biology	Sensorimotor Developmental Problems
	Hypersensitivity to Physical Contact
	Somatization
	Increased Medical Problems
	Problems with Coordination and Balance

continued

Affect Regulation	Problems with Emotional Regulation
	Difficulty Describing Emotions and Internal Experiences
	Difficulty Knowing and Describing Internal States
	Problems with Communicating Needs
Behavioral Control	Poor Impulse Control
	Self Destructive Behavior
	Aggressive Behavior
	Oppositional Behavior
	Excessive Compliance
	Sleep Disturbance
	Eating Disorders
	Substance Abuse
	Re-enactment of Traumatic Past
	Pathological Self Soothing Practices
Cognition	Difficulty Paying Attention
	Lack of Sustained Curiosity
	Problems Processing Information
	Problems Focusing on and Completing Tasks
	Difficulty Planning and Anticipating
	Learning Difficulties
	Problems with Language Development
Self Concept	Lack of Continuous and Predictable Sense of Self
	Poor Sense of Separateness
	Disturbance of Body Image
	Low Sense of Self Esteem
	Shame and Guilt

Attachment, Neglect and Traumatic Stress

Knowing that children naturally want to attach, what prevents the attachment process? One way of understanding the interrelationships between attachment, neglect, and traumatic stress is to appreciate fears that children have in close relationships.

When children have been neglected, they contrast the trust encouraged by parents with their life experiences. Children have had to work to get their needs met! They are afraid not to be in charge of the signals for help. They are also afraid that calm dependence on parents will only result in more neglect. Children who lived with busy orphanage workers or with depressed or drug-affected birthparents learned to get louder, more persistent, more irritating, or more charming, to get basic needs met. Fear of not getting food, attention, and soothing caused a constantly high level of stress hormone, which became a constant template in organizing incoming information. They can push harder and longer for their needs to be met through the combination of earlier learning and the energy level made possible by their hormonal surges from high stress. This constant pushing drives parents into exhaustion. The child does not process the parent's information about love, safety, acceptance, and joy. This child's brain has been organized for hyper-vigilance and survival. When children are unable or unwilling to risk slowing down, it is hard for them to respond to the rhythm of attachment.

When children have been traumatized, they have the same hyper-vigilance noted above. In addition, they are uncertain that parents will be able to keep them safe. They tend to try to be their own parent. They are unavailable for attachment-producing experiences with their parents. They need to control their parents, which neutralizes the lessons of trust that parents are attempting to teach. They are frantic in their plans to keep safe. Often they are still processing past experiences, with plans to re-do the past, rather than focusing on the present.

Because of the distortion of core beliefs about adults and safety, and because of the changes in brain organization in response to survival, therapeutic approaches need to factor in fear, mistrust, and high arousal. Both parenting and therapy have to confront these obstacles to attachment. Proactively, practicing desirable attachment-producing behaviors calms the brain and calibrates attachment signals to safe parents. Methods for doing both of these are included throughout the rest of the book.

Treatment for Severe Attachment Problems

The unattached child who has had opportunities for family attachment and for appropriate therapy, both without positive results, usually requires intensive therapies in order to make progress.

Therapists will allow children to re-experience some of their conflicts in therapy with a different ending. The following description of one session with a boy with severe attachment problems typifies how an attachment-oriented therapist folds in the themes of fear, grief, and attachment.

Chad and I talked with his parents about helping him through some role-playing. In a session with Chad, I pretended to be Chad's birthmother. I lay down on the couch. He had been severely malnourished and abused by his birthmother and her friends. Chad's reaction, which was to control adults, surfaced at once. He lectured his birthmother on behavior. "You should not be drinking and bringing robber kind of men to the apartment," he declared. I appeared bored, so Chad appealed to a power source. "Don't you care about what God thinks of you? He does not like all that drinking and stuff." Chad's tone became demanding and angry. He was entering a state of high arousal. Acting as his birthmother, I told him nonchalantly, "I'll bring strangers to the house at night when I want to. If you don't want them to hurt you, then take care of it…And get your own food." Chad's insistence for two years in his adoptive home that he *could* care for himself evaporated. My statements infuriated him.

Chad, enraged, yelled in my face and ear, "Get off your butt and feed me and my baby sister. I can't reach the bottle!" Then he said, fearfully, "But I still love you! I hope you don't go to jail!" He paused and began to process the meaning and finality of his loss. "There's no hope for you! You never change! I give up on you! You brought robbers in the house so that now I can't even get to sleep at night! I am tired of being scared all of the time!"

Putting on my sweater, the signal that I was the therapist again, I asked him if he would like his adoptive mother, who was in the room. He held out his hands to her, keening and grieving. As she held him, he nestled in. Chad told her how his birthmother would sleep while he was hungry and yell at him when he asked for food. "I needed you from the beginning." He wept and she cried with him. As we were concluding, I pointed out her tears. "You were crying for me?" He was incredulous. "You really do care for me, Mom! You really do care." Then he hugged his mother while she rocked him.

Chad experienced his need for adult protection through role-play, and then had those needs sensitively met by his mother. Of interest was the contrast between his presentation at the beginning of the session and at session's end. "I can hardly wait until I can drive and live by myself," he had said. He had swaggered into the waiting room greeting total strangers. That day, as he left with his

> hand in his mother's hand, he said quietly, "Thanks, Deborah.
> It feels better to get all of that out!"

Working with core beliefs, and using the parent effectively, we were able to help Chad over the period of two years. For children like Chad, it is necessary to push through their façade to help the vulnerable self. This is an example of a therapy session that fits into a traditional therapy hour and format.

When children have such fear and rage that they cannot work in this type of format, intensive therapy should be evaluated. Programs that have sturdy reputations in working through trauma tend to be good bets for such children. A psychiatrist, who is experienced with children adopted after neglect, trauma, and prenatal exposure, is a necessity in determining whether medication is appropriate. Children who are developing bipolar disorder often appear to have severe reactive attachment disorder. While children may be suffering from reactive attachment disorder as well, is important to treat both issues, not just one.

Any therapy that intentionally overwhelms, frightens, or threatens children should be avoided. Rather than creating needs that the parents can meet, these approaches further dysregulate (cause emotional and physical turmoil) and over stimulate children. These approaches do not have the rudiments for a secure attachment: sensitive, attuned parenting. The long-term effects: harsh approaches exacerbate traumatic stress or mood disorders in children. Additionally, children with fetal alcohol spectrum disorder will become massively over stimulated as their more fragile neurologic systems are overwhelmed. As sad parents of a child with FASD told me, "He screamed out his rage at us. But, there were no long-term gains. He hugged us at the end of holding, but now holds the experience against us." Their child saw the "therapy" as a form of discipline. It reinforced his opinion of adult caregivers as untrustworthy.

Intensive programs that can help teach children with stress reduction skills, relaxation, and emotional regulation, at the same time that they work with traumatic stress, are good bets when children are severely impacted. If such programs also have an attachment perspective, they tend to be most successful. ATTACh, listed in the resource section, is a good source of referral for severely impacted children. *Nurturing Adoptions: Creating Resilience after Neglect and Trauma* has detailed descriptions of therapy and home routines for children with mild to severe attachment problems.

CHAPTER 4

Grief and Its Effects

Children do not grieve in the same way that adults do. Since their grief process tends to proceed in stops and starts, it can slip past a parent's attention that their child is grieving. In my practice I find that both parents and I are amazed that sometimes what we thought was a child's true personality turns out to be an unfinished grief process. After progress on grief issues we have had occasion to declare, "This child can focus!" This chapter describes children's grief and a parent's role in assisting children so that they move through grief, as opposed to getting stuck in it. The chapter goes on to describe and suggest help for the grief issues that may arise for parents themselves in parenting challenging children.

Why Do Children Grieve?

Everyone grieves after losing a person he loves. Most parents reading this material have children who were attached to and then lost another caregiver. The normal reaction to the loss of that caregiver is grief. Even if children have left an untenable home life or inadequate parents they will grieve the loss of the caregiver. Children who *wished* to escape an untenable home life or their inadequate parents will grieve longer. It is always harder to grieve losses that include ambivalent feelings towards the person lost. It is especially hard to sort out losses that include ambivalent feelings towards a parent. Guilt and confusion complicate the process of grief. Because children think concretely rather than abstractly, it is hard for them to figure out their conflicting feelings.

Children who are under the age of six have not completed their identities as separate from their parents. They still need their parent in order to feel complete. When children lose a parent to whom they were attached before the age of six, the loss of the child's parent is a loss of part of the child's perception of himself.

When they have lost parents, a major task for children is to find a way to hold onto the positive parts of the parents' identities. In doing so, they regain parts of their own identities. Another major task for these children runs in a parallel way. Children must find ways to distance themselves from the negative parts of their parents' identities.

Former parent figures become shadow figures remaining in the adopted or fostered person's life. These figures can be benevolent and accepting, or they can be threatening and rejecting. Good grief work helps children to retain the positive wishes the parent had for them, helping them to understand negative experiences as an aspect of the parents' functioning, not as an aspect of their own identity. At critical junctures of life, adopted and fostered people wish for a sense of that first parent figure's (often a birthparent's) approval of them. Some of these junctures include adoption proceedings, a girl's first period, confirmation, first communion, bar mitzvah, receiving a school or sports honor, graduation from high school, wedding day, first baby, first job, or college graduation. The birthparent may still be living, but the child goes through a bereavement process similar to that following the death of someone close. The sorting out of information that is part of grief work renders a parent image for children that is realistic about negatives, but includes good wishes for children for the future. Even in extreme situations, this is usually possible.

A child's grief stages vary somewhat from age to age. The variances are detailed in Chapter 8. There are six classic emotional stages of grief for both children and adults. The first stage is shock. After first hearing the news of a separation, the response is a vigorous "No!" They cannot yet process the loss. The second stage is denial. When children are moved too quickly, they sometimes look unaffected because they are in denial. In the third stage, people in grief "bargain," promising themselves, or those in charge, or God, that they will "be good" if only the outcome will be different. Sometimes, if they are not comfortable with verbal bargaining, children will try to change their behavior. In the fourth stage, mourning sets in. Children are sad, irritable, tearful, disinterested in life, and may regress emotionally. In the fifth stage, grievers integrate their loss with their sense of self. They come to believe that they will have to go on in life without the lost parent. In the sixth stage, they begin to reminisce as a way to hold on to their parent psychologically.

Children who are permanently separated from their parents face a mourning process that is similar to children's reactions to a parent's death. In fact, the parents, with their connection and resources and care, are permanently lost to children. The literature that describes children's reactions to a loss of the parent through death is quite relevant to the population of later-placed adopted children, or children in the foster care system who have lost attachment figures. Robert Pynoos M.D. described necessary factors for supporting children's healthy grieving (1997.). Grief can be supported by providing the following:

- information about the loss,
- assistance in reality testing. Most children want to deny certain things,
- assistance in talking about their feelings,
- help in determining what part they played in the loss, (Young children are so egocentric that they are almost always stuck here.)
- permission and encouragement to share their feelings about the person lost to them, and
- presence of a consistent adult, whom they trust, supporting their mourning.

Ways to help children with grief from loss of attachment figures are included throughout this chapter. However, there are other important reasons, beyond the loss of a parent figure, why children grieve.

Children may grieve for themselves after they have been maltreated. After they work through trauma issues, they move into deep sadness, comprehending the terrible things that happened to them as innocents. They grieve the image of themselves as undamaged. If they have brothers or sisters who have also been maltreated, they grieve the maltreatment of their siblings. After placements, they also grieve for the lost potential of their birthparent in the role of parent. If their birthparent is deteriorating, they grieve her humiliating, painful descent. Maltreated children grieve for their lost belongings and lost homes. When placed separately, they may grieve living with their birth siblings. They lose a shared frame of reference when placed away from birthfamily members. Mental baby pictures, retained by birthfamily and shared in storytelling, are often scattered and lost in the moves.

Children moving from other cultures grieve the loss of their culture, food, and first language. They grieve the ease of growing up, uninterrupted, in one culture. Children who are ethnically dissimilar to their parents grieve the natural way that racial competence is transmitted to them by parents of the same race. These factors are discussed in Chapter 6 in more detail.

When adopted children have not been maltreated or placed past infancy, they still grieve at normal stages for the loss of the opportunity to live with their birthparents. Because this subject has been well described in other books, the reader is referred to the Resource List for more information on this particular topic.

Children's Grief Reactions

Parents' Roles in Assisting Children through Grief

Children do not have the emotional strength to grieve alone. They need the reassurance of a sensitive adult who will supply the emotional energy to see them through the grief process. Adults usually do their grief work without breaks, but, even with support, children tend to grieve with stops and starts. Children get "stuck" in grief if they lose the adults who are their sources of comfort and emotional energy. Children get stuck in grief when the grief work includes traumatic separation; children are terrified when thinking about their lost parent, and the last traumatic scene with that parent. When children get stuck, they can "yo-yo" for years, approaching and then avoiding their loss. This is a pathological grief reaction.

It is important for children to be encouraged to grieve and to be supported while they do so in order that they may regain the emotional availability to attach to others, normalize their lives, and enjoy their childhoods.

Recently I worked with a Russian adoptee who still believed, after six years in this country, that she was going back to Russia soon. She planned to meet her birthparents and then to decide whether to live with them. In spite of the facts that she no longer could speak the language and that she had been relinquished in a very clear way, she maintained this magical style of thinking, bargaining about her loss. She had not begun her grief work in order to mourn her losses and accept her American family.

In another typical case, I saw a child in therapy who had weathered two therapists, a therapy intern, and three foster care moves. The child was unimproved by the grief and loss therapy or efforts of foster parents. The losses and attachment breaks had multiplied, with the child still lacking an emotionally committed person to help him start and finish grieving.

Adoptive parents are regularly finding themselves as the first committed person who is capable of helping their child through grief. Dr. Karolynn Siegel (1997) suggests three major factors that help a child through mourning:

1. There needs to be a competent adult to provide support and care for the child. This adult cannot be too preoccupied with his own grief.
2. The child needs to be in an environment in which the child feels able to express painful or conflicting thoughts, feelings, and fantasies.
3. Stability and consistency need to be maintained in the child's environment.

The list is a stunning one, since in the process of moving children into safer homes we are often prone to eliminate all of these factors, at least temporarily. It is only after children have gotten to know and trust their parents that they finally have someone who will supply the emotional energy for them to process losses from prior to placement.

Parents tend to do a great job of welcoming children into families. But, in balance they need to recognize the need for children to grieve. Parents too readily "pooh pooh" their children's belief that they themselves or their behaviors or needs are the cause of separation from birthparents. It is more helpful to acknowledge children's sadness and fear and to use children's questions to invite discussion. Parents need to hear what children are thinking in order to support them emotionally and to help them test reality. An example is in the case of Christopher, a four-year-old adopted after having had good care by his birthmother.

After adjusting to his parents for a few months, Christopher confided that he had caused his removal and placement. In doing so, he was making a clear request for parental emotional support and reality testing. His parents replied that it must worry him. Taking time with him, they sat down. They normalized his reaction by saying that any child would worry about feeling that he caused a placement. They wondered how he had come to such a conclusion. He explained that he had misbehaved for the day-care provider, so that she had called his mother home from work. His birthmother had warned him that she could miss no more work. He had continued to act out at day care, and was eventually placed for adoption.

By taking him seriously, parents could supply other facts, balancing this boy's picture. Parents described his birthmother's earlier interest in infant adoption, her desire for a father for him, and her renewed interest in adoption months before he acted out in day care. Christopher wished that he had not acted up, but decided that his responsibility was teeny. As a result he felt unburdened. He admitted that he had tried the same behavior since the placement, but with a different outcome—an involuntary naptime.

A further discussion occurred, with parents talking about good things that Christopher had done with his birthmother. He remembered ways that he had tried to help. He cried after the discussion, with parents able to dry his tears.

Christopher's example describes some essentials of parental assistance through grief. Christopher's parents supplied emotional support, information about the loss, and assistance with reality testing. These help a child to move through grief.

Parents may need to form an alliance with a mental health professional in order to do grief work. In those cases, parents are still supplying emotional support. The therapist and the parents share roles. The therapist holds responsibility for bringing up difficult issues at a pace that is helpful to a child. Often the therapist uses the parent to provide comfort for their child. An example of this partnering between parent, child, and therapist in moving through grief is seen in Catherine' case.

Catherine came in to see me at age eight, still wishing for placement back with her birth mother. In spite of two years of therapy, with play and family therapy, her presenting symptoms were still loss and trauma. The grief work was only started after she did some attachment work with her foster-adopt mother. Catherine naturally moved into grief work when she felt close and supported. Catherine got the emotional support from her mother to talk about leaving her birthmother. Interestingly, it was not with the second move away from her birthmother, at age five, that she began her story. It was instead with the first move, when she was three. She had still not processed the first move. For five years, she had only been going through the motions in her family relationships.

Catherine shared about her move from her home at age three. She described what the room looked like when she left it the last time, how she felt, where she stood, and why she moved. Catherine cried. Rather than having someone talk to her, she told her own story, with feelings. She appealed for help with the parts of her story that did not make sense. Some of the parts neither the foster-adopt mother, nor I, understood. The foster-adopt mother researched, made calls, and found answers. Rather than have the mother feed the answers to me in therapy, I appealed to the mother's expertise in therapy. As a result, Catherine saw her mother as sensitive, powerful, and approachable. While not all of her questions were answered, many were.

While she did need counseling for loss and trauma, Catherine needed emotional security, named "Mom," first. Secondly, she needed a commitment in therapy that neither her mother nor I would leave her in the midst of the grieving process. I made some commitments to Catherine at the beginning of treatment that I would start and complete her counseling.

Emotional Withdrawal

Grieving children tend to be emotionally withdrawn. They are limited in their emotional availability to attach. It is important to warn prospective parents that children will not supply the majority of work on attachment. Until children get support to move through grief, they do not have the emotional readiness to pick up attachment cues well. Similarly, children who are grief-stricken are at risk for bonding and attachment failures with their parents. The risk is especially great if children shut their parents out of the roles of providers of emotional support, guidance, and nurture.

A complicating factor affecting attachment and grief is how to address the finality of the loss of a parent. In moving through grief, there needs to be a clear way to present the loss as permanent. In foster care situations, there is often a last visit with a birthparent who says things to show the child how important or lovable they are. Instead, the statements can make it difficult for the child to accept the loss. If a prior parent says, "No one can ever really separate us," or, "Goodbye for now," a child can be left clinging to a hope. It is necessary for professionals to help in guiding the "goodbye visit" so that it really is a goodbye. Professionals say directly that it is the last visit and that the child is going to be joining a new family. Prepared birthparents who are able to see past the court process will often give their children wishes for a good future. Birthparents who have met the foster-adopt family have sometimes encouraged their children that the new home is a good home for them. If this last visit has been confusing, it helps to have a debriefing session with the therapist immediately after the visit so that children can understand the limitations on future contact. Any continuing communication contract can be briefly described to children with references to actual paperwork.

In international adoption, children who are grieving birthparents regularly fantasize that their birthparents were separated from them through some mistake. Because they think that it is so obvious that birthparents are not intending to return, adults may fail to explain the finality of their children's loss. Children find it hard to bond to current parents when they are still not certain whether or not they will be returning to previous parents. Conversations to correct misperceptions often seem brutally blunt.

Irina talked about her belief that her birthmother would have realized her mistake and returned for Irina as the reason that Irina did not want to stay in North America. Using facts, I described that the orphanage and her birthparent's home were in the same town. In her five years in the orphanage, she had never had a visit from either birthparent. She had never had a single visitor prior to her adoption. Irina recalled these events as factual. With tears running down her face she said, "So how can I forgive her for leaving me in that place?" Her grief from her life story had been forestalled as long as she denied facts. Now, facing those facts, her grief was real.

Factual information about a loss is an important part of moving through grief. In therapy, it is common to find some denial about certain parts of the loss story. Sometimes if parents are attempting to tell facts, children will perceive this as a loyalty conflict between birthparents and adoptive or foster parents.

Recently, I consulted with a social worker who was moving a young child into an adoptive home. The little girl was leaving a nurturing and competent birthmother. When I asked how the caseworker was telling this little girl that she was being permanently placed, it turned out that no one was accepting this responsibility. The birthparent's plan was to say, "Good-bye," and have someone distract her daughter as she sneaked out the back door.

This would have left the adoptive parents to try to explain the situation. Of course, their explanation would have caused pain and loyalty conflicts for this child, as she was in the process of transferring her attachment. When she better understood the situation that would be imposed on the adoptive parents by default, the social worker took on the responsibility.

It is important to note that in this situation all parties were attempting to do their best. Long-term though, it is most helpful to give the child a sense of finality. Adults tend to shy away from giving information that is painful to children, so they need to remain reality-based in their commitment to do what it actually helpful for children. Even in open adoptions it is important to say that the child's home will change, the name will change, the day-to-day parents change, and so forth.

Irritability and Oppositional Behaviors

Grieving children are known for their irritability. They are grouchy and hard to live with. Grieving children do not want to please or to be pleasing. They are constantly asking for parents to change the environment in some way so that they feel better. However, when the parents make the changes, children still feel bad. Nothing seems right to the grieving child. This exacerbates attachment issues. It is hard to move towards meeting children's needs and feeling in tune when children are saying that nothing feels right.

Children who are moved quickly and/or after traumatic situations, are prone to complicated bereavement, or pathologic grief. Methods for parents to help their children through grief and ideal moving schedules and discussions to prevent pathologic grief are described in *Nurturing Adoptions: Creating Resilience after Trauma and Neglect.*

Why Do Parents Grieve?

The pattern for reacting to and dealing with grief is the same for adults as it is for children. They will experience a series of emotional stages— shock and surprise, denial, anger, bargaining, sadness and resolution. The experience that triggers adults' grief, however, is not the same as the experience about which their children may be grieving.

Unresolved Grief Related to Childhood Experiences

A parent walks through a summary of his childhood while parenting. In the process of determining how to parent, parents reference how their parents did, or did not, parent effectively. Parents who believe themselves to be quite effective are sometimes put to the test in parenting. The following example illustrates a common comeuppance to superiority over one's own parents:

Jim came home tired, but looking forward to an evening with his five-year-old son, Brandon, and his wife. As he entered the house, he heard a voice like his mother-in-law's coming from the bathroom. In his humble opinion, his mother-in-law was mean and self-righteous. She caused emotional pain for his wife through her critical barbs. He enjoyed the 2,000-mile distance between their homes. As he followed the voice to its source, he had an unpleasant stir of apprehension. Opening the bathroom door, he saw a bar of soap hanging out of Brandon's mouth. Brandon' s tears were mixed into a bubbly froth. His wife, usually a kind woman, had a rigid, angry body stance as she held Brandon over the sink. As Brandon wiggled, she smacked at his rear. Looking at the scene, Jim knew issues that he had been attempting to duck for the last six months since placement had come to a head.

"Honey, I'll give you a hand here," he said. "Please go downstairs." He did his best to keep his voice light, since he was so emotional. He knew that there was no way on earth that he would permit his son to be parented in this heavy-handed manner.

Jim's wife cried that evening after Jim described how he saw her parenting. She said, "I always acted like I had a great childhood. Actually, it was hard to please my mother. I am now acting just like her when I cannot control Brandon. Jim, I do not know how to parent in a normal way. And when I sympathize with Brandon, I am sad for myself. Parenting Brandon is the most important thing in my life, and I stink at it. My mother told me that I would be a lousy parent."

In the example above, disciplining her child had re-opened painful childhood issues. This is typical of all parenting to a degree. Many parents find that parenting a child gives them an opportunity to re-work their own childhood issues. It can be a satisfying process, if the issues are not overwhelming for parents or children. When adding an infant to the family through birth or adoption, children's issues are usually not overwhelming. Parents also have lead-time during which they can anticipate and prepare for harder issues like separation, sexuality, peer pressure, etc. When adopting older children, the emotional issues tend to be challenging and are accompanied by little lead-time.

At times, parents do not want to face their own problems. It becomes more convenient to blame a child. While it is true that difficult children can tax parents to the limit, it is also true that difficult parents can tax children to the limit. If children are having adjustment issues, parents may find them to be convenient excuses for punitive parenting.

Parents with childhood issues can work on their issues simultaneously to parenting. Parents can get therapy devoted to their own work. They can work either with their own therapist, or with the therapist seeing the child. This tends to support the adult in parenting well, even while their emotional underpinnings are receiving needed attention.

Parents who have childhood issues may also find that they dissociate. For example, parents with issues of abuse, and especially sexual abuse, may find that they are dissociating when parenting children who have been abused. They sometimes discover that they are losing information. They begin to worry that they are losing their minds. Parents who cannot remember and retain pertinent information about children's histories and about children's behaviors should consider whether this lapse could be due to connections with their own childhood issues. When children become the age that the parent was at the time of abuse, the pressure becomes especially great. Parents sometimes find themselves trying to protect a child instead of working through their own lack of protection as children.

Some parents find themselves replaying the "good cop, bad cop" style that their parents used. Of course, this is dysfunctional. But for parents having a hard time connecting with children, playing a role as the mushy confidante can seem appealing. Sometimes parents would rather be manipulated than unified. In portraying one parent as the "bad cop," parents are telling their child that one parent is insensitive, unfair, and inadequate. The parenting has to be balanced. The logical conclusion for the child is that the tough parent is not safe for attachment. At the same time, the parent who is the "soft touch" does not seem strong or effective to a child. If children can manipulate parents, they know that they are themselves in charge, not their parents. This makes them anxious. It is for these good reasons that parents should avoid "good cop, bad cop" parenting.

Parents whose own parents were too rigid tend to see roles as either being rigid or unstructured. They like to choose the unstructured, since it feels loving. Of course, lack of structure does not bring out the best in children. It is a harmful parenting style for children who need a lot of structure to succeed. Almost without exception, children who are described in this book need high nurture along with high structure. If they want to assure themselves that they are parenting in a kind way, not a rigid way, parents can look hard at the nurturing they are doing along with their structure.

Unresolved Grief Related to Family Building

When parents are helping children with grief work, they tend to feel grief themselves. Parents who care about their children feel some of their feelings. The transfer of feelings as attachment progresses is described below in the case of a newly placed three-year-old, Ivy, and her five-year-old brother, Ben.

The foster-adopt parents were matter-of-fact during the train-ing preceding the placement. Both parents were experienced. The mother was an organized, unflappable woman who listened in-tently while the father took notes for them both. The parents pre-pared unemotionally. But when it was time for placement, the father began to glow. The mother looked like a nurturing earth mother. Her eyes were gentle, her face soft. Attachment began through a good visitation schedule, which also permitted a nice growth in relationship between the other children in the family. About the third week into the visits, Ivy began to grieve. Ben and Ivy were carried constantly by their new parents. Ivy's head barely emerged from her mother's ample bosom. The parents' faces re-flected love and concern.

The mother came into their placement agency with tears. "This is so hard for children," she said. "When we thought about non-infant adoption, we never realized how difficult it was for children. Last night, Ben and Ivy were both missing their foster mother. We moved them into our bed. When the older kids came in to see what the problem was, we told them. Then they started crying. For a while, there were seven of us crying in bed. I don't think that we took over Ben and Ivy's grief, but we felt really bad for what they were going through."

The family in the example above embraced the children's true feel-ings about the placement process. They did not try to avoid their children's grief issues. They also modeled to their other children an acceptance of sadness as a part of life, and a part of their siblings' life story.

When parents have not worked through their own grief, it is much more difficult for them to accompany children into grief work. Rather than having the strength to support children in grief, they find their own unresolved grief facing them. This gives them a disincentive to allow their children to grieve. They give many clues to children not to feel or express grief. Children pick up the clues and internalize the grief instead, which leads to anxiety or depression. Or, they express the grief outwardly in aggressive behavior that looks unrelated to grief. In the following example, a child was anxious and depressed about a move for years. She was reluc-tant to go to her mother, confiding in me about her loss issues.

The mother held a party for the adoption of her daughter just eight days into the visitation schedule of a new placement which was following a disrupted adoption. Her daughter, aged five, was confused and disoriented. She smiled for the camera and thanked the many friends for their gifts. The former adoptive parents were present for a period of time. The expectation was that the girl should be happy. In fact, she was in shock. At the age of sixteen, she describes the party as one of the worst experiences of her life. This type of denial of grief is typical when parents do not want to face the grief of a child. The parent in this example said, "I was never allowed to cry. They called me a bawl baby, and told me to stop feeling sorry for myself. They told me that if life gives you lemons, make lemonade. So, when she acted sad, I gave a party. I think that I paid for that for the next three years."

Parents with infertility issues will often describe that their loss over infertility is triggered by their child's loss. If they have worked to resolve their infertility loss, the new wave of grief is not overwhelming. Sometimes parents say that they thought themselves to have more fully resolved their grief. At the time of placement, they realized that their placement is not the same as giving birth to the child who would have resembled them biologically. They love their child, but it causes them to reflect again on the loss of a biologic child.

One woman said, "I love my son, and would not love him more if he were a biological child. When he was placed, we finally had the baby I longed for. When we faced the losses from his exposure to alcohol, I felt sad again over infertility. I thought of him as he would have been without alcohol exposure. I thought of my loss of the little redheaded child our infertility prevented us from having."

Other families grieve their infertility as part of their adjustment to their child's special needs. They reflect that they adopted a difficult child only after they encountered infertility. At times they wonder what possessed them to move from wanting to parent a biologic infant to deciding to adopt an abused and neglected child with many issues. They wish that they had the easier life that they believe that biologic parenting probably would have provided. Infertility was painful, and their adoption experience is also painful. It seems that something should have been easier. Sometimes parents wish that they could go back in time, remaking a decision. They wish that they could have given themselves more time to make a decision easier to live out. They describe having moved quickly to adopt so that they could be parents. They rue having moved so quickly, since the pain from infertility remains present, and their adoption experience is difficult. Of course, this impacts the amount of energy and enthusiasm that parents bring to family building.

A healthy family-building perspective was described by a family who prepared for their placement. They said, "We waited for about a year after the last infertility treatments. Then we started thinking about how we would parent. I thought that adoption of a sibling pair, adopted after we all knew each other, would fit for us."

Another parent's revealed grief had nothing to do with infertility…

Candice had always expected to meet a man and to build a family with him. She developed her friendships, career, and character…and remained single. She determined at least *not* to be childless! After adopting, she found that some of the sadness of being single was just as poignant. At soccer games, some of the couples talked to her about getting together for play dates with her daughter…but they invited other couples to dinner. She missed having a partner so that she did not have to be "on" all of the time as a parent. She knew that she was fulfilled as a parent, but she became exhausted by her daughter's antics at times. She wanted a break that was built-in. Also, she often wished that she did not have to worry alone about her daughter's future. It would be a comfort to have someone else to be thinking ahead! When her daughter grieved for her birthmother and siblings, Candice felt that she was nobody's plan "A." She comforted and soothed her daughter, but later felt rejected and overlooked. After expressing herself to relatives and close friends, she was delighted to hear how valued she was. "I guess I should not have to need to hear that they think I am wonderful," she said, "but it sure helps."

When single parents have no breaks, except for work, which actually means no breaks, it is common that they think daily about the missing life partner who *should* be there picking up the load. Problem solving so that single parents get breaks, time with friends, and help with the household does not make the loss of a life partner disappear. It does make it feel more bearable. In the situation of Candice above, her brother realized how stretched she had become. He had his niece over after school once weekly for an overnight, giving Candice an evening with friends. Candice's father began to come over once a week to do the yard. Candice found that her daughter did make progress with grief, and, eventually, she herself did, as well. She made it a point to watch out for her own isolation, knowing that it only exacerbated the disappointment of never meeting a special someone.

Grief triggered by unmet expectations of the newly expanded family

Parents have a mental picture of the "wished for" family. It may be vague or well-formed, but it exists. After a placement, the anticipation of the dream family is supplanted by commitment to the real family. If the emotional gratification is great, often parents rarely think of the dream family. But even in the best of circumstances, the dream may emerge occasionally.

Gregg, an adoptive father of four children said, "I miss discussing ideas and books with our children. I had anticipated reading certain children's books aloud. Three of our children struggle with auditory processing. This is minor. We are a close family. All of the children have good character."

In more extreme cases, parents make commitments to children, love them deeply, but find that they grieve for the type of child they had always wanted to parent.

One educator said, "I always saw myself as teaching my children. I wanted to help them with homework, and to enjoy the learning process. My son and daughter spent a long time in the orphanage, and have suffered permanent developmental delay. They hate anything having to do with school. They fight me over homework. Left to themselves, they would have no life of the mind. This is one loss that I cannot seem to get over. It hurts all of the time. It is probably worse since neither child is compliant, and my husband and I have marriage problems. I saw myself parenting a sweet little girl who loved to learn, and who acted femininely. My daughter is a jock. I am proud of her, I love her, and I go to every game. But I cannot get over how differently this has turned out." In this situation, the parent was living a life quite different from her expectations. It helped her to have some counseling so that she could put together her feelings of loss with her sense of her life's purpose and ways to gain fulfillment. After thinking through what fulfilling choices were open to her, she began to volunteer as a story time reader at her library. She felt more at peace with her parenting situation when she set and met some of her own priorities.

If parents unknowingly adopt a special needs child, grief follows. It parallels the process of any parents by birth who learn that their children have special needs. The difference is that some adoptive parents have some additional angst over the part that they played in gathering what may now seem like inadequate information prior to the adoption.

Part of parents' grief process includes the loss of lifestyle enjoyed by parents of typical children. Parents have a process through which they determine whether or not they can parent a special needs child. Especially when children are found to have a permanent disability requiring intensive parenting, like Fetal Alcohol Syndrome, parents wonder whether they can recommit for the long haul. Some parents opt out. Others recommit, usually after some commiserating about how they missed their child's difficulties during the pre-placement phase. This is part of the grief process, bargaining about the loss.

Most parents adopting children with neglect and abuse issues expect to make their children's lives happier than they were before. After adoption, it can be deflating and then depressing to parent an unhappy child. Parents find life difficult with a child who will not "happy-up." Parents of negative children can feel defeated by their child's irritability, negativity, and withdrawal, especially if the children do not permit their parents to comfort them.

A major problem parents face is the relationship between siblings, when the new family member is not compatible with siblings. While waiting for placement, siblings-to-be are often eager for a brother or sister. If the new brother or sister subsequently treats them poorly, it is a source of grief for them, as well as for their parents. Especially if the problem is going to be a longer-term adjustment issue, it hurts parents to see their children's pain. If the new family member turns out to have major developmental and emotional issues, the impact on the brothers and sisters can be profound. Some parents grieve the imposition of an intergenerational burden on the other children. They also grieve the loss of the relationship that they dreamed of between the siblings. If, after their grieving, families go on to rebalance healthily, they often report that the adjustments between siblings are far better than they had hoped. They also find resources that diminish the demands on siblings intergenerationally. More on this in Chapter 11.

Parents Revisiting Grief

Most individuals are about one loss behind in their grieving. As parents face a new loss, they are likely to remember the last loss. A parent who grieved her son's special needs became aware of her unfinished grief over a failed relationship. If the subject matter is similar between the losses, topics people thought were resolved become emotionally potent again. A man abused as a child by his father grieved his adopted son's abuse and his own abuse simultaneously.

Parents who are parenting as couples will usually find that their grief processes do not coincide. It is hard for the sad parent to feel understood when the other parent is expressing far less emotion. It is a surprise to couples when their feelings don't match. However, this is typical. As long as one parent does not try to talk the other parent out of his or her feelings, the advantage becomes that at least one parent is feeling well enough to keep the household moving along.

Some parents will remain in denial over a grievous problem until they feel that there is a resource available for their child.

> A child with serious attachment and behavioral issues came into therapy accompanied by the mother and siblings. After some gains in therapy, the father asked to participate. He had some hope for the first time for his daughter, and so he could endure acknowledging the problem. Previously, it had been so painful that he could not risk more pain with a failed approach.

Like the grief staging listed for children above, there are stages in adults' grieving. At first, there tends to be a denial of the problem. A shout of "No!" or "I do not believe it!" is a frequent part of this stage. This does not mean that the topic is really not open for discussion. Instead, it is simply too much to bear.

> A child who was clearly disclosing sexual abuse and had begun acting out sexually at home had a father who could not believe that someone would abuse a young child in an orphanage. Rather than argue, I did a session of therapy behind a viewing mirror, so that the father could watch the session. As his daughter talked to me about the abuse, he wept for his daughter's loss.

It is important for parents to have factual information in order to move past this stage. It is also helpful for parents to know that things can be done to help their children. The loss is named not to label a child, but as a start towards gathering resources helpful to the child and family.

The second stage of grief is technically known as bargaining. In this parenting context, it emerges as hoping or wishing that the loss will not have its expected impact. Parents commonly believe that pertinent statistics will not apply to *their* child.

Thomas was in a specialized classroom at the time of his foster-adopt placement. His parents were excited by his rapid gains when coming into their home. As the months wore on, his social worker described that additional information was emerging about heavy maternal drinking. The long-term nature of exposure was described to the parents. His parents listened, but were disbelieving that Thomas could be like other children. Later, they described that it was hard to believe that they would have less than a lucky outcome. "We just could not imagine our son as affected as the people in the articles," they said. "Somehow, we thought that once he was adopted, we could help him to cope and that it would be not as bad as we feared. Of course, now we know that he has serious learning and judgement problems. We are there to help him cope, but our love cannot undo prenatal brain damage."

The third stage of grief is processing the loss. The losses and emotions around them occur in domains of identity, lifestyle, community acceptance, and roles. At first the feelings are often angry ones, accompanied by a sense of betrayal. Parents may be furious with adoption agencies, orphanage workers, or an unsupportive school.

During this period parents have anxiety about their child's future and their own. They wonder if they can meet the challenges ahead. Many parents think of disrupting the adoption. When two parents are grieving, with one mentioning disruption, it adds further to anxiety. As these various feelings and thoughts are recognized, parents tend to move into a state of sadness, acknowledging the differences between their wishes for their child and their child's reality.

A great deal of quiet time is essential for this processing, even when parents are facing new challenges from a placement. Parents need set apart time to work through thoughts and feelings, or they remain unresolved.

Without grieving time, they move from denial of the loss to being flooded with anxiety and sadness.

Parents who are considering disruption should give themselves a reasonable length of time to consider whether or not they can go on. Usually three months is a time frame that permits parents to make a careful choice. Many parents are so firm in their initial commitment that considering disruption is not part of their grief.

The last stage of grieving is resolution. The loss is accepted. It may be painful, but parents understand how they can go on with life. They integrate the loss with their identity and that of the family. As new information comes, they can incorporate the information into a reasonably accurate picture without feeling overwhelmed by grief to the same extent, for the same length of time. Once the resolution stage is reached, parents can free up their emotional resources for other things.

> For example, the man who cried for his daughter's abuse was able to plan a wonderful vacation for everyone in the family by the next summer. He describes that he is aware that his daughter has been abused, but that he passed through the daily sadness associated with that loss in about three months.

When grief runs awry, parents can get lost in an unremitting sadness. Their grief seems to color the whole world gray. Anxiety hits hard, since losses and their meaning are not yet determined. Often several old losses unite to compromise progress. At that point parents do well to get mental health help for themselves. If clinical depression has developed, sometimes parents need the help of an antidepressant. Therapy is essential, even if antidepressants are used. With the added energy of a therapist, parents can separate losses, grieve losses, and reclaim their lives.

Summary

Grief is part of losing attachment figures. When children are moved, grief is a natural result, regardless of the quality of care given by the parent figure. Only when children have grieved their losses are they fully emotionally available for attachment. However, some attachment work is necessary, even with withdrawn children, so that children will go to the parents to grieve and to receive comfort. Children do not grieve with strangers. They grieve with people who are known to them, sensitive to them, and consistently available to them. They derive their emotional support from adults. Typically, children are drawn into attachment, move into grief work, and then rebound in both joy and attachment.

Grief is also part of parenting children who have pain in their lives. Parents grieve with their children. Parents also grieve for the loss of their own dreams of how their families would function and how their child would develop. The grief process for the family takes information, time, and support. After parents grieve their losses, they have more energy to find appropriate resources for their child and to make a realistic plan for their family.

In the next chapter, trauma is added to the interplay between attachment and grief.

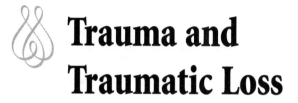

CHAPTER 5

Trauma and Traumatic Loss

When forming attachments, parents and I are often struck by how a child's fear forms a barricade to attachment. Even after attachment is formed, trauma seems to have left its imprint on many layers of children's developing identity—and even on their physiology! Sometimes children's trauma can feel like toxic waste in family life. Understanding trauma, calming traumatized children, reducing trauma's toxicity in children, and moving beyond a trauma-impacted worldview are among the considerable challenges for parents and affected children. Techniques and attitudes that assist in these tasks are described in the rest of this chapter and will be continued in Chapter 9.

What Is Trauma?

Kimberly and Allen did not know a definition for trauma when they met Ginny. But both parents were focused on trauma after six months of placement. They researched to find answers to questions like, "How can she keep going without sleep?" Ginny, at age four, took two hours to go to sleep. She woke up in the night. She was also awake in her bed when parents got up in the morning. She gazed and smiled at strangers. She also smiled as she grabbed toys from her little brother. A sudden noise made Ginny jump and tremble. She either screamed or laughed when someone got hurt.

When they called their caseworker for a referral for help, the caseworker agreed with the parents' assessment, "Our daughter is the poster child for trauma." They added, "We were told that since Ginny was nonverbal, she would have little memory. That is clearly not true. Maybe she can't tell us what happened, but some part of her remembers. Dying is the biggest theme in her play. And what typical four-year-old sneaks a steak knife to bed to protect herself?" These parents identified related symptoms, putting them into a cluster that was telling. It helped them to go get appropriate help.

The following paragraphs give some technical information about trauma, giving parents access to the same information that professionals are using.

Parents find the terms *trauma* or *traumatic event* used precisely by mental health professionals. The American Psychological Association describes a traumatic event as "an event that is outside the range of usual human experience and that would be markedly distressing to almost anyone." (APA, 2000, p.468). In the entire lifetime of people in our culture, about 50 percent of women and about 25 percent of men are traumatized. (The rates are higher in high-crime areas. Women have higher exposure because of their higher rate of sexual assault.) Trauma is followed by specific, high-stress symptoms that have lasting effects on key areas of functioning. Those symptoms are called *posttraumatic stress symptoms*. When mental health professionals use the term *trauma*, it is not used lightly. If parents hear the term, they should catch the implicit information carried with it—that the event has left its indelible mark on their child.

Competent parents in safe communities reduce their children's exposure to traumatic events. However the cocaine and methamphetamine epidemics in North America have dramatically compromised parental competence and community safety. Children today enter care with more exposure to violence, higher rates of abuse, and traumatic levels of neglect. An enormous change in the foster care and adoption field has occurred as these traumatized children enter families.

Children who are adopted internationally are also a changing population. According to statistics from the Immigration and Naturalization Service, the rate of international adoption has increased at least 10 percent for each year since 1992. A decade ago, two thirds of the children adopted internationally came from Korea, a country where children tended to be cared for in foster homes and where they tended to have access to good medical care. Now, more than two thirds of children arrive from institutional care settings in countries with poor nutritional and health care resources. According to Dana Johnson, M.D., a pediatrician with many years of experience working with children adopted internationally, of the children adopted to North America from Eastern Europe, the rate of traumatic exposure is high. In a sample studied by Dr. Johnson, of the 30 percent of children who have several serious problems, trauma was a common denominator (Johnson, 1997).

People who have been traumatized show its impact in four areas: lowered control over regulation of their moods; exaggerated startle response (evidence of overdeveloped "fight or flight" response); emotional numbness; and physical symptoms such as stomach aches or unexplained pain that tie back to trauma. Children demonstrate changed patterns of thinking and specific behaviors associated with trauma—they organize their world as if it were hostile.

- They are hyper-alert.
- They show helplessness in problem-solving.
- They have trouble organizing information.
- They move from hyper-arousal into fighting or aggression; or they move from hyper-arousal into dissociation; or they move from hyper-arousal to panicked recoil.
- They are oversensitive to stressful stimulation. When in a shocked state, they may actually look insensitive.
- They are ashamed of their helplessness, and try to cover it in some way.
- They experience emotional numbing. It is unpleasant, like feeling "dead."

- They have physical pains, with a questionable basis.
- They show a decrease in auditory processing—the ability to understand what is being said—when exposed to reminders of trauma.

When children are first coming into a home, some of the behaviors above can be evident without any trauma. It is normally stressful to adjust to a new family, culture, or language. Within months, parents are able to detect the presence of trauma, even when adopting children for whom they have no history. Over-arousal, dissociation, or both, remain high. Children often begin sharing their fears with parents, especially after a frightening reminder of trauma or nightmare.

Parents of adopted children have a more complicated parenting course today than they used to have, by far. As children come into new families with more complicated trauma histories, parents are contacting their agencies more frequently for referrals to services. Parents regularly describe the surprised reactions of experienced adoption workers to traumas reported by children.

In response to changing populations, foster care and adoption agencies have had to move into high gear, providing post-placement services to deal with more serious mental health needs. Some agencies complain that since their international programs are self-described as independent adoptions in-country, the agency only functions to facilitate. They resist taking on ethical and legal liability. Other agencies do provide post-placement help when asked, but worry about frightening prospective adoptive parents and international connections if they discuss potential problems openly with prospective parents.

Indeed, some prospective parents find that the stories they report of their children's suffering are unwelcome, that connection with parents with similar problems is not provided, and that parents are not supported through their agencies. Other agencies are stepping forward to meet the extra challenges of foster and adoptive children and families by requesting training, learning resources, and providing post-placement help.

Diagnosing Post-Traumatic Stress Disorder

About 30 percent of people exposed to traumatic stress go on to develop a chronic condition known as posttraumatic stress disorder, PTSD.

Since the most important protective factor for children in preventing the development of PTSD is the quality of continuing attachment from the caregiver at the time of trauma, parents reading this book are likely to see their children affected (Perry, 1999, p.5) (Zeanah, 2000, p. 202). The diagnosis of traumatic stress is found in the *Diagnostic and Statistical Manual*, DSM-IV-TR. You will find this diagnostic criteria on page 364-66 in the Appendix, and parents who believe that their children may be suffering from PTSD are encouraged to read that formal definition.

A parent-oriented checklist is as follows:

1. Children have been in an extraordinarily frightening situation that filled them with fear and dread—to the extent that they may not have been able to move or talk.
2. They are having dreams that cause them to wake up in terror. They seem to be recalling parts of a real experience.
3. They have tantrums or shut down in fear over incidents that remind them of the traumatic event.
4. Children complain of someone trying to harm them, and may seem to see that person's face through the window, in a crowd, etc. The "someone" is related to the trauma.
5. They act blank at times, and seem to lose their place in time. They are frightened rather than daydreaming.
6. They rage after being exposed to something that reminds them of the frightening situation—hitting, punching, and seeming to fight for their lives.
7. They have symptoms of being on high alert—not getting asleep easily or sleeping through the night, jumping at sudden noises, watching for clues of danger, concentrating poorly.

It is obvious by looking at this criteria that traumatized children will be demonstrating, rather than discussing, their traumatic exposure. Children who have been traumatized may not be able to recall events in a descriptive fashion. Often, however, the memories are stored in what is called *behavioral memory* (Brown, Scheflin, Hammond, 1998, p.21). That means that they will act out relevant events, with little understanding of what they are doing, or why.

A little boy, age four-and-a-half, who had been moved at eighteen months of age after he wandered for a time on a busy highway and had experienced several near misses with cars, played out the event three years later. He put a boy doll on the road, brought a policeman, and showed himself being taken away to a new home. He played this repeatedly, but could not "remember" this as part of his placement story. He said that he did not know why this "picture" kept coming into his head. "I hate the picture and the feeling," he said.

Children who are traumatized after having a background of deprivation and neglect are particularly vulnerable to developing posttraumatic stress disorder (PTSD). Rather than "being used to it," in a way that would show resilience or coping, children and adults are over-sensitized. They become even more stressed by additional stressors and traumatic reminders. An exaggerated startle response in children is one example of this over-sensitization of the body to new stress after previous trauma. It is important to note that *extreme deprivation and neglect are earlier traumas.* (Briere, 1992; Friedman, 1997).

Children's emotional states are disregulated and poorly moderated. In children who had early trauma, those memories tend to be stored in the part of the brain that was developing at the time. When they recall the memory, they recall the memory in the same way a child would, which is in the same overwhelmed way that they stored it, and with little cognitive input. When very small children are hungry, they are all the way hungry. Their brains have not decentralized as an adult's brain or older child's brain is capable of doing. Adults can get a little hungry and de-centralize that feeling successfully. Children who have reminders of the traumatic event often have a difficult time due to this overwhelming way of remembering. Children remember traumatic events in much the same centralized way that they were stored. (van der Kolk, 1994). They often respond to day-to-day events in this same overwhelmed and poorly modulated way.

Children may suddenly lose their place in time and space, responding to some reminder of trauma as if the trauma is happening in the moment. This is a result of physiological changes to the body post-trauma. "For some individuals with PTSD the sympathetic nervous system appears to over respond to a variety of stimuli even many years after having experienced an overwhelming trauma. The individual continues to act psychologically and biologically as if the danger is still present even through the event may have occurred in the distant past." (Southwick, Yehuda, 1997). Children are at particular risk if they do not get help in de-sensitization from the reminders of trauma, or if they are not buffered from high stress situations.

How Trauma Impedes Attachment

In order to guard against more negative, traumatic events, children organize their world as if it were hostile. One of the ways that they defend themselves is through friendliness to strangers. Rather than believing in the safety provided by their parents, they feel at the mercy of any adult around. Children know that it goes better for them if adults are favorably disposed to them. Children control the total strangers by acting overly friendly and charming.   Their indiscriminate friendliness can fool parents during pre-placement visits. Parents think that they are seeing a child who is open to a family. Instead, after placement, parents find that the charming smile masks fear.

Trauma causes a child to be certain that more bad things will happen in the future, and that adults will be ineffective in preventing these insults. Children who are thinking about life in this way are not likely to trust new parents. When they do relax and begin to depend on parents, they are afraid to risk trust for very long at a time.

Trauma causes numbing of emotions, as well as rapid shifts in emotions. Children are either not feeling much, or they are feeling far too much. This makes it difficult for children to receive the signals of love, appreciation, and care that their parents are conveying. If they are having night terrors, they become stiff, cool, or explosive, literally overnight. In order to avoid these unpleasant extremes, children may try to use dissociation. Or, they try to control much of their environment—parents are part of their landscape. When children are putting all of their energies into control, they are not working on trusting or attachment.

Even though children are not as responsive after having been traumatized, attachment work still comes before trauma work. There is some evidence that attachment helps to calm some of the over-aroused parts of children's brains, which in turn helps them with trauma. Eight-year-old Melody's story follows a typical order: work on attachment, then on trauma, and finally on grief.

Melanie came in with her mother to see me. Her life included having witnessed a lethal assault, having been sexually assaulted, and having functioned as the scapegoat in her biologic family. She had had a failed adoption, as well. She did not have the cognitive resources to work on trauma, yet was having flashbacks. At home, her mother had learned many ways to control Melanie's frequent, oppositional acts. However, Melanie stayed dissociative, cool, and remote, unless she was screaming. In our first sessions, I told her that before working on trauma, it seemed best to make her a happier, more comfortable girl. Melanie liked the notion that we should help her to be happier.

I told Melanie that her job was to get close to Mom. I compared her to a gecko in the room, who got too chilly to be able to move. I told her that she needed to bask in her mother's love, like the gecko would bask on a warm rock. Looking at a thermometer, Melanie decided that she would like to feel nice and warm inside instead of still and cold. Her mother hugged her, snuggled her, tickled her, and joked with her until Melanie felt nice and warm—about 82 degrees, she decided. When Melanie got chilly, still, and distant at home, Mom used their common language. "You look about 55 degrees, Melanie," she would say. "Come warm up!" Her mother began to rock Melanie twice daily. They dropped all outside activities in order to slow life down. Mom rubbed Chapstick on Melanie's lips, which she loved. It helped Melanie's motivation that she had to call my voice mail to report her progress on a nightly basis.

Only after Melanie learned to relax and depend on her mother, was she able to talk about the horrible events that were on her mind. She needed a person of refuge to walk through the trauma with her. She also had to be certain that she would not feel stuck in the endless remembering of trauma. She felt that her mother could be trusted to help her calm down, move through, and endure her trauma work. As Melanie worked on trauma, she reached for her mother automatically, knowing from experience that her mother was there for her. She grieved for the lack of protection that she had gotten from her birthparents. After the trauma work was largely finished, Melanie showed an expansion in her attachment and in her outside interests. The screaming absolutely stopped.

Melanie's mother developed competence in helping her daughter to overcome trauma. She learned techniques and timing in the sessions. After all, the mother, not the therapist, was available at 2:00 A. M. when Melanie had nightmares. Melanie's mother learned to note a particular look as Melanie was getting frightened. She intervened quickly, pulling Melanie close. As they sat together, initially she could not feel much or talk much. Within about ten minutes of closeness and comfort, her feelings would begin to return, as well as her speech. She described in a halting way what triggered a memory for her. She hid her face in her mother's shoulder and listened to reassurances until she felt better.

After six months, Melanie found that she was able to reassure herself most of the time. She breathed deeply, as if sitting with her mother, and used the same words. When she discovered this, she asked to go on her first overnight at her girlfriend's house.

Meeting basic needs for comfort is always a good place both to begin and to come back to when helping children through trauma. Slowing down the pace of life is key. Traumatized children already have more than they can deal with. Reducing outside exposure helps them. Some children are so accustomed to a high level of arousal that they crave constant, excessive stimulation. This is not conducive to healing from trauma. More on this is covered in Chapter 9.

When Trauma Is Part of the Child's Identity

Some people think that something about them keeps drawing trauma to them. They confuse the life event with their own identities. This is easy to do, since trauma is so insidious in the way in which it distorts beliefs. An example is Ahmed's case. He looks successful on the surface, but is a miserable teen due to his belief that trauma comes to people he loves:

Ahmed was working hard cleaning the home. A 4.0 student in the seventh grade, Ahmed had finished his homework. He avoided his parents after cleaning. His sister, whom he loved dearly, had left for a school program at a boarding school. Her learning differences had resulted in school problems. In the year before she left, the two of them had engaged in ugly verbal battles.

Amhed came into therapy trying to understand the meaning of his birthparents' traumatic deaths. The losses intersected with a new loss. He was afraid to grieve the loss that his sister's school placement represented, and the older losses that it brought up. He could not bring himself to lean on his parents. "I'm afraid that the stress will be too much for my parents," He said. "I've been having dreams that I will lose them too. Everyone just sees the outward person, the son of respected parents. No one else is like me." As we talked, he described how stress had killed his aunt, who was his caregiver after his birthparents' deaths. "I'm the kind of person that these things happen to. Doesn't it seem like more than a coincidence that every parent figure has died? I don't want to die, but I probably will, too."

When his mother came into the therapy session, she assured him that she was strong, physically and emotionally. Ahmed gave lip service, but was a long way from accepting this as a new truth. As he left, he talked about his plans for the afternoon—he planned to work around the house. "Well, Ahmed," I said, "orphans have to work." At that, Ahmed stopped, and said through tears, "I don't like that...I don't like hearing that!" His mother said, "Then just be our son. You do not need to earn your keep! We want to take care of you." She pulled him close to her as he broke into sobs. "This has been hard on you, too," she said, referring to his sister's leaving.

"Ahmed wonders if it should have been he who left," I mentioned.

"Just because he was adopted and she was born to us?" His mother said. "Of course not. I love you both. You are my son—always. Just like she is my daughter—always."

"Didn't Ahmed go to boarding school?" I asked.

"Yes, Ahmed, you went to boarding school after your aunt got cancer. In that country, children whose families had money often sent their children to learn languages, like English. You only came home occasionally until we adopted you."

"I am so mixed up," he said sadly. "I keep thinking that because of me you will die, or that I am the one who goes to boarding school, not her. I think that I was somehow to blame for my parents' and aunt's deaths."

In the vignette above, Ahmed's identity includes trauma's contamination. His beliefs include the following...

- He believes that the traumatic event occurred because of something about him. "I am the kind of person that things like this happen to."

- He connects cause and effect between events that are unrelated, except in his history. His boarding school placement and his sister's were for different reasons. He has exaggerated the impact of the latter, expecting disaster.

- He has guilt and shame about the traumatic events, in part because he sees himself as causative.

- He is looking for omens, attempting to control the out-of-control events in his life.

- He experiences a "nothing feeling." It is a feeling that makes him feel empty and awful.

Because Ahmed's trauma happened later in his childhood, and because he had good nurturing after his losses and his adoption, and because he had had a course of therapy during primary school, his brain had been reasonably calmed and well-organized until the recent trauma triggers. Trauma triggers are reminders of the trauma that cause an emotional response similar to the one at the time of the trauma. In his case, his impression that he is beginning to resemble his deceased father turned out to be a trigger, as did his sister's departure for boarding school.

In identifying with his biological relatives, Ahmed was identifying with their tragically foreshortened lives. He believed that the same fate awaited him. He needed help in being able to identify with parts of his parents' identities, but to form distance from traumatic parts. Sweet words to him began with this phrase, "You are different from your birthparents in these ways." They came via another biologic relative. As Ahmed was able to express his feelings, he felt grief. He said that this felt better than the "nothing feeling."

Children who have lost parents traumatically process ways in which they feel vulnerable by identifying with birthparents. These must be balanced by ways to hold onto their birthparents.

A child who finished her work completed an exquisite dance with lyrics to describe her relationship and life with her birthmother. This dance was shown in therapy, and to her father and mother exclusively. It allowed her to accept both her birthmother's death as well as her continuing approval and influence on her life. In her therapy, she was permitted to work through which parts of her birthmother's story she needed to embrace, and from which parts she needed to distance herself. The result allowed her a peace that gave her more authentic emotionality. She described herself as being able to get rid of the "nothing feeling," most of the time. She believed that she would live, carrying an intact image of her birthmother in her mind. She was free to attach, develop, and relax.

When Your Child's Trauma Triggers Your Own

When parents have themselves been traumatized, they usually think that their experience will assist them in understanding a child's trauma. Parents do not usually anticipate the re-emergence of their own issues. In a confusing twist, extended high stress can renew traumatic stress symptoms. Sometimes issues are not similar, but prolonged high stress brings out symptoms from issues that had been carefully processed years before.

Previously traumatized parents wonder later whether they were re-enacting by adopting. In re-enactment, people find a similar experience, attempting to master the situation in the present tense. It is a high-risk way in which to work out a psychological problem. These situations often unravel, ending in disruption, or in highly dysfunctional families.

How do parents know if their trauma has been triggered? Since most parents are adjusting after a placement, some symptoms of difficulty are normal, especially with international travel. Confusion and disorientation should be on the wane after the first six weeks of placement. Signs that are classic red flags of resurfacing trauma reactions are night terrors, intrusive thoughts of doom, and hyper-vigilance. If parents are becoming numb, distant, angry, harsh, and insensitive, the damage is mounting.

Parents with traumatic stress symptoms cause confusion and alarm in their children. Children will tend to develop a disorganized attachment style with this type of parent figure. If parents are having symptoms and a child is already in their care, an immediate course of therapy is necessary. The outcome does not have to be disruption or dysfunction. Often simultaneous treatment helps get the parent back on track, able to meet the needs of their child.

Sometimes parents find that certain aspects of a child's history trigger their issues, but that those aspects can be avoided. One child found that she could disorient and immobilize her parent by screaming. Her mother gave her anything that she wanted to stop the screaming. Her parent stopped the manipulation by putting on airplane mechanic ear protection when her child started up. The screaming did not affect her mother, so the girl gave up the behavior. Before she gave up the behavior, the little girl tried harder and louder for two weeks.

Another child's sexual abuse issues triggered a parent's memory. While she supported the child's therapy, she was not present during the disclosures. The toxicity of those descriptions would have rendered her ineffective for comfort and support.

Parents who have been traumatized have to watch their own stress levels carefully. Regular hours, sufficient sleep, processing time, and pleasurable activities all help parents to keep their own internal regulation. Limiting the demand for emotional support from outside the family is necessary. After trauma, children and adults have a threshold to stress that is lowered. Participation in parent support groups should be selective. Having a small group, with known stories, is preferable to having new stories at every meeting. Avoiding traumatic stories, which play off the parent's own, helps keep the parent's boundaries intact. Sometimes parents do much better with an adoptive or foster mentoring partner than with a group. They can get support in this manner, but minimize their risk of exposure to toxic information.

Some parents find that it helps to have the same therapist as their child's therapist, asking for time for both of them. A careful therapist can help arrange attachment-oriented techniques and behavior shaping with the parent's vulnerabilities and strengths in mind.

For example, a parent who could not endure her newly adopted child in her lap did a lovely job using attachment techniques while sitting next to her daughter. They worked in front of a mirror, which the child watched, receiving positive facial expressions from her mother. This child also was sung to, read to, and snuggled. After a four-year follow-up, this nine-year-old girl has never complained about lack of lapsitting. Her anxiety level is only slightly elevated. But previously, as a five-year-old, she had complained that her mother did not like her. The mother had been avoiding her daughter's frantic hands and insistence on full body contact, which triggered traumatic memory. When freed to do things differently, she warmed to her daughter and formed an attachment.

Trauma's Influence on Normal Learning

The stress hormones that ready the brain for quick response actually damage the brain's capacity for normal learning over time (Perry, 1993). The brain prunes away structures that it is not using, as it builds connections that it does use for survival. When curiosity, achievement, and positive relationship building are ignored, children do not develop them. The brain structures that support these capacities actually get reduced. Research studies show that very extreme deprivation and other forms of trauma result in abnormal brain scans.

Traumatized children are hard to teach. They are hyper-vigilant and hyper-aroused. Often, they are misdiagnosed with attention deficit disorder. If they do have attention deficit disorder, they can also be hyper-aroused. It is tough to treat both successfully. There is a need to both stimulate the brain, and to calm it, in different areas.

These children lack concentration. They tend to be inflexible in learning. Often they are not sleeping well, so appear as grouchy students. If a trauma trigger is hit during class, the child might dissociate for the next couple of hours, completely missing the lesson's main point.

A child traumatized by sexual abuse could not get past the letter "m" in the alphabet. Every time she came to the letter, she dissociated. After a visit to the class, her mother noticed that the key word for "m" was "man." The alphabet pictures circled the classroom walls and appeared on a poster. The "man" bore an uncanny resemblance to her daughter's abuser. The teacher was an excellent and no-nonsense educator. She had a "moon" pasted over the "man" within a half-hour. The child resumed her progress through the alphabet by the end of the day. Successful education takes such adaptations and teamwork.

When children flood with anxiety, their ability to tell about what is happening inside of them is diminished. Sometimes they become aggressive, responding to all of the flight and fight energy that anxiety brings. They are the children who need the most structure given in the most nurturing manner. Instead, they often get the least nurture, with school systems using a tough, harsh approach. Traumatized children need a calm, consistent, and nurturing approach in order to learn best. They do much better with a teacher who knows them well and can see when they start to get anxious. The teacher can often intervene with support before the child becomes aggressive.

Traumatized children have more trouble with sequencing when they are especially upset. They also have difficulty with memory. Verbal instructions just do not stick in their brains. If teachers know this, they can repeat directions without shaming children. Or, better yet, they can write directions on the board for all to see.

Traumatized children do best when school visits to the police, fire department, and other disaster drills are minimized. Some children may need to stay home those days. Other children will do better having a parent accompany them on a field trip. Some accommodations in procedures are important and work well. For example, officials who overstate safety issues to make a point can reduce a child's feeling of competence.

> A second grader, who had heard that another child's life might hinge on her response during a disaster, was terrified that she would freeze up when she had to pull the emergency release on the back door of the bus. Since her traumatic incident, she had had several instances of freezing. She had nightmares about the bus driver, the lever, and wrecks. Assigning her an older "lever partner" was the solution reached in five minutes by the transportation director and therapist. Unlike their non-traumatized peers who blissfully live in denial, children with exposure to disaster need to believe that they are reasonably insulated from danger.

How Does Trauma Impair Social Skills?

Children who have been physically and sexually abused are the children's research population with the highest aggression scores (Mash, Barkley, 1998, pp.563-573). Such children tend to have fewer friends, simply because potential friends are afraid of getting hurt. Within eighteen months after sexual abuse, girls show a decrease in their social acceptance by other girls (Putnam, 1999).

It is difficult for children who are frightened to learn games, to share, and to involve themselves in the flexible give and take that friendships require. Children who are emotionally numb often wear the matching look on their faces. Other children veer away from that face because it looks unfriendly. When traumatized children play, their play themes can be fascinating, but unnerving, to other children. Children may give them attention, but not acceptance. This only accents their perception that they are different and inferior to other children.

Their mood regulation necessary for keeping friends is poor. Children who act out their feelings aggressively may lack friends. Children who hold their intense feelings inside may do better with friends. However, they pay a price for holding in feelings with increased anxiety and depression. Recall Ahmed, from the first section. Ahmed was popular, but complained that no one really knew him. He thought of suicide. His biggest restraint in considering suicide was concern for his parents.

Some children have had such little empathy shown to them during abuse and neglect, that they internalize brutality and lack of empathy. While this is not typical of all traumatized children, it is common.

One boy, who went on to develop a loyal, protective and kind character, pulled a cover off a heating vent and tried to stuff his toddler brother's legs into the duct work during a family session. Through the tangle of six adult arms, the brother's howling and both parent's directions, I could hear the boy laughing at his brother's distress. "You are so funny," he chortled. His speech mimicked a drunken person. The incident had happened within a few seconds. Like other traumatized children before treatment, he

> moved instantly from the idea to the action phase. He did not
> inhibit his impulse. His hyper-vigilance gave him information
> that the screws on the vent cover had not been replaced, a detail
> that most children would have missed.

Lack of empathy combined with impulsivity make adult supervision worth battle pay. It is no wonder that play dates are made warily. Parents find that "going outside to play," is not safe for some traumatized children. Left without structure, they will play out themes of victimization and dominance.

Some traumatized children do well with initial friendships, but they are so intense in their friendship styles that they wear other children out. They are acting with high levels of stress hormone in their bodies. Visiting children ask for some breaks and calm down periods. Until traumatized children improve in their level of arousal, they have a hard time feeling the same need for a balance of quieter activities. Often they hound the visitor for more intense play. The guest gives in, but avoids future invitations.

In an interesting twist, these children routinely express the belief that someone can tell by looking at them that they have been abused. Since adults know details about them, they assume this to be true. They do not know, nor have they been told, that these adults have read their histories. So a surprising number of children think that personal information must be discernable. It has been quite reassuring to children to realize that there is nothing transparent that shows this information to other children or adults.

As girls move into the third and fourth grades, they are expected to match the body language and voice tones of other girls. If girls are not able to do this, they risk being ostracized by cliques. While good schools work to interrupt cliques, it is helpful for traumatized girls, especially, to learn to match the facial and body language of others. It helps them with social acceptance. It is more difficult for children to do this matching after trauma, since the body is not in regulation. Many children can learn to do matching, even if they have not healed from trauma or remain hyper-aroused after treatment. The skill set is a learned one. After children have learned the skills, they can use them when motivated. There is more on this topic in Chapter 12.

Coaching children on friendship skills helps to ensure the development of these skills. Working with specific strategies helps children to key into situations in which they are likely to miss signals, or misread signals.

> One boy, who constantly kicked others accidentally, realized that he did this when he was uncomfortable after other boys bumped him. Instead of an automatic kick, he learned to give a friendly push on the shoulder. The push was typical of boys his age. It was rehearsed until it came naturally.
>
> A girl who wanted to talk about spooks, hauntings, death, and decomposition agreed to interview several slightly older teens, who advised that these were topics that would label her as "messed up." She saved these topics for therapy and for her mother—an accepting soul who visualized little.

Helping children to develop empathy works much better than a punitive system for aggressive behavior. As children feel sensitivity shown to their needs, they are more likely to show sensitivity to others. Often children can work backwards. As they describe the injustice to another, they can remember how they felt when someone did something similar to them. After finding their feelings of disappointment, parents can ask them if they want to pass that feeling along. Sometimes, provocatively, I say, "Now you are acting just like the person who stole your stuffed bunny when you were little. Are you feeling good?" The child usually adds with a long face, "No, not very. I didn't know that was what I was doing." They identify with the child they wronged by remembering their own losses. Then, they can move to restitution more easily. Restitution is a necessary part of caring for a friendship. In the long term, aggression towards friends is reduced by the improvement of empathy towards themselves, and empathy towards their friends.

How Parents Can Intervene to Help Their Children

When children have been traumatized, they are afraid almost all the time. This is an important concept to grasp. Fear is the reason that parents need to go back to the basics when dealing with their traumatized children. Forming attachment and strengthening attachment come first in working with frightened children. Children learn through attachment work that parents are connected, that they will protect, and that they will comfort.

If parents imagine turning off the sound in their homes and trying to imagine the ways that their children would be reassured, they have the amount of reassurance that children receive reliably. Traumatized children have reduced auditory processing ability when very frightened. Words must always be accompanied by pictures, smells, touches, or role-plays in order to help. Which works better? The father who calls, "You are fine," as the child goes into his dark room, or the father who walks into the room ahead of his child, turns on the light, and says with a smile and reassuring touch on the shoulder, "You are fine." Little is conveyed about parent protection through words alone. Verbal discussions work only after children begin recovering from trauma.

I must emphasize that parents' first job is fostering closer attachments in their traumatized children. Techniques for attachment are described in Chapter 8. Teaching children the protective value of a family and parents overlaps the formation of attachment. Parents can describe their jobs, interpreting their behaviors to children as they do their daily tasks. For example, parents ask children to walk with them around the house before leaving for a trip. As the parent closes and locks windows and doors, the parent describes how seriously he takes his job to keep the home secure. Parents can show children their checkbook, and describe how they budget for cartloads of groceries. Without giving detailed financial information for the benefit of the entire fourth grade, parents can still share their careful plans to feed their children. These types of practical plans are reassuring to children who have been traumatically neglected or abused. These children worry about very basic needs getting met.

The nightmare most common and the worry most prevalent in traumatized children is that they will be taken from their parents. This theme is recurrent. Parents must demonstrate ways that this can be prevented. Rather than a global reassurance, parents should describe the systems that are in place to prevent this. Sign-out procedures at school, block watch programs, patrol patterns of neighborhood police, immigration procedures that prevent unwelcome visitors, security systems in the home, are all topics that help children.

As in any horror movie, the worst fright is the one after the trauma, just when the person feels safe again and has let down defenses. Since "getting taken" is a common fear of children, it helps to find out what children thought happened to them. In child welfare cases their removal from the home was usually frightening, and it happened more than once. Often children are unaware that the Child Protective Services person was a "good guy," authorized to help. Or, they think that the police were mad at them during a visit that resulted in their leaving home. Many children are waiting for the same events to occur again. Learning why caseworkers or police officers came to the home in the first place sets the stage for why they would not come back again. This can be described in a sequence of pictures. Adopted children who have spent years in the system are surprised to learn that they no longer have a caseworker. Parents now make their decisions. This tends to be an "ah-ha" moment for children who expect people outside of the family to make decisions about them.

As children try to let down defenses and relax, they wonder whether it is safe to do so. Reassurances based on practical facts are helpful. Some parents are reluctant to make strong, predictive statements of safety. If children ask if the house is safe at night, their parents respond with, "Probably, but you never know in this day and age." This is not helpful. Instead, say, "Yes!" If parents are perceived as weak, then children have to remain hyper-vigilant. Part of the meaning of a family is that the family commits to keeping their children safe. This fundamental quality is accented in parents who are intervening on behalf of their children.

Since traumatized children are not well-regulated in their moods, parents should set the tempo in the home. They can help children slow down when they are becoming emotionally overwhelmed, racing faster and faster. They can provide structure and reassurance when children are slipping away into dissociation. It takes enormous reserve for parents, since they are using their own bodies' breathing rate, their touch, their voice tones, and their verbal content to re-regulate children throughout the day. If parents are moving too fast, they cannot help their children. Effective parents sit down, without television or the telephone, making themselves available to their children for calm down. They can invite their children to join them, since the time has already been cleared.

Some children use frantic over-activity as a way to express their terror, or to try to block out information. In the vignette that follows, brothers use this together. Often siblings have used frantic over-activity as a way to endure overwhelming events like domestic violence, physical abuse, and physical fights in drug houses.

James was grinning and poking at his brother. Timmy, ten months older, resisted briefly—he really did want to please Dad at this picnic. He took a sidelong look at James's tight body. Timmy's body became a mirror of James's...and they were off. Their pulses were high; their bodies revved up. They had evolved their own way of dealing with too much danger and tension. They became so wound up in their play that they could block out the people around them. Even though this "Welcome to Kindergarten" family potluck picnic contained no dangerous people, the boys stayed wired for danger. James felt scared and out-of-control. He could not control or scan this many people. Besides, that one guy had a full beard and a ponytail like...James could not stand the sudden memory that began to emerge. With a heart rate of 150 beats per minute and a plastered smile, he poked Timmy into their old "block out domestic violence" routine. The kindergarten teacher made a note to talk to the parents about screening for attention deficit disorder with hyperactivity. After an early exit, the parents went home to make a plan for the upcoming year that did not continue the pattern of frantic over-activity as a means of coping.

When kids whose brains have been wired for survival and danger enter safe homes, they continue looking for the dangerous elements. Their triggers, or reminders of danger, are essential for parents to know. Parents who do some detective work note that, like the children in the vignette above, their children may be afraid of men in flannel shirts, or who have beards, or who wear glasses. If parents know the reminders, they can desensitize their children, help them form a strategy of avoidance, promise to stay between the frightening person and their child, or take other reasonable approaches.

After the first two months of school, James' and Timmy's dad bought a beard, flannel shirt, and put a pillow under his shirt. The children had to approach him ten times, until they felt better. This was done with a lot of giggling. Then, they made "the bad guy." They stuffed the shirt and some jeans with some newspapers, and made a head out of a stuffed paper sack—complete with a beard. Masking tape held him together. The kids jumped on him, kicked him, remade him, controlled him, mimicked remembered insults, and eventually ignored him. By the next school event attended by parents, the boys were sure that they would not be confused by their classmate's father. "It is your choice." Their dad said. "We can either make the stuffed man again, or use the time to kick the soccer ball."

Kids with severe symptoms of traumatic stress usually need crowds and day trips limited. Some children feel better wearing a hat and sunglasses when outside of the home. They feel more protected and hidden.

It is uncommon to make much progress against stress reactions like dissociation, fighting, or frantic over-activity until the child has some alternative tools to use. Parents can take their child's pulse and feel their shoulders, both of which serve as barometers for escalating tension. If children are filling with the extra energy for fight or flight, parents can give the child an outlet for the energy, as well as help her to calm down. Children can do 150 jumping jacks, run in place for five minutes, or run up and down a hill. If the child is not already too overexcited, parents can ask their children to do some deep breathing; name collections of things; smell a good smell; get a drink of water; or have the child cozy his head into the parent's lap, arm, or shirt for a while. Frantic over-activity is a sign to me that a child is preparing for the flight that comes with hyper-arousal's fight or flight. Children are simply working too hard in life when they have to use this as a defense.

Children who have begun a behavior due to stress are not above using it for control purposes at home or school. If children choose not to use the techniques that can help them, parents can make them pay for the privilege of using the old way.

> For example, James and Timmy began giving evening baby sitters a horrible time because they were scared. When they were only a little scared, they continued the behavior. The solution was that they had to pay the sitter an additional fee when they acted out. The sitter got extreme duress pay. Soon the boys were trying harder to use their calm-down techniques.

Since it is wearing on adults to deal with certain behaviors, fining children either with money, extra jobs, or earlier bedtimes helps to curb outrageous behavior. After parents have permitted adjustment in the home, and after therapy is well under way, parents can put in these disincentives for acting out. Parents can say, "You can do 50 jumping jacks to help that feeling and come get a snuggle, or you can go to bed ten minutes early for each minute you play that way. It's your choice."

Practice preferred alternatives to acting out when children are not stressed. That makes it much easier for them to use the preferred behavior when they need to, since they have practiced when they were feeling good.

> For example, Mantze, age six, vomited and tantrumed when Mom left the home for a few hours, leaving Mantze with a kind, familiar, and long-suffering family friend. Her mother felt that Mantze was re-enacting her abandonment in a subway station at age two, over and over again. Verbal reasoning had not helped at all. Mantze practiced going to an agreed-upon calm-down spot, with a book and a nice-smelling pillow. Her mom went outside

the door and came back in the house in a few minutes. As Mantze practiced sitting in her spot, she got praise. Mantze practiced this quite a few times, and received continued requests to practice, which she found inconvenient. Her mother said that she was not certain that Mantze was strong enough in the new behavior. Mantze insisted that she was certain that she did not have to practice further—her mother could leave! After many practices over two weeks, her mother went out while Mantze stayed with the plan. When she began to slide a few weeks later, Mom insisted on more practices, saying that she did not want Mantze suffering stress. She settled herself, rather than enduring interruptions in her days for boring practices.

In a final touch, the mother had also bought a tan, generic cereal for Mantze's breakfast, instead of the expensive brand with multicolored letters. Mom explained that her consulting work hours were reduced—from doing so many practices. She had to balance the budget.

Children often create reenactments or symptoms of traumatic events that are vivid and controlling. After de-sensitization practices give alternatives, and when children continue to use symptoms for control, parents should make the outcomes as dull as possible.

Some parents use their own extreme moods to signal their children to practice control. This rarely works for traumatized children, who get further out-of-control. Some children may dissociate when their parents get very angry with them, and will show worsening symptoms within a few hours or days. Parents who use the threat of expulsion from the family will only undermine their child's safety. The short-term improvement that parents see for a few days is at the expense of long-term progress. It is a signal to the child that the parents may not be strong enough to help their child. Parents who find themselves threatening their child in this manner should obtain professional support immediately.

Children removed from birthparents because of neglect and abuse often worry that they may parent like their birthparents. Using the concept of learning, parents can tell their children that they will learn parenting skills. That way, they will not lose custody of their children. Sometimes children will say to me, " I wish that my birthmother had had a mother like mine. My mother could have taught her the right way." Or, "When my birthmother had trouble, my mother could have helped her, if she had been there." In figuring out the factual basis of events, children loosen the identification with the traumatic end to their birthparent's caregiving.

Maintaining Attachment after Trauma

But what if parents had their child in their home, and had an attachment, at the time of trauma? Parents have immediate steps that they can take to improve children's outcome. Immediately after an incident, physical closeness to their parents helps children to depend on their parents. Parents should provide for physical needs in a comfortable way that promotes dependence and prevents isolation. For the first few days after a traumatic incident, parents and children should be virtually inseparable.

A young teen, who had been molested at a sleepover, was interviewed by the police and sent home sometime around dawn. A few hours later, she told her mother to go on to work. Her mother started out, turned around, and came home. She later said, "She was in no condition to know how she was doing. I needed to be home." She was right. As she entered the house, she saw her daughter, sitting wide-eyed and in shock on the sofa, with the curtains drawn and the lights out. Proximity is essential in maintaining attachment after trauma. Newly traumatized children need expressions of care and compassion that help them believe that they are not alone in their pain.

Unless children have empathy shown to them, they internalize the insensitivity that was shown to them or someone else during trauma (Pynoos, 1997). A new ending, with empathy, is put on the trauma story when parents hear their child's story, hold them close, and tell them how terribly sorry they are that it happened to their child. Often the parents and child cry together, which allows the child to internalize a sensitive, caring voice. It restores empathy for themselves, and allows them to feel empathy for others.

Children need to convey what happened to them. In working through the process of description, the first step is to find out what they wish had happened instead. For example "I wished that the tree would have fallen the other direction away from our home." Or, " I wish the car had not turned into us, but had stopped." Drawing the "wished for" event helps younger children to feel a little better. Children can also describe how they want things to go in the future. One child, working at the beginning of his trauma work said, "I would have a rule that no children could be separated from their mothers at the hospital. And only one doctor could feel the mass, not all of the student doctors." It gives children a sense of justice and control to talk, draw, and act out their wishes. Parents can encourage the statement of wishes.

Next, helping children to form a simple story line, with what happened first, second, and third, allows children to move from the beginning to the end of the event. This helps children not to get stuck in the middle of the event. They can describe where they were, where others were, and what they were thinking and feeling. This is work done best with pictures or role-play. It also helps to find out from children "the thing that they could have done without," in the words of Pynoos, an outstanding researcher in the area of children's trauma (1997). There is often some particularly painful detail that happens after a traumatic event.

One girl describes how her friend's notebook was tossed in the trash after emergency workers cleaned an accident scene. She felt that the notebook symbolized her friend; she was thrown in the trash.

Often children want to undo that symbol in some way. Finding out what reminders of the event are painful to children is another important task. Avoiding those reminders, and later having plans to de-sensitize, helps to bring down anxiety.

Parents should get immediate professional help after a trauma. The opportunity to prevent posttraumatic stress disorder is best with prompt treatment. While the standard advice is to wait, the research does not support this at all. Immediate intervention for children is proactive.

A child who had been sexually abused by a female cousin came in for treatment because she was angry with her mother. At the end of two sessions, she looked fully into her mother's face and said, "The icky feeling is gone now. I have felt icky since it happened. It's gone!" Children are angry with parents when they have been hurt and their parents cannot help them with distressful feelings. Parents can help foster attachment by acting powerfully on behalf of their children by getting treatment.

Advice mentioned in earlier sections helps maintain attachment after a new trauma. Parents should maintain a slower pacing, increase comforting rituals, expect a regression in development, give more support for tasks that requiring concentration, show more protection, provide extra time for rest, and keep the home orderly.

Children need a sense of order and predictability in the home when things have become unpredictable. A quieter, uncluttered home and schedule help children to have the space and time to think things through.

Finally, children often feel powerless after a trauma. Give children choices and options after traumas, as long as they are not choosing re-enactments. Help them to see the many areas of their lives over which they still have control.

Preventing Toxic Reactions in Parents Dealing with Children's Trauma

Some parents are so attached to their children that they become deeply disturbed by the traumas their children are reporting. They begin to experience the horror of the incident, along with other symptoms of hypervigilance, lack of concentration, and intrusions into dreams and thoughts.

While symptoms like this are normal for a few days as parents process what happened to their children, parents can develop the profile of a traumatized person themselves.

Parents can start to insist that the world revolves around their child's trauma. They want to focus friends and groups on events designed to right the injustice done to their child. While in itself this seems laudable, when this is a symbol of traumatic stress, nothing is ever good enough. The story of their child gets told over and over again. The efforts for change are subsumed in the need to tell of the overwhelming suffering. Such parents are clearly caught in the middle part of their child's story. They cannot permit themselves to move on to the present.

Parents in this position need to immediately back out of their child's trauma work. Interestingly, these are parents who are usually intrusive and somewhat harmful to the child's work. Parents having problems with toxic reactions bring up the child's trauma at home when the child is relaxed and happy. They may attempt to add to the scope of the child's story.

Parents who are very interested in the dramatic should be aware that they may become pathologically interested in their child's trauma issues. Other parents, who handle normal life changes with difficulty, may be overwhelmed by the child's trauma. In both of these situations, parents should be up front with the treating therapist. They will do best to sit out of the sessions. Surrounding themselves with a positive, regulated, familiar, and healthy environment will help them to stay stable, which benefits their children.

Why Seek Help for Traumatized Children?

"Why do we have to talk about all that old stuff?" A parent posed an excellent question at a conference recently. He added, "Why open up a can of worms?" Before I could answer him, an experienced adoptive parent from a panel explained, "So the kids don't have to *think* about it all of the time. That's why we talk about it!"

Until children have worked through trauma, it keeps intruding upon everyday life. It is a silent shaper of everyday experiences. An example of this shaping of perception is in the example which follows:

Cynthia was mad and snotty. It was the last week of school. She was finishing the first good school year of her life. The teacher *liked* her! Cynthia's mother called, confused and wanting to bring her daughter in to see me, because Cynthia was so difficult. As Cynthia and I talked, she mentioned that her mother had scheduled something so that she would miss the final two hours of school, the time children would just be saying, "Goodbye." Processing with Cynthia, I mentioned that this was, "Goodbye for now." She was going to see the teacher over the summer, and could stop into her classroom the next year.

"Yeah," Cynthia said, relaxing and looking cooperative for the first time. "It is not like my teacher is going swimming!" Cynthia's sister had drowned two years before, after Cynthia was moved to a foster home. Cynthia felt keenly that she had never had a chance to say "Goodbye" to her sister. She was superimposing some unfinished trauma and grief on a normal situation that had a related theme.

Professionals and parents work on trauma and loss so children can move on to think about other things, more typical of childhood.

Trauma therapy has three stages of treatment (Pynoos, 1997). In the first stage, the child is stabilized. Even though it feels like parents are going against the tide, they still work on attachment. Both parents and therapists are aware that until trauma is treated, attachment will be impeded. Children have extra security, comfort, and predictability in everyday life. Dependence on safe parents is encouraged.

The second stage is trauma-focused. In that stage two major tasks are undertaken: correcting distorted and destructive beliefs, and desensitization to trauma-related memories. Grief is a prominent theme in this stage.

In the last stage, children disconnect from trauma and grief and reconnect with the present (Pynoos, 1997). During this stage, major tasks are developing strategies to deal with trauma triggers and developing coping skills in life. Typically an additional increase in attachment occurs near the end of this stage. Children are less frightened and have much more energy to put into relationships, including ones with their parents.

In the final stage, children show more independence, which is true independence based on trust.

The children who have not worked on trauma maintain trauma-contaminated core beliefs. These beliefs distort their developmental perspectives of themselves and others. Girls and boys who have been sexually abused regularly worry about whether their bodies were damaged, whether a foreign object remains inside of them, or whether others will feel compelled to similarly abuse them if the abuse is discovered. They believe that they are sexually irresistible, or that they should be treated like an older person because they have met the sexual needs of an older person. Commonly, they pair victimization and dominance with sexuality. They believe that something about them caused the abuse. Typically some disturbing beliefs are very specific, like, "He would not have abused me if I had not called him 'stupid.'" Global reassurances do little to dispel these specific beliefs.

In order to protect themselves from prosecution, abusers will sometimes say things like, "Your mother knows what I am doing. She does not care." Or they might say, "Your parents will be very angry with you if they find out." There is an interruption of the protection by the parent. Unless some specific work is done, children will believe what the abuser has told them. They then lose confidence in the protective function of adults in other areas of their lives. This occurs even after they change caregivers. Unless they can risk examining some of their beliefs, many of these beliefs remain fully operational and unexamined.

Without treatment, trauma's disturbing beliefs and images can gain momentum as the years pass, rather than recede. For example, researchers note a "sleeper effect" in damage from sexual abuse. As time goes on past the sexual abuse, children have more marked impairment with social relationships, show disruptive behavior, have concentration problems, and show poor frustration tolerance (Putnam, 1999). As the brain readies itself for quick response to a dangerous world, it loses its adaptability to function in a safe world.

Severely impacted children may need intermittent treatment for many years. They have a form of posttraumatic stress disorder that functions like a chronic illness, with flare-ups and better times (Marsh, Barkley, 1998). Other children maintain their gains, coming back in at particular developmental stages to consolidate gains and to get ready for the next developmental tasks. Typically, when children are about eleven, their brains begin to develop abstract thinking, and children do well with a check-in. At thirteen or fourteen, before teens are entering romantic relationships, another check-in is good. Prior to leaving home, around seventeen, is another good check-in time. Many children become skillful at knowing when they should come in. They will tell their parents that it is time to make an appointment. This is typical of a successful working relationship with a therapist.

Researchers are showing decided improvements for children who receive therapy for trauma when compared to children who do not (Foa, Keane, Friedman, 2000). Because of the clarity and consistency of these studies, I recommend counseling for all traumatized children even if children do not remember trauma.

 The Impact of Cultural Change

How do parents communicate their love to children who are frightened of them and who cannot understand parents' soothing messages? How do children bridge the distance between the cultures of two families in open adoptions? How do parents and children ease the beginning stages of sharing their lives, becoming close families after coming from opposite sides of the world and speaking different languages? What steps should be planned to assist families in forging strong cultural identities when they come from culturally and racially dissimilar backgrounds? These good questions are addressed in this chapter on the impact of cultural change. Sensitive parents must assist the developmental progress of children not just through their transition into the family, but through their identity work as they enter the larger community. In open adoptions parents are assisting the identity work of their children as they negotiate their ties to a different family system with different rules.

Open Adoption

Since the early 1980's there has been an increasing trend toward more openness in all kinds of adoption. The spectrum of openness in adoption today is a wide one, ranging from occasional contact by letters sent back and forth through a mediating agency to the establishment of close, extended-family relationships involving regular visits. Most open adoptions, however, fall somewhere in the middle of this spectrum. In domestic infant adoption, more and more expectant parents are being given the option of selecting specific prospective parents from profiles prepared for an agency or private adoption facilitator. Often, these matches are made several weeks or even months before the child is born, and relationships between expectant parents and would-be adopters begin to build over that time and are expected to continue throughout the child's growing up years. Where once children placed out of abusive or neglectful homes were separated completely and permanently from contact with birthrelatives, today, more and more professionals are supporting the value for children of some level of careful, supervised contact with their families of origin. Even in international adoption, once a bastion of permanent secrecy, there is a growing trend toward some level of contact with birthfamilies for children adopted from some countries. Most mental health and adoption professionals conclude that, in the long run, openness in adoption is healthier for all members of the adoption triad—birthparents, adopting parents, and children who were adopted. Openness in adoption is hardly a panacea, however. It brings to adoption its own set of challenges.

Issues Affecting Children

Adoptions permitting children and their birthfamilies information about the other's wellbeing are sensitive. While listening to children and birthparents and other members of birthfamilies, it is abundantly obvious that they never forget each other. They often have strong needs to know information about one another, either through direct contact or an exchange of information, particularly when the adoption occurs not right after birth, but following a period of time when the child has actually been parented by a member of his birthfamily. Sometimes this means an open adoption is the best arrangement. But given this standard, there are mitigating considerations that can dictate a different course. Parents who are readers of this book are likely to be parenting children with challenges. Some adoptive parents will also have experienced situations which may challenge their attachments.

Children who have had attachments to previous caregivers will need some information or contact with them after placement. They are not able to complete their grieving without this information. However, when children are forming new attachments, sometimes the openness rocks the child's attachment processes. The problems fall into four major categories.

Sometimes the child feels that the current placement is not permanent when exposed to previous caregivers.

Josh, a five-year-old, who had been with his birthparents for the first eight months and then with grandparents for two years, showed anger, sleep problems, and cruelty to other children when visiting with his grandparents. He needed to have a holiday from the visits for a while. He could not sustain the gains that he was making with his parents. Instead, he began to make cruel comments to his parents like, "You cannot make a baby inside of you. You had to steal me. I do not want to live with you." Some of the damage from moves and neglect in his first home showed in his contempt and disregard for others' feelings. A break in the visits with grandparents helped him to stabilize. "I am doing great," Josh said. "I am ready for kindergarten. I am a great son, and I love my parents. I get confused sometimes. Why do I act like that? I get a feeling like I don't need parents, and I am not going to do what they say!" While the visits in this case did resume at a slower pace, a holiday was needed so that Josh had the energy for other developmental demands. On a deep level, his basic security in his family was jeopardized with contact that reactivated issues of neglect and grief.

Sometimes there are safety issues that involve trauma that the child has not shared with anyone.

> One sexual predator, who was a birth grandfather, walked into the child's foster-adopt home without knocking and sat down. Though the parents appropriately set boundaries, the child still had doubts that his parents could protect him. He did not disclose sexual abuse for four years after placement. When the therapist helped him feel safe from the grandfather, he disclosed sexual abuse.

Sadly, this is not an isolated case. Some children have erotic, sexualized trauma bonds with former caregivers or relatives. They test by asking to see these people. They miss them, but are terrified of them. I have seen no benefit for children in visiting people with whom they have trauma bonds. Asking to see them is often a form of re-enactment. Should visits take place, inevitably the child blames the adopting parents for not keeping her safe.

Children may have been raised in role-reversing families, in which children meet the needs of adults if they want to get their own needs met. Even after children develop healthier relationships, they are prone to move back into earlier patterns.

> One girl, who was four, visited with her birthmother regularly. It was a relative placement prompted by the birthmother's drug and alcohol problems. The girl had nightmares, masturbated constantly, and was oppositional after visits. The little girl cried, saying that her birthmother needed her. "She is lonely. I have to go help her," she said. Her own needs for safety and love were forgotten as she contemplated her birthmother's needs. After a discussion about what children need, she said, "I do not know why I think that I have to take care of her. When I am with her, I feel like I have to do it." Visits were decreased, and the mother began to monitor the discussions between her daughter and her

birthmother. She interrupted comments like, "You will never forget who your real momma is, will you? I will get a job, get into treatment, and come back for you."

When children are expected to take care of adults' emotional needs, emotional damage to children occurs. Visitations should not include a leeching of emotional energy from children.

Children who are not safe in the custody of parents can benefit from continued contact when carefully guided.

One girl, age ten, had been her birthfamily scapegoat. She received little love from her birthmother, and she wondered why. She wrote to her birthmother, asking about this, and also requested some baby pictures. The adoptive mother got her the address, using my office as the return address. The birthmother wrote a loving letter back, affirming the child, but saying that she had been too much under the influence of alcohol to explain why she acted this way. In her letters she included some baby pictures, and promises of a gift and a letter from a birth sibling, which never came. This helped the girl to process some of the information about her relationship with her birthmother. She felt less guilt and shame. She also was able to determine through the letter that her birthmother was intelligent and a good writer. She noted the lack of follow-through on promises. This type of reality-based contact was very healthy for this child. As she said to her mother, "I know that she just can't parent, but I care about her and want to make sure that she is still alive."

In continuing contact, parents can often pick out the loyalty bonds that children have.

For example, in the above scenario, the child did not know how to address her birthmother. Just write, "Dear Mom," her mother said. The daughter had a hard time when reading the letter aloud to her mother. She read, "Dear mmmmm," slurring the word.

Her mother just laughed, saying; "I know that she is going to say, 'What?' if you write, 'Dear Birthmother.' I do not care. I know that I am your mom." The letters comforted this girl when she missed her "first mom," the term that felt most comfortable for her.

When children are placed away from their siblings, continued contact is necessary. Sometimes families who are compatible spend day trips together. Other times, shorter events work. If a child has disrupted out of one family, planning to have contact with siblings must include these rejection issues.

One foster mother went over-the-edge with her foster son. She screamed at the boy constantly, and placed his belongings in garbage bags for the move. The pre-adoptive mother had asked that she help her son pack. Several days before, she described for the foster mother the damage to self-esteem of moving belongings in garbage bags, so she brought suitcases for the move. The transfer of the boy was accompanied by a ranting chorus of his damage to their family. Rather predictably, the tirade moved on to the pre-adoptive mother, after she defended her son. In spite of the intense feelings of the adults, visits with the siblings proceeded, because all children needed the contact. After some trial and error, they found it best to meet at places like roller skating rinks and parks. Meeting in homes seemed to accent the rejection themes for the children.

Openness in adoption, even in challenging situations, can be extremely helpful in assisting children with their grief, giving them information about loved ones, and in helping them with identity formation. Safety and developmental issues must be considered, so that the contact builds, rather than dismantles, a stable sense of family. It has the advantage of giving children information that is reality-based, rather than wishful. It gives children a framework, so that they are not looking for fantasy birthparents into the future. Instead, they have facts and events that shape a realistic view of all their relatives.

Issues for Adoptive Parents

Parents sometimes note that their initially welcoming feelings about the benefits of open adoption are altered through painful experiences in the adoption process.

One family, in describing their slow start in attachment, said that they were numb by the time that they had successfully adopted. Four times they had endured being selected by expectant parents considering an adoption. After faithfully following the pregnancies and coming to view the birthparents as extended family, the birthparents chose to parent their children rather than follow through with an adoption plan. In the most heart-wrenching situation, they had acquiesced to the birthmother's wish for them to take "their" son home from the hospital even though necessary papers were not yet filed because of a holiday. They returned "her" son after the long weekend. Open adoption seemed ethically correct to them, but emotionally dangerous. It threatened their sense of entitlement. They were anxious about another devastating loss.

Both parents were slow to warm to their daughter, and noted that they were holding back emotionally. Comments from a wise grandparent, who mentioned that their infant daughter seemed sad and that they seemed afraid to love her, helped these parents to examine their attitudes. In retrospect, they say that they missed the joy of the first months. The openness in their adoption scared them. "I hate that I am saying this," the adoptive mother said, "but I feel that I am going to do all the work of raising my daughter for someone else. I did not start out this way. I used to be a proponent for open adoption, but I am not dealing with the emotions well. I am afraid of the birthfamily."

In this situation, the adoptive family had some work to do. They did write a letter in which they described their own pain-filled journey. They did not renegotiate the open adoption agreement, but they let the birthparents know how difficult a time they had been having. They were careful not to blame these birthparents for their own issues of entitlement, but they were honest about their struggles in this area. This resulted in a letter of reassurance from the birthmother, who also spoke to the birthfather, sending along his confidence in them as parents. By not needing to present themselves as completely strong, mature, and faultless, they allowed for a natural process in a relationship. They allowed the birthmother to meet some of their needs.

In another situation, a birthparent in an open adoption went swimming with the adoptive parent, who was a single mother, and her daughter. While it went well, the adoptive mother later sat in my office and wept. "I felt that I was so old. April deserved a young, fit mother. I did not look like any of the other parents in the pool. I looked like her grandmother. April thought that this visit was great! She can hardly wait to do more things with her energetic birthmother. Maybe I am the wrong parent for her!"

In fact, the mother was a great match for her daughter's needs. But she did need to do some honest rearranging of her attitudes. Her poor body image had been a factor long before she adopted. She criticized herself physically, applying it to her adoptive parent status in the same self-deprecating way she applied it to career and other life situations.

When she could think more clearly, she knew that she was not comfortable with trips every week with the birthmother. She needed to be clear about her own limits. The birthmother did not have good boundaries, so the adoptive mother needed to think reasonably about the type of contact that was in April's best interests. Her solution included doing more fun things with April, like the outings that she craved, while maintaining the normal contact in the open adoption agreement.

Language and Country

Parents adopting internationally should learn some basics of normal child development and some language from their child's original culture. They should also get honest feedback about themselves from someone from that culture. Parents who do so avoid major problems like those in the next vignette. When children tell the story of coming into their new country, they all tell me that they were afraid on the airplane or train. The comfort and competence that children feel in their own culture is lost as they enter a new surrounding. Li Fu-tze described the following, after she had English command.

At age four, Li Fu-tze had learned to behave herself around adults. She averted her eyes and tucked her chin when addressed. She was a polite and respectful girl. She was too old to be adopted, she thought, so was surprised when called in by the orphanage director, who told her a confusing tale about a father who was in China to adopt a sister. It took Li Fu-tze a few minutes to realize that the man in the room was the "father" being referred to. Through the translator, he said that he was her new father, and that her mother would be back to get her. She was attempting to understand this, when the translation included the request that she look up at him. She politely refused. The translator began to prompt her in a wheedling tone. She looked at the man, as she was told. He gave her an intense look of longing. She wanted to ask what was wrong with the man. She was quiet, as a good child should be, and she was confused. Was it some kind of a test?

Long after the event had faded from her memory, she was told that she would be adopted. She had always called an orphanage worker Momma. She expected that her new momma would be the worker, or at least Chinese. She had wished hard. When she met her mother, she knew that she was doomed. Her mother had blond hair. In China, only witches had blond hair. She was being tricked! Back at the hotel, no one understood her as she yelled, bit, and fought. Her mother attempted to calm and subdue her. Li Fu-tze glared at her. She had no problem with full eye contact. Her chin was high. She would not go down without a fight!

Li Fu-tze was renamed Kelly. In therapy, she wondered whether her poor adjustment to her parents had started with this unfortunate beginning. Her mother said, "I bleached my hair to look younger and more appealing to a small child! It had the opposite effect. When I finally got the translator to come to the hotel to find out what she was repeating, it was, 'Don't hurt me! Don't eat me!'"

In transcultural adoption, the meaning of things changes. Children are not able to exert control over their lives through language, which frustrates and confuses them. In the situation above, the parent got off to a poor start with an extremely frightened child. New parents formed an opinion of the child as a hard child who needed heavy control. Actually, she needed reassurance and a tender touch. Once home, her father conveyed much of his information with looks—loving, warning, angry, inviting—and all lost on Kelly. She continued to look down when addressed by her father.

Learning normal child development in a particular culture is important not only for parents in the initial adjustment period, but over the course of years. Transculturally adopted children have to be able to feel at ease with two cultural groups.

One girl adopted from Korea as a small child said, "My new boyfriend is Korean. When I am with his relatives I know how to act. All of the culture camps and language lessons paid off. I am comfortable with my Korean identity, even though I left Korea when I was a baby. My parents also took me back to Korea. Now I am grateful that they made the effort."

In another situation, a woman had her nails manicured and painted a bright red before she left to adopt two children in Tashkent. Her new daughters had never seen red nails before, and conjectured that she must have gotten them from the blood of children she ate. In their folklore, orphans were eaten by witches. Many children report being warned in the Russian or former Soviet bloc orphanages to close their eyes at night or the witches would come and peck them out. Within two days of placement, one daughter had attempted to run away in an enormous outdoor market. The mother told her husband that it was obvious that the other daughter hated her.

Children being raised without parents are particularly prone to common childhood fears of being eaten by monsters or witches. With just a few props like nails and hair, new parents can embody a child's nightmares.

Sometimes parents find themselves in situations that seem incredible from the point of view of their own culture. Some children are told that the birthparents have finally arrived to get their child. I have heard this explanation a number of times about preparation for children in countries in the former Soviet Union, in which there is no tradition of adoption. One orphanage worker advised parents, "Never tell this child that she was adopted. It will kill her Russian soul." She answered their logical question about language by explaining that because their daughter was largely nonverbal, she would not question why they were talking a different language. Some children have come into the country angry with parents. Working with a translator, children have wondered, "Where were you? Why did you leave me in the orphanage?" It makes for a confusing beginning for parents and children.

Older children usually do not want to be adopted out of their culture. In children's stories, it is usually the adults who are describing North America as the great place to be. Their part tends to be one of hearing the adults' excitement, and being confused and afraid. Children who are old enough to remember their wait for adoption tell me that foremost they yearned for their birthparents to come back for them. After that, they hoped for someone who looked similar to them and who spoke their language. Often they hoped for a caregiver who was a relative, especially if they have been visited by relatives. Leaving the country brings these childhood dreams to an end. In some cases, attitudes that children formed to fit into their culture are not adaptable to this culture.

One mother said that she expected that her daughter would need to be placed into an adult group home in the future. The mother said, "If somehow she could have gotten medical and mental health care in her own country, she could have lived independently. By adding the challenges of language and the differences in attitudes and life skills, it is too far of a stretch for her to succeed outside her country of origin. She was too old for us to bring into the country, given the other issues that she had to face. In spite of severe sexual abuse, she often wishes that she could have stayed in the country in which she was born. But she does not speak the language now. She has no friends here, and does not have current prospects to make any. After eight years, she cannot accept American societal rules. She argues with them, and refers to the Russian way in the institutions as the correct way. She does not believe that she has to make a living for herself.

"Our son, adopted to America at the same age, had a family background, and thus brought with him fewer emotional issues. He has adapted. At the time of adoption, he understood the concept of family, and he had had less abuse. He had enough energy left to make the adjustments to a new culture. He is still learning though, and seems a couple of years behind boys his own age."

When children are learning a language, the language represents not just a code, but a conceptual map with cultural meaning. As the language is learned, it forms a conceptual map for sorting incoming information. That map is not erased as children learn the concepts and language of a new culture. Instead, the second language becomes a map on top of a map. These children never really perceive an absolute reality being spoken. Instead, their perceptions alter how they hear and interpret what is said to them. Children adopted internationally will have some of the shaping from the first language map in their concepts. It is important for parents to understand this as a quality not only of language development, but conceptual development.

Many children are detailed in wanting to know why their country did not want them. Frequent comments from children adopted from Eastern Europe are, "Do the people in that country know what is happening in the orphanages? Why do the people treat children so badly in the orphanages? Don't they care about us? They treated us like garbage!" It helps children to hear that most people do not know about the orphanage abuses. Or that often parents are so poor that the only way for them to feed their children is "abandonment," which is the only form of placement available to parents. Some older children appreciate seeing the report from the Human Rights Watch on Russian orphanages, which validates their beliefs that a great injustice was done to them (Human Rights Watch, 1998).

The attitudes toward institutionalizing children with disabilities or allowing the State to raise a child can be discussed in terms of the culture. In Eastern Europe, the attitude that the State can do it as well as the family still prevails. The attitude towards disability issues in other countries can be discussed, and how that affected the child. Discussing the economic realities of countries, as well as the tradition of adoption in the countries, are both topics that give facts and bring resolution to children. Most children want to know why their country did not want to keep them. These are loss issues that need to be processed like any other grief. Children expend emotional energy and require longer learning spans when moved from culture to culture. Confusion and loss are normal parts of the experience. When parents foster children's positive ties to both cultures, it is a way to mitigate these losses. It also helps their children to forge strong identities.

Religion

Some children shift religion easily, taking it as part of adjustment to their family and culture. Other young children already have deep spiritual beliefs, and they struggle with their changing religious identity. Even when children are not moving between countries, there is a movement between subcultures when moving between devoutly observant and casually religious families.

Questions that children express include, "Was my adoption meant to be?" "How could God care about me after what I have been through?" "Is God mad at me?" "Would I worship the same God if I were in another country?" "Are my birthparents going to heaven?" "Is it my fault if they do not?" "Should I be two religions?"

John, a boy born in Colombia, was adopted by a Jewish family. He began to resist going to his Hebrew classes and asked to go to Catholic Youth activities. John's older brother and mother talked at length, wondering whether John was meant to follow a Catholic religious faith because of his birth culture. In a therapy session, the mother asked if I could explore the issue with John. John matter-of-factly told me that the three most fun kids in third grade were Catholic. He wanted to be a Catholic because they played baseball at CYC. He would be just as happy if the group was named Jewish Youth, as long as baseball was part of the religious program!

It does help to ask for the obvious in these matters! Nevertheless, children may want to explore how their identities would be different if they followed their cultural faith.

Very painful occurrences can happen in moving between families.

One girl was sexually predatory and felt a deep disgust for herself. While in her foster family, she gained a sense of God treasuring and forgiving her. This was something precious that she referred to regularly. It was her strength when she felt lonely, angry, and sexually predatory. When the foster family decided not to adopt her, she moved into a treatment home, which was also quite religious, although it was jarring, since she had two mothers in that family. Her previous denomination had precluded this. However, she did adapt, and went from being Catholic to Protestant. It was a change, but after some confusion and distress, she again found herself stable spiritually.

When she was placed for adoption, she was placed in an atheist family. It had been difficult to find a family, so her beliefs could not be honored. In order to please the family, she was quiet about her beliefs. In the first therapy session, her new parents made fun of religion of all types as well as of the former caregivers. This girl lost one of the mainstays of her life. She was put in the position of gaining a family at the expense of loving and feeling loved by God.

Because of the necessary separation between religious belief and government, government placement professionals tend to avoid talking to children about their spirituality. The tendency to stay away from religious topics makes it difficult to advocate for children who have strong beliefs. It also makes it difficult to help children whose trauma has caused them deep spiritual questions. For children who believe in a loving God, loss of faith in a loving God is part of the classic damage from trauma. They describe being confused between life and God. Parents should be aware that children with broken attachments have difficulty believing that God could find them lovable and acceptable.

One teen, who had developed multiple personalities from severe abuse, could not memorize a Bible verse at her Christian school. The verse content was that God would not test a person beyond what they were able to bear. She described her crisis of faith, "Deborah, you know that it was more than I could bear. I did not bear it and broke under the strain! I am going to flunk Bible. I cannot write the verses."

As we talked, we discussed that suffering was not necessarily "a test," but what happens in this life. For example, people in America who suffered from high rates of tuberculosis did not finally "pass the test," or learn the lesson, thus giving us a lower tuberculosis rate today. Looking at the verses, it was clear that the teacher had interpreted the verses in an optimistic way that led students to believe that they had a magic ticket for safety in this life. Our discussion led to this young woman's re-examination of texts, and her restored belief. (She did not flunk Bible.) While it certainly was not my choice to make her believe or doubt, it does help to sort through beliefs affected by trauma, or others' denial.

Often children feel outside of normal religious beliefs, since their life experience requires deeper answers to questions of faith, suffering, and trust. Further discussion of this topic is contained in Judith Hermann's book *Trauma and Recovery*, on the Resource List.

Parents without belief in God or an afterlife sometimes find themselves wanting to preserve their child's beliefs. They ask, "How do I assess or discuss the beliefs?" In talking with their children, a few concepts are particularly important. Children often feel that they have a relationship with God. Parents can ask how children talk with God. What kind of a feeling does God give them? When do they talk with God or feel that God is close to them? Children talk about God as they might talk to parents about a close friend whom the parents have never met. Parents can go on to ask what helps sustain that relationship. Does going to a religious service keep the relationship growing? What about speaking to an adult with strong faith? Has the child been reading through spiritually instructive books with an adult? Night prayers, or morning prayers, and readings from children's versions of scriptures are woven into the fabric of daily life in families of faith. Parents whose children have a faith can help to build these experiences into the life of their child, continuing the development of their spirituality. Parents without religious beliefs can talk with adults with religious beliefs, in order to identify spiritual developmental processes that can be nurtured. Parents can talk through this type of information with clergy, who tend to be approachable and helpful.

Race

The African-American community continues its tradition of fostering and adopting at a disproportionately high rate. The Hispanic communities and Pacific Islanders have used extended family placements to care for children within their communities until relatively recently. In spite of these efforts there are African-American, Hispanic, Pacific Islander, and multiracial children who are waiting for placements in the U.S., and who need parents more than they need to be race-matched. The result has been a widely debated, but upward trend towards transracial adoption in the U.S. A large percentage—in fact, the majority—of international adoptions have always been, and continue to be, transracial.

Transracial adoptions have been successful, as studies have shown. The children adjust well. Yet people who grew up in transracial adoption give valuable information about what went well, and what did not go so well. Adults raised transracially offer several suggestions for parents adopting transracially:

- They want to be raised in a community that has others of their same race.
- They want to feel comfortable with traditions, attitudes, and people of their own race.
- They experienced love and acceptance, but were sometimes hurt by "color-blind" attitudes of their parents.
- People of the same race can expose and transmit attitudes and traditions from within a family context.
- Instead of talking about racial issues, children see them modeled. When parents cannot model, they have to find other ways to help their children to feel competent and esteemed as a minority person in the culture.

One African-American family adopted a baby whose birth parents were also African-American. After the baby was born, they noted that the baby was especially light-skinned. Since the birthmother was light, and often newborns are light, their questions about parentage were met with some reassurance by their agency. By a year, the family was looking for connections to the Hispanic community, since it was clear that the baby's father had been an Hispanic man. As the mother told me, "My daughter will be viewed as an Hispanic or mixed race person in our society. I know little about the Hispanic community. My husband is a pastor and much of our life is centered in the African-American church. We have started monthly potlucks in our home in order to bridge to other Hispanic and African-American families."

There is a comfortable anonymity to blending into one's surroundings. Children and adults feel a constant, low level of stress by being the only person of a particular race in their school, on their street, or in the grocery store. Even if they are "accepted," the word itself points out the difference factor. Someone else has the choice of accepting or not accepting. In their making the choice, often the naturalness of an everyday interaction is changed. People in the grocery store often feel the need to stress their acceptance through extra attention, when the family just wants to pick up a gallon of milk.

Parents often select homes and social circles that seem personally comfortable, sometimes at the expense of their transracially adopted child's comfort. Parents who decide that it does not matter if their child will be the only one of their race in the community should spend days in a part of a city in which the parents are racially different. They will find that race does matter.

Parents who are part of the Caucasian majority in North America cease being a Caucasian family when they foster or adopt a minority child. Children feel most comfortable in a multiethnic surrounding because their family is multiethnic.

Parents need to have advice from minority adults in order to perceive the implications of certain experiences on their children. Parents' blind spots make identity formation harder.

> One African-American woman who had been raised by white parents mentioned that in her rural, nearly all-Caucasian college, leering young men at parties referred to her as "exotic." She translated that term, accurately, into a sexualized one. Her reasons for selecting her college reflected the standards of her rural, Caucasian parents, who gave her no guidance around the racial prejudice she could experience when meeting certain Caucasian, male students. Her parents had never been exposed to the sexual implications for young, African-American women. They had no in-depth relationships with other African-American women in order to learn how to prepare their daughter. In their rural, white community there were no other African-American women.

Having difficulties in finding one's identity is common both to ethnic minorities in North America and adoptive families. Both groups have identities attributed to them by the majority culture that can be distorting and confusing. Finding one's own identity is a more difficult process when teens or young adults are members of both groups. Parents enhance ways to help young people find who they are, as they define themselves, by exposure to information, discussion, and experience with members of the same race or ethnicity.

Parents do best to live, worship, and educate their children in communities that are as diverse as their families. Even if the parents feel stretched, children can develop identity more naturally. So many identity clues are modeled instead of spoken that children and teens need close contact with other minority adults. Some children who come into the country through international adoption find themselves perceived in a way that does not reflect their identity.

> One girl complained, "My teacher keeps calling me African-American. I am an American from Colombia. I have told her, but she wants to argue with me, saying that my ancestors were from Africa. She is missing the point. I am from South America. People think differently about race there. I know, since we have been back to Colombia several times. Why does she suggest report topics like civil rights, when she never asks the other kids to do them?"

Other children from Brazil, Marshall Islands, or India have a complicated sorting task, finding that they are perceived in a manner different from their self-perception. Parents and children often have to work on ways to word corrections, and times to ignore or speak up. The tempting notion for white parents is to say that it does not matter. But it does matter in terms of being authentic in one's identity. Children have already lost some information about themselves, just through the process of adoption. It becomes important for them and for their parents to retain accurate information that allows the full potential of growth in identity.

For more guidance on this topic, parents may wish to read Gail Steinberg and Beth Hall's *Inside Transracial Adoption* (Perspectives Press, 2000).

CHAPTER 7

Other Complications for Attaching

The previous chapters described ways that attachment is affected by children's negative or positive experiences with caregivers and safety. This chapter describes organic factors that complicate the formation of attachment or may coexist with or be mistaken as being Reactive Attachment Disorder. As this chapter stresses, symptoms may belong to several diagnoses. Each of the diagnoses listed below has grassroots groups advocating for early intervention and treatment for children who need help. This undeniably saves many children from suffering from delayed help. Yet some advocates seem enamored by their particular diagnosis, becoming overly inclusive. They miss factors critical to the diagnosis of other conditions that share symptoms. The material in this chapter gives some basic information on several problems that regularly overlap attachment problems. While not meant to help parents to diagnose, it does lead parents to relevant specialists if parents seem to see their children reflected back in the diagnostic criteria.

The sections on Attention Deficit Disorder and Learning Disabilities include their specific attachment-related challenges and some techniques helpful in working with children with ADD and LD. The sections on Fetal Alcohol Spectrum Disorder and Alcohol Related

Neurologic Defect will provide parents ways to lead to their children's strengths when working on attachment or empathy. Some of the methods help explain the ways in which children's brains are functioning, and how to work around their limitations. Parents will note that many of the suggestions not only in this section but throughout the rest of this book fit the needs of children with prenatal exposure to dangerous substances.

The mood disorder descriptions are helpful for parents who are wondering if something else might be causing some of their children's attachment problems. Ways to determine what might be a mood disorder as opposed to an attachment problem or traumatic stress are described, as well as what to do if parents believe that their child might have a mood disorder.

The chapter closes with discussions of Autism and Asperger's Syndrome. Parents whose children are autistic do best to have an individualized assessment and plan for them with attachment formation as part of the plan. Parents whose children may have some autistic-like symptoms after early deprivation may be especially interested in these sections.

ADHD

Children with Attention Deficit Disorder, or Attention Deficit Disorder with Hyperactivity are estimated be in the range of 3 to 7 percent of the school-aged population (Barkley, 1997). With a history that includes one birthparent with ADHD, the rate of ADHD in children rises to 57 percent (Barkley, 1997, p.37). The rate of Attention Deficit Disorder rose to 65 percent after *any* history of malnutrition in a large study from Barbados (Galler, Ross,1998). In the Barbados study, the total population showed an Attention Deficit Disorder rate of fifteen percent, which is high. Nevertheless, the fifty percent difference was shocking.

The rate of ADHD in adopted children has been reported at about 20 percent. That rate will reflect the changing demographics of adoptions, with more children being adopted from poorer countries. Caseworkers talk frequently about high rates of ADHD, or ADHD symptoms, in children who are in the foster care system. The rate of ADHD in traumatized children has been between 28 percent to 38 percent, with the understanding that more than ADHD is being measured (Putnam, 1998). Russell Barkley, a recognized expert on the topic, reaches the conclusion shared by other researchers: ADHD is not a factor of home environment. In North America, a small percentage, about five percent, of the ADHD total is from brain injuries. This includes malnutrition. Typically, ADHD develops as a result of abnormalities in the development of the prefrontal-striatal regions of the brain, the causes of which are probably under genetic control (Barkley, p.35-37).

Children with ADHD fall into six subtypes. However, common traits are

- The children's brains do not sustain attention on the main point of an activity or a conversation. Life for them is like a three-ring circus, not a center stage.

- Their brains seem to get "stuck" on a particular topic, or in a particular behavior pattern. They tend to spend too much or too little time (as above) on a task or activity. They have a hard time moving from one activity to another. They make the same error many times in a row.

- They have a hard time planning for the tasks that require self-control or thinking ahead. Planning ahead and rehearsing self-talk to guide oneself through a situation tends to be harder for them.

- Sometimes they miss the personal implications of their action. For example, they may get involved in hitting the piñata, missing the implications to the girl that they stepped on while fixed on hitting the piñata.

- Long-term goals work less well than do short-term reinforcements for children with ADHD. They need frequent reminders and bridges to keep them on track. Natural consequences end up as natural disasters.

- Self-regulation is poor. Others need to help the child regulate.

- Many of the children have mood shifts with the ADHD.

- Children often know what to do, but their bodies impulsively react with motor activity before they think.

Parents can get very tired when parenting a child with ADHD. They end up supplying the control that their child cannot generate. Since attachment formation takes so much time and energy, ADHD represents one of the issues that further depletes parents who are trying to form attachment.

Parents who are trying to present a secure, positive, and nurturing presence in the home find that their constant vigilance about listening and looking for their child's next impulsive act leaves them overwrought and grouchy. Coping with impulsivity is an area that defeats parents. Parents say that they are failing to teach their children impulse control or how to learn from experience. Parents become too tired to try again.

Living with ADHD takes patience. For example, a child who is sitting on a couch next to a coffee table will begin to kick the coffee table. The parent will stop the child. In a few minutes, the child will start again. The parent will correct the child. In a few minutes the child will start again. The parent will correct the child…and so forth. Parents who have accepted the ADHD will simply move the table.

Russell Barkley has said, "ADHD is not a disorder of knowing what to do, but of doing what one knows. It produces a disorder of applied intelligence by partially dissociating the crystallized intelligence of prior knowledge, declarative or procedural, from its application in the day-to-day stream of adaptive functioning." (1997, p. 314.) Because of this impairment in "executive function," children with ADHD do best when seated close to the executive. Children with ADHD should sit front and center in the classroom. They have an easier time watching the board and the teacher when those items are precisely in front of them. Similarly, they should sit right next to the parent at dinner. They do best sitting close to the parent doing homework begun at the agreed-upon hour. Background noises from the radio or television are not on when parents want children with ADHD to attend to anything besides radio or television. Children do well with very specific instructions and lots of smiles. Catch the child with ADHD doing a great job. Compliment him when he is paying attention, being considerate, thinking before acting, etc.

Children with ADHD have a hard time with the give and take in relationships, because they are not well-regulated. This also complicates the part of the attachment work that includes knowing each other and valuing each other. Some of this reciprocity in relationship is undeveloped, not because children are unwilling, but because children have a harder time with synchronicity with others. In turn, this impacts empathy, since children do not stop to consider the feelings and interests of others. Children with ADHD have to be slowed and brought back through situations, so that they can form patterns of responsiveness to other's feelings.

Parents who have children with attention deficit disorder hope their child will be one whose condition improves through the teen years. A large number of children do show improvement as they mature. Of the children who do not, training them to stay within circumstances that respond to their strengths can help them to select work and study environments with routine, structure, and systems of organization.

Children with ADHD also have a high rate of learning disabilities. However, the learning disabilities alone do not cause the same issues in self-control, planning ahead, impulse control, and applying experience that are common to those with ADHD.

Children with ADHD can be misdiagnosed as having attachment problems. While children frequently have attachment problems and ADHD together, a good assessment for ADHD helps with differential diagnosis. The child with attachment problems and trauma has symptoms of fear, intolerance of closeness, and lack of empathy that a child with ADHD alone does not have. The therapeutic dose of stimulant medication helps children impacted by ADHD, as does counseling. Parents find that the combination of medication and counseling conserves some of their energy, helps children to function better, and leaves more time for attachment work.

Children with ADHD are able to benefit from the grief, trauma and attachment suggestions and techniques in this book. Parents will find that the high structure and high nurture techniques that help with attachment and recovery from trauma also bring out the best in children with ADHD and/or Fetal Alcohol Syndrome.

The Resource List has some information for the group Parents with Children with ADHD. There is a wealth of practical information available for parents. The topic of best parenting for children with ADHD is so broad, that practical techniques solely for ADHD cannot be covered as a separate issue in this book. Many helpful books written with parents in mind are available on the topic of ADHD. Parents will also find help in dealing with educational issues in resources for ADHD.

FASD/ARND

Fetal Alcohol Syndrome is a birth defect caused by the exposure of the unborn baby to alcohol. The diagnosis of Fetal Alcohol Syndrome includes permanent brain injury. The syndrome includes facial anomalies, low birth weight or low weight-to-height ratio, central nervous system neurodevelopmental abnormalities, and a pattern of cognitive and behavioral abnormalities not explained by other factors (Institute of Medicine, 1996). Fetal Alcohol Spectrum Disorder means that some of the characteristics of the syndrome are apparent in the affected person.

FAS is defined below and in the appendix. Readers will see the term FASD (fetal alcohol spectrum disorder, defined below, used in place of the previous term, FAE (fetal alcohol effects). FASD is best understood as a spectrum disorder with a range of impacts in key areas. Parents will still see good information under the former term of "FAE." The take home message is that even without the diagnosis of FAS, there may be a range of impacts. Individuals with FASD may be more or less severely impacted than someone with FAS.

ARND means alcohol-related neurologic defect. Definitions for FAS and ARND are in the Appendix of this book. Julie Bledsoe, M.D. Director of the FAS Clinic at the University of Washington, suggested that readers will find these concise descriptions helpful:

Fetal Alcohol Spectrum Disorder (FASD) is an umbrella term describing the range of effects that can occur in an individual whose mother drank alcohol during pregnancy. These effects may include physical, mental, behavioral, and/or learning disabilities with possible lifelong implications...Each year, as many as 40,000 babies are born with FASD, costing the Nation about $4billion.

Fetal Alcohol Syndrome (FAS) is a birth defect syndrome caused by maternal alcohol consumption during pregnancy. FAS is characterized by: Growth deficiency (height or weight less than or equal to 10th percentile:

- A unique cluster of minor facial anomalies (small eyes, smooth philtrum, thin upper lip),
- Central nervous system damage (structural, neurological, and/ or functional impairment),

• Prenatal alcohol exposure.

Partial FAS is a diagnostic classification for patients who present with:

- Most, but not all, of the growth deficiency and/or facial feature of FAS,
- Central nervous system damage (structural, neurological, and/ or functional impairment),
- Prenatal exposure.

Static encephalopathy (alcohol exposed)…This diagnostic classification is for patients who present with:

- Central nervous system damage (structural, neurological, and/ or significant functional abnormalities),
- Prenatal alcohol exposure.

Neurobehavioral Disorder (alcohol exposed) is a diagnostic outcome classification for patients who present with:

- Central nervous system dysfunction (mild functional impairment with no evidence of structural or neurological abnormalities).
- Prenatal alcohol exposure.

Outcomes such as ARND, Static Encephalopathy (alcohol exposed), and Neurobehavioral Disorder (alcohol exposed) are far more prevalent than FAS or partial FAS.

In general, the central nervous system damage/dysfunction observed in individuals with ARND or Static Encephalopathy (alcohol exposed) is frequently as severe as those observed in individuals with FAS (FAS Diagnosis and Prevention Network, 2009).

When parenting children with FAS or FASD, parents find that children's brains often do not work the same way two days in a row. Also, the brain seems to have dead ends. Messages just do not get transmitted. Parents input the same way, but sometimes the receiving systems in the child are down, even if they were working yesterday. Mood problems occur when these children become overwhelmed. Or, because of gaps in the brain, children may react to an event hours after it occurred. Children have difficulty generalizing from one similar situation to the next. The brain does not recognize them as similar.

Often children get into trouble as being provocative, when they are just unable to recognize a situation as similar. "Do not play ball by that window," does not translate into not playing ball by the next window. These children do not know how to think abstractly. Time, money, math, and amounts are hard for them to fathom. People with FAS and FASD have trouble "translating hearing into doing, thinking into saying, reading into speaking, feelings into words"(Malbin, 1993, p.13).

There is an interruption in comprehending cause and effect relationships. They have to be memorized, like a script. Children will not foresee how the events follow and relate. Or, they may be able to foresee them one day, but not another. Subtle differences in the relationships already memorized can make the relationship unrecognizable to a child with FAS or FASD.

Babies with FAS or FASD are usually "hard" babies, not easy going. Parents need support right from the start. Parents find that their fragile, easily stressed child needs tremendous support in order to do well. Parents report that their children have difficulty with daily living activities. Difficulties establishing sleeping patterns, toilet training, and personal space are especially challenging.

Parents of kids with FAS or FASD are challenged not only by the disability, but by never knowing how the day will go. Because their children's brains do not work the same way from day to day, every day dawns a mystery. Yesterday's learning is not necessarily here today. It makes it hard for parents to settle down into a consistent pattern. Parents who do not mind repeating themselves make great candidates for parenting children who have Fetal Alcohol Syndrome and/or Attention Deficit Disorder.

In forming attachment, parents of kids with FAS or FASD have found that the attachment-producing techniques listed in Chapter 8 work well for them. Children do respond, attach, and develop empathy. But difficulty with emotional modulation has to be considered in terms of the degree of brain damage, and not necessarily in terms of either development or control. Due to their brain injury, some children become terribly overstimulated in surroundings. Consequencing them simply adds to the stimulation. It is better to simply calm the child down, recognizing that adding more words, more pressure, and more ideas will change things—it will make a bad day worse!

Issues of trauma, grief, and emotional reciprocity do need work in children with FAS or FASD. Parents and therapists have to use role-plays and pictures for much of the work. Some children do not necessarily ever understand fully the concepts of "why" things happened to them. They can express their own feelings though.

> While I was doing grief work with a child with Fetal Alcohol Syndrome, she cried over her birthmother. Her grief at losing her, and of her developmental differences was cried out, "Why, why did she do this?" While she could not comprehend the concept of addiction, she did grieve effectively and move on. Her question expressed the injustice of having such painful experiences. Later, she referred back to "when I was so sad over missing my birthmother." She acknowledges that she is still angry some days about the alcohol's effects on her hearing and her ability to make friends. Therapy allowed her to express feelings as feelings. Some feelings were put into words, but some were not. They were expressed with gestures, facial expressions, and sounds.

When children are working on issues of personal space and conflict resolution in the home, parents and teachers should try to use the same modality to practice as the child will use in real life. For example, work on personal boundaries is rehearsed by role-play. That way, doing is practiced by doing. Hearing about boundaries may not connect with doing. Some FAS children follow verbal information if they repeat what is said. That way, they get to input into their brains again. If they are readers, it allows parents the chance to help them with lists. They can read them and self-prompt. It helps to have some pictures alongside the listed prompts.

While children and teens with FAS/FASD may seem like pleasant conversationalists on abstract topics, they lack the ability to translate that information into practical life. They tend to do well with concrete information applied to specific topics. They have hundreds of templates memorized for how to respond to situations. So instead of learning "why," children are taught mantras of "what." "What are the rules for the car? What are the rules for the phone? What do we do with recycling?" Some of those "what" techniques are used with attachment and safety issues. "What is the job of the mother?"

The lovable answer might be, "To hug me, to buy me food, to take me to soccer, to lock the house at night, to smile at me, to be your artist!"

Children with FAS or FASD perform almost astonishingly better with structure. Again, the type of parenting that seems to bring out the best in children with attachment issues is also the type of parenting that benefits children with FAS, FASD, and ADHD.

Before adopting or fostering children, some parents report being told that their child is "a little FAE." While parents are expecting some learning problems, they are shocked to learn their children have problems as significant as the full syndrome. Sometimes these children have a normal intelligence quotient, or even above. Their functioning shows an inability for them to use this intelligence in areas that require judgement or prioritization. When parents are looking into the future for their children with FAS or FASD, they worry whether their boys will fall into the criminal justice system or whether their girls will be starting families too young and without parenting capacity. It can be difficult to chart a safe path for children with FAS/FASD.

Parents improve their abilities to protect by joining existent advocacy groups and by early diagnosis. The diagnosis is enormously helpful in buffering children with known judgment defects, a result of the brain damage. If children have the effects, but not the full syndrome, children may not get advantage and protection afforded through Special Education classes in schools. Parents who have children with FAS or FASD have years of high alert parenting. Getting cooperation from the school and good respite care is a must, so that they can decompress. Parents expect that they will be helping their adult children transition into the next phase of the life cycle.

Dr. Ann Streissguth and her colleagues have written a book that describes some of the ways to prevent secondary problems in children and adults who have been prenatally harmed (1997). Among findings reported in their book were the following:

Adults with FAE have as high a rate of dependent living as those with FAS, but lower rate of problems with employment. Of the 90 patients over 21 years of age, seven lived independently and without employment problems.

Of 415 individuals with FAE/FAS over twelve years of age, with the median age of 14.2 years, the following problems were experienced:

- mental health problems, over 90 percent;
- inappropriate sexual behavior, 50 percent;
- disrupted school experience, 60 percent;
- trouble with the law, 60 percent.

Some of the protective factors that Dr. Streissguth and her colleagues found that improved outcome were

- living in a stable and nurturing home for over 72 percent of life;
- begin diagnosed before the age of six years;
- never having experienced violence against oneself;
- staying in each living situation for an average of more than 2.8 years;
- experiencing a good quality home from age eight to twelve years;
- being found eligible for Division of Developmental Disabilities Services;
- having a diagnosis of FAS (rather than FAE);
- having basic needs met for at least 13 percent of life.

Rather than labeling and limiting children's capacity, a diagnosis afforded much-needed special treatment. In the sample above, only 11 percent had a diagnosis before age six years old (1997, pp. 32-37). It is not uncommon for a child to have FAS or ARND, ADHD, Posttraumatic Stress Disorder, Reactive Attachment Disorder, and adjustment issues of grief and loss. The medications for ADHD often do not work as well as they do for children not prenatally exposed. Some parents have found that medication to help their FAS/FASD children sleep at night is beneficial to protect sleep for the rest of the family.

Parents also find it necessary to shelter their alcohol-effected children from an early age.

As one girl with ARND said, "Why is it that other people know that a guy is a dirt bag, but I never know it until months after? What is wrong with me? My brother cried when he heard some of the things that I had done. I feel really guilty now, but when my boyfriend said that my dad would not mind if we drove the car, I felt like it was fine. When he said not to tell about having sex and that I wouldn't get pregnant, I believed him. Well, he was right about not getting pregnant. I didn't. I did get a bad disease from him." This girl was developmentally about seven years old. She could not discriminate between true friends and cads, in spite of a good, well-taught value system. She did not connect the information in her value system with the experience as it was happening. She did feel shamed later, but it did not help her to predict future cause and effect.

When children have FASD, parents find that their children look better than they can perform. In a support group, a teen with fetal alcohol effect read fluently and spoke articulately. But her self-care skills were that of an eight-year-old. A trip to the grocery store was so stressful that she was unable to buy groceries. Parents' oversight needs to be vigilant, since the young person is so suggestible. School personnel tend not to be as alert as they should be, since the child often looks chipper and bright.

Because their children can slip through the cracks in a school system, especially those kids with a near-normal intelligence, parents feel appropriately pressured to get systems to work for their children, and to keep their children safe. The diagnosis that helps parents procure special services for a child can be viewed in a derogatory manner. Unsophisticated teachers or caseworkers have questioned, "Why do you think this mother *needs* this label? It seems that she is labeling a bright, active child. I spoke to him yesterday, and he was perfectly normal!" After this type of interaction, an additional challenge to parents is to avoid foul language.

Parents who are parenting children with prenatal exposure will find specialized resources on the Resource List. Parents need support in order to avoid the exhaustion of informing teachers and setting up systems single handedly. Children with FAS or FASD will need to have significant changes in their environments in order to live as successfully as possible. Their brain damage is permanent, so learning situations will have to be altered for success. Parenting feels risky to parents who are parenting a child with FAS or ARND, especially if their child looks typical. Joining a coalition of parents helps to share some of the risk and to borrow from the solutions of others.

Learning Disabilities

Children with learning disabilities often need some additional help in working through their placement history. This can affect attachment in that children have a harder time working through tasks of grief work when they are having difficulties understanding sequencing or getting the meaning out of language. Additionally, parents may think their children are willfully defiant, when their children are simply so barraged with words that they are extraordinarily frustrated. This can place a strain on the parent-child relationship.

After parents have given clear information about the facts of their child's placement, they get caught by surprise if children are still confused. If children have learning disabilities, processing issues come into play, causing a need for repetition or a different style of giving information.

A parent who dedicated time telling his child's placement story found that the boy was not retaining either facts or the relationships between facts. By working with the lifebook using a simple annotation under the pictures, they did better. They further refined the sequence into four simple pictures, connected by arrows. The boy looked at the four pictures and said, "So that's what happened to me." His learning disabilities had prevented him from organizing the volume of information coming at him. He had to have the basic concepts separated out clearly. Only after they were separated out, could he gain the main points. He went on to ask basic questions, this time with a framework that helped him to organize incoming information.

Learning disabilities can be easily mistaken for some of the issues that are oppositional issues. Children who hear what parents have to say and act like they do not care, may not have decoded speech. Children who need few words and simple phrases are often given many, many words as parents over-explain. Children with alcohol effects get more confused, not less. A communication gap can emerge that makes reciprocity between parents and children difficult. Often children begin to get angry and aggressive.

"Why doesn't she tell me the truth?" a girl asked angrily. Her mother, who had talked for ten minutes, just gaped at her. "You never answer my question. You go on and on and on!" the girl continued. Her processing style needed a simpler approach. "What part do you understand? What part is not clear?" Those are great questions before parents move forward.

Good perceptual testing is helpful if parents discern that children are simply not processing well. Children may need testing by a neurodevelopmental psychologist when they are saying things like, "You never told me that! You lied; you said the opposite to me. I do not remember you telling me to do that. You told me to take the laundry basket to your room, not downstairs." Clues come from children who cannot follow three commands. If they cannot remember, "Please do x, then y, then z," by first grade, it is a red flag.

Learning disabilities interfere with attachment by making communication more difficult. Children and adults can become confused over the meaning of the misinformation. It is harder to get on the same wavelength, when the signals are crossed. Once diagnostic work is done, parents find it easier to identify and work around processing problems. Parents stop personalizing, and children have lessened shame and frustration.

Mood Disorders

This section is included as an aide, but with a caution against do-it-yourself diagnosing. Currently the diagnosis of bipolar disorder is "trendy." Since many of the symptoms overlap those of traumatic stress and attachment disorder, diagnosing bipolar is made with restraint by the most skilled psychiatrists. However, I have had the unfortunate experience of having clients get both a diagnosis—"rapid-cycling bipolar"—and a prognosis—"just wait until your child destroys the house"—from other parents in chat rooms on the internet. This is not helpful to children or families. This section gives parents basic information about mood disorders so that they can consider whether this plays into their child's difficulties with attachment and self-acceptance. If parents feel that mood disorders may be part of their child's clinical picture, it is vital that they add to their team a child and adolescent psychiatrist experienced in adoption for diagnosis, medication consultation, and treatment planning.

Celebrations or losses cause people to move to one end or the other of the mood spectrum for a period of time. For example, falling in love causes euphoria. Losing a loved one causes depression. Some people experience these mood extremes without events that would be expected to cause such mood shifts. During clinical depression, people are at one end of the mood spectrum, even without predictable causes like recent bereavement. People with bipolar disorder swing from this depressive state into an exuberant elated state. They have little in-between time in which life is steady, enjoyable, and simply pleasurable.

Mood disorders are genetically based, and are a biological dysregulation. Because of the biological dysregulation, pharmacological treatments are the primary line of intervention (Nathan, Gorman, 1998, p.240). A leading view is that the vulnerability for mood disorders is inherited, but may not be activated unless there are particularly stressful life situations or family environments. Most readers have children whose passages have been through stressful conditions, leaving parents to recognize that their children's dysregulations may already have been activated.

In addition to the heritable quality of mood disorders, a fascinating series of research projects are linked showing that mother-infant interactions alter brain physiology by selectively reinforcing particular neural networks. Mothers who fail to respond to infants' distress do not allow for neural development that leads to regulation of moods (Mash, Barkley, 1998, p.218). Other researchers have noted how depressed mothers and their children spend a great deal of time matching one another's negative moods. These children are developing neural pathways that are developed to reflect helplessness, lack of pleasure, and hopelessness throughout life. Some of the specific work for parents in the later chapters of this book gives children different experiences with parents, allowing new pathways to form. Of course, the earlier these experiences occur, the better, using to best advantage the plasticity of the developing brain.

It is difficult to separate the mindset of depression from other negative beliefs that children have after maltreatment. Depression has an underlying triad of negative assumptions about oneself, the future, and the world. Children who have been traumatized and who have attachment issues share these fundamental negative beliefs.

Depression and bipolar disorder can make attachment problems worse. In fact, Michael Bloomquist describes a common theme of difficult attachment and behavior in toddlers and young children with ADD and mood disorders (1996). While bipolar may be getting extra attention in children, depression in children is probably being underdiagnosed. Both of these get specific treatment in the sections below.

Depression

Depression in children has many causes. As mentioned above, there are biological dysregulation problems that are well-recognized. About half of the children correctly diagnosed with depression meet the criteria of at least one other mental health diagnosis. For example, there is a common overlap between depression and anxiety.

Children with depression have a number of common traits:

- She may not seem to think clearly: grades slip, time frames become confused, and assignments get lost.
- He is usually irritable. Irritable moods occur in about 80 percent of depressed children and teens.

- She seems to isolate herself from friends, and has trouble relating to friends when she is in groups.

- He describes himself in negative terms—as a failure or worthless, and describes the world as negative—the world works against any of his efforts anyway.

- She cannot find pleasure in life's activities. Nothing seems fun anymore.

- He may have sleeping or eating problems—eating or sleeping too much or too little.

Lydia, age thirteen, had been moved into her adoptive home at age five after having been sexually abused by her foster father in the foster home. Her foster mother told the placing agency that they could not adopt Lydia, since she was not attaching to her father. Lydia had already had prenatal exposure to alcohol and drugs. She came into her adoptive family with a diagnosis of ADHD and poor attachment history. Within a few weeks, her savvy foster mother knew that symptoms pointed to sexual abuse and asked for an assessment, which confirmed their suspicions and led to therapy.

Over the next few years, Lydia did very well in her attachment work and in her trauma work. She no longer met the criteria for ADHD. When she came in for her preadolescent work, she was also doing quite well with her gender development and adoption issues. Through an open adoption agreement with her birthmother, more medical information was received, including the diagnosis of severe depression in the birthfather.

A crisis call came a year later when Lydia was having an impulse to take all of the medicines in the house. She was stopped only because she left her bedroom door open with all of the pills in sight, while she got water to wash them down. Her parents were stunned. She had only been difficult for a few weeks! They thought that she had been going through teen rebellion with irritable behavior, dropping grades, and isolation.

Lydia could not quite explain to me or to herself why she felt compelled to take pills that night. The force of the feeling frightened her. "I just thought of everything that I had been through, and how happy everyone was that I had always coped so well, and I got sick of it. Why should I have had to cope? I am sick of working so hard. I thought that all of life would just be like this—boring and stupid."

Lydia immediately responded to an antidepressant medication and counseling, and showed good success with friends and self-esteem within three months. At two-year follow-up, with monthly maintenance appointments, she continues to do well, and has not been plagued with more suicidal thoughts. Her parents suggested that she discontinue medication, but she declined. "They really don't know how close I came to killing myself," she said. "I know it was wrong, but it seemed like the only thing left." Lydia is highly creative, and enjoys composing music and designing fabrics in her spare time. She is rarely bored.

The above example illustrates the impact of clinical depression. This is a not atypical illustration of a teen who has many complicating factors that interplay. I do not believe that therapy alone would have helped this teen's biologic dysregulation.

Children who are depressed should be in therapy that includes work on thinking patterns and behaviors, also called cognitive-behavioral therapy. Depression can make it difficult for children to attach to parents or to maintain their connections. Nevertheless, attachment work is undertaken, since children need parents in order to cope with depression. Medication is often considered for a period of time for older children. It helps them gain and maintain the energy and cognitive clarity to take advantage of the therapy.

Bipolar Disorder

Bipolar disorder has the depressive end of the spectrum, as described above, but also swings into extremes on the other end of the spectrum. It is important to note that while the other extreme of bipolar is an elevated mood, the mood may not be the expansive, cheerful version, but may be an irritable mania, lacking joy.

"Actually, I have come to hate it (the mania), too," one successful professional told me. "It drives me to stay up. I have to keep moving. My mind is full of thoughts and the connections between the thoughts. I have the energy to execute the science concerning those thoughts, and I am brilliant. But I hate that the mood won't let go of me. I want it to let me alone. I want to stop working, stop thinking, but I can't."

Depressive features were listed above. Some indicators of the mania in children and teens are described as follows. Mania often shows its start as a child's mood becomes excessively elevated over an event or a person. There is increasing and out-of-proportion enthusiasm for the upcoming event or person. Children may feel that they can do anything, displaying a grandiose element. While many children are not reality based, this takes on new dimensions. Teens may take on too many challenges. There is a sense that they view themselves as central to the universe as they take on these activities. They seem unheeding of the risks of many obligations, or of their increasing chaos. Older children become more interested in sexual activities. People with mania may have a decreased need for sleep. When manic, children or teens will talk on and on, often with theatrical gestures, irregardless of whether others want to listen. Or, they become irritable, giving ranting speeches full of hostility. They may move into assaultive behavior. Children can be agitated, expressing a need to pace and move around. Like children with ADD, they cannot screen out other stimulation very easily.

Children with bipolar disorder (BPD) often are confusing because they do not have such clear-cut cycles as an adult. Their moods tend to swing without a set pattern. This can be confusing when children are recovering from traumatic stress or reactive attachment disorder. In both of the latter cases, the children tend to cycle in progress. Bipolar can look like this same cycling. Until parents or therapist know a child well, they may guess that there may be more grief or trauma work to do, when actually the child is showing the cycling from bipolar disorder. Because children with BPD tend to be self-centered, showing limited empathy during mania or extreme depression, they can resemble children with lack of empathy due to reactive attachment disorder. This is especially true if children are not assessed over a period of time. Bipolar children do have empathy when not at the extremes of each mood spectrum.

Of course, children with bipolar disorder may also have reactive attachment disorder and ADHD simultaneously. These are not uncommon pairings. The rate of serious mental illness in maltreating parents is very high. Their children are not only high-risk from genetic factors that make him vulnerable to bipolar, but are high-risk for attachment problems and one type of ADHD.

Children with BPD can have rages, with destruction of property and danger to other people in the family. Bipolar children are rigid about being moved from an activity as are children with ADD. Bipolar children may rage for 3-4 hours over a parental limitation whereas the child with ADD tends to calm in about 15 minutes. Raging can look the same as the rage that is seen with severely attachment-disordered children.

The sense that comes from talking to children with bipolar disorder is that their mood takes over them. At times, younger bipolar children will maintain that the event merited their out-of-control action.

"I got mad," a boy explained. "That is why I threw that hammer at my sister's head. She should know not to make me mad. I told her that I wanted the swing next. Besides, I missed her head and just hit her shoulder. She keeps making a big deal out of it." This is a typical thought process for a young child with bipolar disorder. This boy still has periods of closeness with his siblings and parents that are not yet affected by this mental illness. At other times, he shows no empathy or regard for anyone but himself.

The example below describes the need for getting to know a child before making a diagnosis:

Willis looked bipolar or attachment disordered to his mother and stepfather. He had been adopted at birth, with little information about birthparents provided. (The attorney explained that he had "purged" his files when the family went back for non-identifying information.) His adoptive father had died suddenly when he was ten. He was now fifteen, showed little attachment to his mother, and had unpredictable moods. He seemed excitable and manic around his friends, and was ugly in manner towards his parents, ranting on and on over simple issues, sullenly refusing to discuss his issues or go to counseling—until he started to yell and rage before a family get-together one evening. He screamed out that he did not want to see these relatives since one had repeatedly sexually abused him until he was nine years old.

Parents were worried that Willis would not get help if they made the request, so I called Willis. Willis did come in to work with me after I personally invited him. He agreed to meet with me three times initially. He found our work and relationship valuable, so went on to work weekly for a year and one-half. He would not go to school for approximately one month during the beginning of treatment. He was depressed and described that he was concerned that he would cry at school. He refused any medication, but did agree to make nightly calls to my voice mail to report on any suicidal gestures. He came up with an alternative plan to finish his classes, so he went with this program. He prosecuted the relative with the help of his stepfather. For the first year of therapy, he refused to engage in any work on attachment. "I do not want to be close to my mother," he said. "Only a stupid person would have missed what happened to me. Why would I want to get close to her?"

In working through the issues of loss from abuse, Willis recognized his own distance from his mother as one of his losses. She and his stepfather did not press their advantage, but stayed consistently nurturing. Willis began to bridge some of the memories from his early, happy years into his present conversations. Willis also worked on adoption issues and did get records from the Court with the help of his stepfather. These actions meant love to Willis.

> Willis' moods returned to normal range. He finished high school and moved back into a close relationship with his mother—which he had enjoyed up until the time of his abuse. Appropriately, he kept some areas of his life private. In follow-up, he told me that he had stayed home after high school. He chose to work in their family business for a couple of years before starting community college. He was developing the type of age-appropriate closeness to his parents and peers that is normal for a young adult.

This is a typical case, fortunately with a good outcome, in which a teen had major mood problems without being bipolar. While bipolar disorder would have "explained" the moodiness and lack of empathy towards his mother, it was the wrong diagnosis. I have worked on other cases without having the advantage of a teen blurting out the problem, but instead hiding it. It is critical to know a child well in order to rule in or out other problems that are causing mood disturbance.

Bipolar disorder in adults occurs in about one percent of the population. However, the risk of suicide in bipolar patients is 10-15 percent (Nathan, Gorman, p.240). It is a serious illness that can have a lethal prognosis. Medication is a necessity. The relapse rate in one study of teens was 92.3 percent when medication was discontinued, compared with 37.5% for patients who continued medication (Nathan, Gorman, p.241). A combination of medication and counseling gives the best outcome.

There is a move to medicate bipolar children earlier. A mood stabilizer is used routinely. Parents who ask for medication during the depressive part of the cycle may receive antidepressants. Antidepressants are often a clue that children have not just depression, but bipolar, since children become extremely elevated in response to the medication as they swing into mania. Often these children have histories of maltreatment, attachment issues, attention problems, drug and alcohol exposure, and learning issues, when professionals are attempting to tease out the possibility of a mood disorder. The truth is that all of these issues are interrelated with mood issues. When children are not making the progress in nurturing homes and good therapy and continue to show mood disturbance, a mood disorder may be compromising their progress. When children are tried on a mood stabilizer and show positive results, that may be the clearest proof that they have a mood disorder.

The sections above illustrate the complicated nature of isolating one of several problems that have some of the same symptoms. Parents and professionals are often working on several tracks simultaneously since it can be impossible to isolate variables. It protects children when professionals consult about children with professional groups, and get alternate opinions. Professionals who mistrust their own favorite diagnosis are always considering what other factors should be considered in the treatment plan. Good treatment plans are pinned to good diagnoses, but keep the door open for contingencies.

Autism

Autism can be confused with attachment problems by parents. Parents of autistic children know early that there is "something" wrong—but sometimes they have not figured out quite what. Certainly attachment is not forming as expected. Attachment in many autistic children does not develop until elementary school years, if at all (Zeanah, 2000, p.301). Preschool children may have a strong bond to an unusual object like a wind-up car or an eggbeater, instead of to parents. Autistic children do not seem attracted to human faces. They get stuck on the stereotypical movements of their bodies or objects. For example they may like watching objects twirl or their fingers playing. Their developmental milestones are delayed, and the beginning of speech used for social purposes is slow. Other social non-verbal gestures that are normal to infants, such as headshakes, nods, finger pointing, tend not to appear. "About 75-80% of autistic children are mentally retarded, with about 30% falling within the mild to moderate range and about 45% falling with the profoundly mentally retarded range" (Zeanah, 2000, p.302). Children with autism experience stressful sensory overload when exposed to normally stimulating amounts of touch, eye contact, noises, and movement. They vary in which areas are most poorly tolerated. They may have a seizure disorder as well.

There is consensus that autism is a form of developmental delay with some evidence mounting of a chromosomal abnormality affecting abnormal functioning with the hypothalamic-pituitary-adrenal axis. There is no shred of evidence that parents' behaviors have any contribution in developing autism, which is a change from earlier, now completely dismissed assumptions from the beginning studies on autism.

Children with autism do not have the jumpstart that other infants do, who are wired to respond socially, and who find human faces interesting. Instead, children with autism have diminished interest in social interactions, including speech and gestures. They have heightened responses to stress. They seem to see the world in slices, rather than as a whole. This makes independent living very challenging for older autistic people.

Early intervention takes advantage of the plasticity of the brain in the first few years of life. By stimulating brain development, professionals and parents hope to see many more children with sturdy life skills. Instead of allowing highly stressed children to spend their first formation years in self-imposed deprivation, stimulation pushes them into the development of competencies and builds toleration to stress.

Autism has been well-studied as a disorder. The resultant educational programs are well-developed to assist with social relationships, including attachment and responses to family. Educational programs to help children with language communication are specifically developed for children with autism.

Families with children adopted from orphanages often find "autistic-like" behaviors in their children. These behaviors began as a form of stimulation when no other stimulation was available. Rather than preferring finger-play to social relatedness, which is the case in the child with autism, institutionalized children had no options for social relations. They still prefer the familiar as they come into their new homes, so shut out parents, going back to solitary activities. Parents interrupt these autistic- like behaviors, substituting their care for these behaviors, as the example below shows.

Colby, age four, fell asleep by rapidly banging his head back and forth on the sides of the crib. He pushed away from his parents when they attempted to stop this bizarre-looking behavior. They had adopted Colby from Bulgaria the month before, and were eager to meet his needs. After consulting their child development book for four-year-olds they were on the track of teaching him independence in falling to sleep. As we talked in my office, I encouraged them to meet some of Colby's earlier needs by rocking Colby to sleep every night. Colby did enjoy rocking, albeit stiffly.

When frustrated, Colby crawled a few feet away from them and banged his head on the floor. When outdoors, he banged on the cement sidewalk. They were wondering if they should use natural consequences. Colby, in fact, had a large expanse of scabs on the side of his head from this dubious attempt at natural consequences mixed with a dollop of parental exhaustion. He banged his head at least a dozen times a day. I asked the parents to intervene when Colby head-banged, cuddling Colby and expressing compassion, even though he resisted at first, preferring head banging. Within less than a month, Colby stopped banging his head on the floor when frustrated and began to look at his parents instead. He occasionally did rapid head turning to fall asleep, but not with the same vigor.

At age eight, Colby came in for a few sessions with his parents. He told me that he remembered rats coming into his cot at night in the orphanage. He rapidly turned his head to get to sleep and to shut out the experience. He remembered getting bitten by rats, and could show matching silvery scars from the bites. After talking about this, his rapid head turning stopped altogether.

Research has shown that as children adjust to their parents, behaviors labeled as "institutional autism" diminish and social behaviors flourish. Parents ignore or provide substitutions for some of the minor behaviors, like picking and finger-playing. Others parents interrupt the repetitive behaviors, since they are preventing the development of positive patterns. Children who want to pick during sessions with me are stopped from this activity. For example, since I want them to interact with me rather than the upholstery on the sofa, I alternately teach them other ways in which to calm anxiety, like taking deep breaths or holding their parent's hand.

Pediatricians or family practice doctors are the recommended first stop for parents with questions about autism. Physicians regularly refer for an assessment by a multidisciplinary team in order to assist with an early intervention plan. Support for parents and siblings is an essential part of the plan.

Asperger's Syndrome

A diagnosis of this form of autism is more easily missed, since children with Asperger's syndrome (AS) have normal or even high intelligence. Asperger's syndrome is actually considered a type of non-verbal learning disability by some professionals, since the children are not affected in overall cognition. Children with AS have a desire for social relationships, but have brain impairment that prevents competencies in learning how to relate. Their empathy is limited. For example, a child or teen with AS may lie down on a sofa, with others having to sit on the floor. He cannot understand why others are irritated by this behavior. The person with AS regularly talks at wearisome length about an interest of theirs without being able to determine that others are impatient when listening. I once fell fast asleep in my chair in an unsuccessful effort to conceal my boredom during a speech on an arcane subject by an adult with AS. As I came to, the adult expressed concern that I had missed a critical piece of the discussion and prepared to repeat it.

Children with AS tend to have poor motor movements and speech patterns with peculiarities—including being excessively grammatical. These are children whose parents worry that they have attachment problems as a primary problem. In fact, the children do have a poor capacity to build a healthy attachment, since they lack empathy and the ability to understand how others' feelings and events interrelate. However, the attachment issues are secondary to the AS limitations. Parents notice that children with attachment problems but without

Asperger's do seem to understand emotional issues over time. They may be limited in their ability to respond. Children with AS do show attachment to their caregivers. Over time, it is apparent that they have serious problems in understanding the feelings of others.

Children with serious deprivation in their backgrounds often seem similar to those with AS if there has been permanent brain damage. Children with serious deprivation are also likely to have some motor issues, like AS children. Again, over time, it is apparent that empathy and emotional awareness are growing in the children from deprived settings. It may not develop in the optimal way it would have without deprivation. Grabbing and "me-first" behaviors are resistant to change after extreme deprivation, but children will be upset if another child is hurt on the playground. The child very impacted by AS will be interested in the emergency and wonder why no one still wants to have a party after the ambulances leave.

Lack of social awareness and empathy are startling gaps in the developmental profiles of children with AS. In children with serious mental illness, including severe attachment problems and traumatic stress, it is consonant with an overall pattern of disturbance. Children with developmental delays due to deprivation again have lags in social awareness and social skills. Again, these delays are part of an overall slower curve of development with specific problems due to experiences of lack of care. In AS poor empathy and social relatedness are sharp dips from the rest of the developmental curve. There is a helpful book for parents interested in this topic listed on the Resource List: *Asperger's Syndrome* by Tony Atwood.

Summary

The brain that is dysregulated or has been damaged through exposure to toxins is the brain that is also trying to respond to emotional cues and attach. So therefore there is no surprise that organic and emotional factors are interlocking and interdependent. Parents might easily despair at the complexities of some of the issues. When that attitude seems to loom, it makes sense to take a step backward in order to consider what parents actually do know. They know a lot about their child, and already have used information to benefit their child. Learning about organicity is not an end to itself. Its usefulness to parents is in the way that information is used to help their children to move towards a happy life.

> One boy who had a rare organic syndrome made a book with me called "What I Need for a Happy Life." In listing these basics again, we found that the keys to a satisfying life were in his hand already. School and moods were still difficult, new educational challenges had to be overcome every year, but the important factors like friends, a loving family, spiritual aware-ness, and a way to have income were attainable.

Taking a long view gives children and parents a perspective that differs from the daily pressures that come with organically based struggles. Instead, it focuses them on what children need in the long haul. Children with parents who love, train, and advocate for them already have advantages for the long haul.

CHAPTER 8

Emotional Development: Promoting Attachment at Every Phase

A ll development is sequential and adaptive. Physical development unfolds in an orderly progression. Children first creep, then crawl, walk, run and hang from their knees or do cartwheels. Similarly, emotional growth unfolds sequentially and in stages. When early stages are stunted through exposure to trauma, the emotional unavailability of caregivers, and physical neglect, that child's psychological wholeness is compromised. Adaptive behaviors, which may become maladaptive later, will develop to compensate for lack of stimulation, care, human contact and love.

Healthy emotional development unfolds in a supportive, interactive, loving environment with a consistent caregiver who meets the child's needs. A child who lacks this positive environment will develop a personality equipped to cope with indifference, abuse, or neglect at the expense of healthy emotional development.

Children who arrive in their permanent families later in childhood, commonly from multiple foster care placements or institutional care, often have developmental delays. Loving touch, rocking, cuddling, bathing, encouraging direct eye contact—just some of the basic building blocks of early nurture—may feel unfamiliar or even threatening to them. These children benefit from the planned support by loving and consistent caregivers to help them access and move through the earliest stages of emotional development that they may have missed.

When a child's emotional needs are vastly incongruent with her chronological age, parents may find it challenging and confusing to find ways to integrate their new child into the family. But not only is it possible to support their new child through the necessary stages and phases of emotional development—it is well worth the effort. Parents must be encouraged to enjoy meeting their child's early needs for nurture. Doing so is taking a positive step toward ensuring that their child does not become a desperately needy adult later on. The most successful parents are those who use highly nurturing approaches in parenting *any* children, including those who have had a tough start.

What does planned support by a nurturing caregiver look like? Andrei's story describes the dynamic start, using a highly nurturing approach.

Andrei's vigilant scanning stopped at the sight of the woman in blue. She had a quiet smile. She was here again! She had brought him some little cars and played with him yesterday. She had whispered to him like they had happy secrets. Who was she? With a curious and coy gesture, he waggled his fingers and looked at her from the corner of his long-lashed brown eyes. In his short life, lived with preoccupied caretakers, he felt his first sense of peace coming from this attentive and sensitive person.

He came close to this woman, nestling into her backwards. He noticed the woman's hands— her touch felt soft. He held his breath and could feel her warm breathing against his back. He looked at those gentle hands, and grinned. He seemed to remember something quite wonderful from long ago. The feeling made him put his fingers in his mouth and suck a little. Then this woman produced, not a toy, but a bottle of sweet apple juice. She scooped him into her arms, sat right down on the floor, and fed him. He felt himself arrest from the wandering, searching anonymity of the past three years. He was drawn forward from his dazed state, and found! He focused, pulling his eyes all of the way up to his nurturer's eyes. Sucking in a smooth rhythm, he gazed into her kind face and began to know her.

Chronological Age versus Emotional Age

Andrei's mother was correct in assessing his needs. She met him on the developmental schedule that fit his emotional age, not his chronological age—accepting and enjoying his beginning stage of emotional development. There does come a time when it is too late to bottle-feed in spite of unmet needs. For example, children entering adolescence are simply too long and self-conscious! Luckily, Andrei was only four years old—and quite within the age range for meeting early needs.

Parents can identify the emotional levels of their child, choosing direct and appropriate support to help fill in gaps. The following sections describe the sequential phases of emotional development in children and the tasks of parents in each phase. Vignettes (drawn from direct experience) illustrate the use of supportive techniques and their outcomes.

Phase I—Welcome, Precious! Or, No Place in This World for Me!

Adapting to a Hostile or Welcoming World

How is the baby greeted upon arriving in this world? Is it with "Welcome, precious!" or with "The timing could not be worse!" Is the atmosphere surrounding the baby's presence tempered by concern for his needs and those of his parents, or is he thrust into the chaos of an overwhelming situation?

In Phase I of emotional development, children decide whether there is a place for them in this world. They begin to relate specifically to respond to a hostile world or a safe one. They develop social tendencies or avoid social interactions. It is in this phase that they prepare for the work of the next phase, which includes forming an *exclusive* attachment to someone. In institutional care, the world does not provide enough predictability or nurture for children to do their Phase I work, so they may remain emotionally "stuck." Adoptive parents who recognize this loss and take steps to support their child's primary need to feel safe and welcomed into the world are taking a monumental step toward ensuring their child's emotional growth and health.

Attachment is a relationship and a learned way of relating. In Phase I, children get ready to form an attachment, providing that there will be a consistent caregiver in the next phase. The attachment cannot be secure if children are without enough sensitive care or enough food, warmth, and stimulation. Sleep patterns, eating patterns, interest levels, curiosity levels, frustration control, and anxiety regulation are all emerging during this first period of emotional development. Parents play critical roles in helping their children become comfortable in their bodies, in buffering them from overwhelming feelings, and in protecting them from frightening events.

Tasks of Parents in Phase I

The task of the parents in this phase is to help the child form a healthy pattern for getting needs met consistently, in a safe and nurturing environment. Meeting basic needs like diaper changes, timely feedings, and comfort for body distress promotes this healthy pattern. Additionally, the parents reward their children for their curiosity, new achievements, sunny smiles, and affectionate gestures. Parents respond sensitively, helping children to stretch out their positive moods.

Vignettes of Children in Phase I, Helping to Form Trust and Regulation

What happens if parents are not able to start their tasks in Phase I and babies have already determined that there is no place for them? What do babies look like and feel like? How do parents respond? Sarai's story describes a situation in which a parent starts over again, coaxing trust and regulation a little later in infancy.

Sarai was born a month prematurely in India. Her birth was induced so that her birthmother could avoid the last month of pregnancy. Sarai was small by any reckoning. She had huge eyes that seemed to reflect the planet's ambivalence to her arrival. She ate poorly. She startled easily and cried hard and inconsolably until she finally stopped crying at all. She arched her back when workers held her. Her body language and her photograph accurately told her story, compelling her new adoptive mother into immediate travel. "I knew that she was ready to give up," she said. Even now, when her mother shows her daughter's placement picture and tells this story, she becomes choked with tears. Sarai made the trip home from India at ten months of age, but her large, sad eyes held that wordless question, "Will I remain here or not?" for many months to come.

Four months of her mother's predictable and consistent feeding, diapering, sleeping, and bathing routines paid off. Sarai started to sleep better. She inhaled her mother's scent while she drank her milk. Feeding was never smooth, but more food seemed to go down and stay down. The feeding problems seeming less like resistance, and more like suck-swallow weakness. She started to snuggle. Granted, it was still more of a cling than a cuddle, but it was definitely an improvement over the arched back. Over the next seven months, she began to ignore some things around her rather than stiffening with dread. She played on the floor, looking up occasionally for her mother's eyes and the eyes of others.

She smiled. She got interested in back-and-forth games and laughed during peek-a-boo. She was completing the tasks of Phase I at 21 months old.

With consistent and sensitive support from her adoptive mother, Sarai was completing several key tasks in Phase I:

- becoming physically regulated,
- stretching positive moods,
- developing social skills,
- signaling pleasure with eye contact, facial expression, and body,
- learning about her world (in a way that was not based on fear),
- learning a "back-and-forth" or reciprocal social style,

- using the adults to reduce stimulation,
- checking with adults' faces to gain information.

In the vignette above, it took several months until Sarai moved into a pattern that helped her to calm. The next vignette, Will's story, describes the transition of a little boy who moves from lonely anxiety to childlike dependence on his parents. Like Sarai, he lacked a welcome into the world. He entered the family walking and talking, but not any further along in the development of healthy emotional patterns.

Will moved, AGAIN, days before his second birthday. It was his tenth foster home! The new foster parents were given no preparation visits. They were shocked that after knowing him just three days, their birthday gifts for him were all he got. His life was looking like one of the grimmest stories from foster care: massive neglect, prenatal drug exposure, and a staggering number of placements. But instead of pulling another losing hand in this placement, he had just been handed four aces. His new parents, brothers, and sisters were a treasure box of fun and nurture. And his new social worker shared an iron resolve with his foster parents. He would not be abused through further foster care moves!

At placement, Will held onto his coat, even indoors, cleared his dishes, and dressed himself. He did not seem to be aware of parental love and care. Will scanned family faces to check for trouble and then dropped his gaze, missing smiles and invitations for play. He was a solemn boy, who seldom smiled. His developmental milestones were months behind his peers.

Will's parents drew him within the circle of their nurture. They kept his days consistent, so he had the relief of knowing what came next. His mother stayed home with her children, not with the house. She sat down with the children, reading and smiling for hours. Woven into every day's life was nurture by his parents. Soon, he loosened his tight body control during a rocking time with his mother. He and his brother laughed with glee during a bouncing bedtime routine, as run by his father. Will checked his brother's face to figure out whether things were really as fun as they seemed. Will's own laugh began a couple of seconds behind his brother's. His brother played, ran, and loved with abandon. Will followed suit. It seemed safe! Will's father began to make a bed for Will by hand. Will watched the bed in process. When it was finished, he slept well in it.

When he became legally free for adoption, he stayed in his family. He felt safe within a few months in his home. He developed a gorgeous smile, which he flashed on request for his family. He knew he was good-looking! When Will forgot his coat on a log on the beach—like any child would do—he and his dad ran back for it together.

Will finished Phase I tasks at 46 months of age. He had the cognitive maturity of 42 months, expressive language of 36 months, and the motor coordination of 40 months. His was the emotional progress typical of eighteen-month-olds with a healthy start. His achievement was remarkable. Over the years, he has continued his progress through subsequent emotional phases.

With the highly nurturing focus of his foster-adopt parents, Will completed several critical tasks in Phase I:

- learning to depend on adults as reliable,
- entering into the fun and nurture of his family,
- regulating himself for a predictable world,
- signaling when he had a need,
- relaxing in his safe home.

At the same time, Will's parents' tasks were

- supplying a predictable home so that Will could relax,
- emphasizing that Will was safe,
- teaching Will how a back-and-forth, or reciprocal, relationship worked,
- drawing Will out so that he could learn to play,
- using "cues" for promoting nurture.

Will's early experience of the world had "wired" him to respond to an indifferent and always changing world. Will was "rewiring" his brain—

and transforming into a social, fun-loving little boy. While babies do not form an exclusive attachment during this Phase I, they are affected if they lose the caregiver. They are also affected by negative events like abuse or deprivation (Briere, 1992). Maltreatment derails the building of trust. It causes the loss of developmental milestones in the short run and higher anxiety in the long run. High anxiety makes for a jittery, wary, hyper-vigilant baby or child, which makes the development of a positive relationship with parents much more challenging.

Prenatal drug and alcohol use can impede the formation of trust and regulation. Parents of children with Fetal Alcohol Syndrome often describe that their babies were "different" as newborns. The babies have difficulty getting comfortable in their own bodies. Changes in routine are atypically upsetting to drug-exposed babies and children. They tend to have difficulty establishing regular sleeping patterns. Notice in the previous vignette with Will how carefully parents worked to provide consistent and predictable patterns, necessary factors to help prenatally exposed children.

The next vignette highlights the same factors, but additionally describes the effects of moving a baby, depression in the birthmother, and transitions into adoption.

Damien came into foster care with two strikes against him: he was drug-exposed and had been neglected by his depressed birthmother. Martha became his foster mother when he was four months old. She noted that he could hardly hold up his head. His poor muscle tone could have been due to effects of alcohol and drugs and/or no stimulation. The caseworker said that his depressed birthmother had taken him to bed with her. They dozed, he fussed, she fed him, and they dozed again. Martha thought that Damien looked groggy. When she tried to wake him up, he startled and then cried inconsolably. He got so upset that he could not eat.

Damien slept lightly, but he slept a lot. He had learned to doze with his birthmother. He was underweight. Martha turned his head towards her and gently made eye contact when he ate. He began to smile. (Martha thought it was gratifying that his eyes were *open* now when he smiled!) She stroked his cheeks, palms or the soles of his feet to wake him and to get him to eat—especially when he dozed off after just an ounce of food. Once Martha got Damien on a regular schedule, he woke just once a night.

Martha had a friend who supported her with encouraging phone calls and visits. She needed the support, since Damien was a hard baby to take places. Damien became over-stimulated away from home, crying inconsolably. Martha limited herself to shorter trips, stretching Damien's tolerance by continuing to take him out.

Damien had been visiting with his birthmother, but visits stopped with her relapse. She entered a dual diagnosis program for addiction and depression and made a plan for adoption.

Martha started the careful transition of Damien into his adoptive family. The fetal alcohol testing showed that he had Alcohol-Related Neurodevelopmental Disorder (ARND). Structure and a gentle transition were essentials in keeping Damien's developmental and emotional progress.

Damien at nine months old was not yet exclusively bonded to Martha. He was social, "talked" to Martha, crawled over Martha's feet, and pulled himself upright! He was still more easily startled than are most babies. It also took him longer to respond or to calm down if he got upset. He could not screen out background noise.

Martha knew from experience that the adoptive family would fall in love with him and want to move him quickly. Since the family lived only ten miles away, they were able to do the transition properly over a two week period. First the parents cared for him in Martha's home with her there. Then Damien started to go to their house with Martha. After a couple of days, Martha stayed home while they took Damien for longer times and naps. When he went overnight, he took his own bed with him for good.

At the final "goodbye," Damien put up his arms to his mommy, not to Martha. Martha had made a lifebook for Damien, which included pictures from his birthmother. At the final "goodbye," the parents took a picture of Martha for the lifebook. She was waving, crying, and smiling.

In this emotional stage for Damien, Martha's tasks were

- helping Damien with clear differences between sleep and wakefulness,
- keeping Damien regulated while stretching his capacity for new stimulation,
- giving the adoptive parents a successful start,
- developing Damien's curiosity about his world and social interactions,
- learning and working with Damien's limitations,
- getting support for herself.
- using infant stimulation techniques.

At the same time, Damien's tasks were

- developing better sleep patterns and eating patterns,
- becoming playful and social,
- becoming a more interested baby without becoming overwhelmed,
- allowing more stimulation into his life.

Techniques and Cues that Promote Readiness for Attachment

In the vignettes above, the parents took advantage of Phase I nurturing techniques that help children bond to their parents or primary caregivers. The word *cue* describes an action that, when used with children, seems to promote a bonding response. Cues are signals that seem to be hardwired into children's brains. They, in turn, signal back to parents that the children are bonding. It is gratifying to parents to receive the signal. It helps them to form a relationship with the baby or child, which is the essence of attachment.

Cueing for Attachment at Phase I

- During bottle feedings, gently move the baby into eye-to-eye contact, holding the baby on the left side.

- Maintain predictability in daily schedules.
- Have skin-to-skin contact.
- Bathe with the baby and child, for a delightful way to bond. (When children have been sexually abused, the parents should wear swimming suits.)
- Rock the baby and dance with the baby and child. Use movement to help cue the baby to respond to the parent.
- Sing or talk to the baby or toddler, giving pauses for the baby to respond. Dr. Berry Brazelton (Brazelton, 1980) has demonstrated a voice pattern that is especially alerting to babies, which looks and sounds like the musical notation below:

60 beats per minute

Repeat the above two lines, giving space for the baby to build in excitement and to vocalize at the end of the pattern.

Speak, rather than sing at the indicated pitches. Hold the baby in a face to face position. Chant the voice pattern while smiling. The baby will begin to "lock-on" to gaze, moving arms and legs, trying to respond. Slower responses just mean more repetitions.

- Nurture the nurturers. Ask someone to cheer on parents, supporting them as they do a good job with the baby.
- Use helpful self-talk, such as "I am doing a good job with a precious, but more difficult child or baby."
- Babies and children who have been passed around or who have been in dangerous homes develop a brain that is on high alert. Maintain a predictable home with few excursions.

- Feed this baby or child on demand. Parents are trying to form a pattern in which the child/baby calms and believes that her needs will be met.
- Rouse the passive, dissociated baby/child who prefers to stare off alone. It may take longer to alert these children/babies and to get a response. Try cueing much longer.
- Stay with the yelling, inconsolable child. Avoid leaving him or her alone for long. Adult care helps this child not to feel so out-of-control and alone.
- Limit childcare. When it is absolutely necessary, try to arrange for the care to be in the child's home.

Indicators of Disruptions in Phase I Emotional Development in Babies

- The baby does not "settle" into napping, eating and sleeping schedules after an initial six-week period.
- The baby appears overly stimulated or too passive.
- The baby arches her back instead of snuggling into the parent.
- The baby who is three months or older may not have the ability to socialize with the parent. During feeding time, the little one does not make eye contact, nor does he or she smile, babble or track the parent with his or her eyes.
- The baby may overfeed or irritably underfeed.
- For the baby moved in the months after birth, there is a loss of the last developmental milestone.

Indicators of Disruptions in Phase I Development in Toddlers or Older Children

- Children show little or no ability to stay with the parent.
- They do not use the parent as a safe base of protection during new experiences.

- They try to take control of all food and eat without the parent's help.
- There is little or no eye contact.
- Children use their own methods of calming to go to sleep, including head banging, rocking and other forms of self-stimulation.
- Children shut down emotionally and do not look for adults when distressed.
- Children do not know how to initiate or maintain play with parents or other children.
- Children do not mold to the parent when carried.
- When carried, they do not reach for the parent or seem to look for the parent's expression.
- Children may be averse to the parent's touch, a signal that they have rarely been touched before or were touched inappropriately. (This is especially common in children from orphanages.)
- Children are hyper-vigilant to their surroundings.
- They overreact to negative stimulation.
- Children do not fall asleep or stay asleep easily.
- Children show rapidly fluctuating mood changes. Crying and rage seem out of proportion to the circumstances.

Summary of Phase I

In Phase I of emotional development, babies determine whether the world is safe or hostile to their social and physical needs. They learn how to signal in order to get their needs met in their worlds. They begin to develop social skills. Their brains become "wired" either for a predictable, interesting, and nurturing world or to attend to crises with quick, short-term responses and a period of dissociation (Perry, 1993). The brain establishes more neurological connections in order to help it with the type of world the baby will experience. It prunes away connections that do not seem to be needed. As a result, children learn to be either curious and social or anxious and wary as they prepare to move to Phase II.

Phase I Checklist for Emotional Tasks

These Phase I emotions and behaviors are evident in a child or baby who is completing Phase I:

____The baby/child often watches the parent as she moves around the room.

____The baby/child calms down with the parent's interventions most of the time.

____The baby/child prefers being with the parent to being alone.

____The baby/child smiles back at the parent.

____The baby/child seems to like the parent.

____The baby/child reaches out to the parent.

____The baby/child likes to play little games with the parent.

____When upset, the baby/child looks at the parent, distressed and crying, and expects the parent to help.

____The baby/child snuggles into a parent's embrace and is beginning to hang on when carried.

Phase II—The Sunshine of My Life

In Phase II children form exclusive attachments with their caregivers. When there are no obstacles to attachment, they tend to move into this phase around 6-9 months, leaving it at 16-20 months. (There is a normal variation of several months.) For a time during this phase, the baby may not want to be separated from the parent—even for the parent to leave the room. Their world momentarily crumbles if the parent disappears. However, by the end of the phase, the baby believes that the parent can be counted upon to return. The belief in the parent's reliability fosters the child's belief that he is worth returning to.

Babies or children move into Phase II ready for attachment. They perfect skills that they will use for the rest of their lives in forming attachments. There is a strong sense of attunement in children and parents who are forming positive attachments when in this phase—they feel "in-sync."

Children who are attached in a positive, secure way feel comfortably insulated from the world. They show an ability to regulate overwhelming emotions when using the parent as helper and comforter.

This is the stage in which people talk about their child having some "stranger anxiety," or separation anxiety. The baby wants his special person, who is usually his mother.

Tasks of the Parents during Phase II

This is the first phase in which good, nurturing caregiving by a series of people will not substitute for one caregiver. This child or baby needs to have a consistent adult with whom to attach. Her caregiver needs to devote at least six months of steady caregiving in order for a child to move through this phase successfully. This is a stage in which the parent can give a child a lifelong gift—the ability to trust and depend on people who merit trust. The parent needs to

- meet the basic needs of the child,
- be emotionally available to the child,
- stay physically close to the child, avoiding overnight trips and long day-care hours.

Caregivers who are traumatized, depressed, emotionally threatening, physically threatening, or using substances tend to transmit an attachment style to children that is marked by mistrust and confusion. (See Chapter 2: Types of Attachment.) On the other hand, caregivers who are sensitive, competent, and consistent form an attachment that is positive and secure. Children cared for in this way have a resulting optimism about relationships that can be traced to this phase. Even if later calamities occur to disrupt a personality, completion of a positive, secure attachment in this phase yields emotional benefits that can help offset the damage.

Vignettes of Phase II Children

How do parents help children to move into Phase II? The vignettes that follow describe these transitions in the relationships between parents and children. The first vignette, Mai Yin's, describes a situation that is considered nearly optimal. It still requires specific work on the parent's part.

Mai Yin was a daily delight to her foster mother, Chen Rui. Chen Rui, her husband, and their two boys reveled in Mai Yin's smiles and dear ways. They savored time with Mai Yin, knowing that in a matter of months she was returning to the orphanage to meet her adoptive family.

Mai Yin had been discovered on a subway in China. She was well-nourished. Her birthdate, indicating that she was three monhs old, had been pinned onto her warm bunting. After a short time in an orphanage, a private agency arranged for foster care with Chen Rui. Now Mai Yin was part of the family. Mai Yin sobbed if she had to be babysat. Even when she did stop crying, the sparkle in her eye was gone until her family members, and especially her foster mother, returned. Mai Yin was well attuned to her mother. She looked to her mother to find out how she should feel about a new situation. Her mother's facial expressions were a guide to their shared world; her mother's words named items worth attention; and her mother's body was a comfort when she got tired or overwhelmed.

When Mai Yin was fourteen months old, she returned to the orphanage. With formality, her foster father handed her to the orphanage staff, with her foster mother and two officials looking on. Mai Yin began to scream. She was handed to her adoptive mother, Mary. Mai Yin responded by batting at her mother's face. She continued to scream the next day. Mary got the message— she was the wrong mother! Mai Yin looked Mary right in the eye and howled. When Mai Yin was not protesting, she seemed to shut herself down. Mary found this as concerning as the scream-ing. She consulted with her agency representative who came up with a plan. Mary's agency interpreter sent word that that they had a gift for the foster family. Using that opening, they described their urgent need for assistance from the foster mother.

Mai Yin was exhausted when she saw her foster mother. Mai Yin seemed angry with her, but did calm down after a few hours. Over the next two days, Chen Rui brought Mai Yin's belongings and showed Mary familiar childcare techniques. Mai Yin even played with Mary. Mai Yin did protest, but did not panic when Chen Rui left. Mary was able to comfort her daughter. She used skin-to-skin contact with Mai Yin. She held her in the way Chen Rui had showed her. She used the clothing and feeding items that Chen Rui had brought. By the time they left China a week later, Mai Yin was beginning to bond to Mary.

Twenty friends, twelve relatives, and fifty balloons met them at the airport. Mai Yin stayed in her mother's arms. Her grandmother was noble. She stated that she could wait until Mai Yin fell asleep before holding her for the first time. Within six weeks, Mai Yin resumed her progress in Phase II, in which she showed an exclusive and attuned relationship to her mother. She searched her face for clues about her world. She shared little gestures of delight. Mary saw no sign of attachment difficulties.

When Mai Yin was twenty months old, Mary could leave her for five hours with little trouble. She knew that her mother would come back to her. When she saw herself in a mirror, she blew kisses to her own reflection. She believed that she was loveable!

Mary's tasks in helping Mai Yin through Phase II of Emotional Development were:

- helping to transfer Mai Yin's exclusive, secure attachment from the foster mother to herself,
- reducing Mai Yin's stressors to help keep her from moving into a shocked, or dissociative state,
- learning child care methods familiar to Mai Yin,
- using skin-to-skin contact, smell, play, and feeding to promote attachment,
- using her adoption agency to smooth a difficult situation.

Some children will move from Phase I to Phase II for the first time as toddlers or school-aged children. Until they enter a family, children who have lived within orphanages their entire lives have not had anyone with whom to form attachment. They will be entering Phase II for the first time. Other children will have previously had an attachment to a parent figure. They may move into their new home in grief and shock, resisting or withdrawing from bonding attempts. These children need to be coaxed back into Phase II, re-building a bond with a new parent.

Children who have already had a positive, secure attachment may be able to transfer this attachment to new parents. However, since there are different types of attachment, children may be trying to transfer trauma bonds or, avoidant, disorganized, or ambivalent attachments. (See Chapter 2).

Mai Yin's vignette describes transferring a positive, secure bond. James' story is more complicated. James is transferring his disorganized attachment style, with his parents moving him into a positive, secure attachment style. His story is a typically difficult rebuilding after multiple foster care moves and prenatal exposure.

James was moved into foster care at the age of 33 months. His aunt had become his caregiver sometime in the first year of this life; exactly when, she was not certain. His birthmother had come and gone from his aunt's home, bringing drugs and domestic violence in her wake. The aunt never could turn away her sister, in spite of resultant domestic violence that brought in the police and further Children's Protective Services intervention.

James was puzzling to caseworkers when he was with his aunt. He cried for her, but could not cuddle with her. He always wriggled off her lap during hugs. He grew anxious when he was too close or too far from her. Sometimes he would run towards her calling her name. He veered off before he reached her, yelling, "Let me alone!"

The aunt herself was puzzling. She cocked her head, seeming to listen to something that no one else could hear. She could not talk about her family without long pauses. It required prompts to help her get back to the subject. She smiled when topics were terribly sad. Sometimes she froze in place for a few moments.

On evaluation, James was described as having a disorganized attachment to his aunt. He did not recognize his mother. James was in Phase II with his aunt. He had an exclusive attachment to her. However, it was impossible for him to obtain coherent clues from her about their world. She also provided little help in modulating his negative emotions. James was learning her style of leaving, emotionally, when things became stressful. He showed the anger from the violence that he had witnessed in aggressive behavior.

At age 33 months, James moved into foster care with Ned and Carolyn for what was to become five months. After just six weeks they were sure that they were not a permanent home for him. He was unnerving to their other children. He hit them, hard and erratically, in play—grinning while they cried. The dog ran out of the room when he entered. Decoding his speech impediment, Ned and Carolyn realized how frequently he swore at them while smiling. He substituted *tr* for *f*. Their patience at being called "truckers" wore thin. He greeted everyone who came to the door, asking to leave with strangers.

At age 38 months, James arrived in his permanent home with Marlys and Luis, the foster-adopt parents of his older biologic sister. She was bonding well, but his parents expected that James might have more difficulty. In the visits, he began to relate to Marlys in much the same way as he had to his aunt and his foster mother. He seemed to be more open to Luis.

James seemed frenzied when he moved. He ignored his adoptive parents, focusing on new toys. On the first day, he hit his sister; she hit him back—and got his dessert at dinner. He threw a tantrum, spitting and head butting for an hour, when parents followed through on basic compliance. He had night terrors.

His caseworker appraised the situation and referred the parents to therapy as a form of coaching, helping them to help James to bond and to cooperate. Luis liked having a game plan so that he and Marlys could work together.

Marlys' and Luis' first job was to get adequate sleep. They were too tense and tired to begin techniques. Calling on grandparents, they got help. The grandparents were honestly concerned about disruption, and glad to know of practical ways in which they could help. Marlys' mother took three vacation days to watch the children while Marlys slept and caught up on phone calls. Luis's parents watched the children on the weekend while both parents slept, talked, and organized. With the household chores current, Marlys and Luis could go to bed right after the children's bedtime. James had night terrors, which Luis and Marlys handled by alternately getting up nights. They found that they were still getting enough sleep by alternating nights. After a week of catching up on sleep, they began going to bed two hours after the children, but continued to alternate nights. Grandparents continued to help weekly with childcare and errands. Marlys' mother quietly paid for a year's worth of weekly housecleaning. Only after they got rest, did Marlys and Luis begin techniques. Luis wrestled with James every morning and night. James lay quietly on his father, relaxing, in between rounds. Luis counted slowly, gradually extending the time that James relaxed with him between rounds. He began to seek out his father's touch. Marlys, who had been staying home, took over the financial reporting for their family business. That freed Luis to spend more time with both children. Marlys liked the office calmness three afternoons a week.

Marlys needed the help of their therapist to persuade James to begin cuddling with her. After drawing pictures to show the sequence of what would happen and gaining his agreement, the therapist arranged James in Marlys' lap. James was praised for being a strong family boy who let his mother's love into his heart. "Can you stay in her lap until I reach the count of ten?" she asked. He arched in panic, needing reassurances. He was not restrained. After several tries, he did make the count of ten. He was praised and rewarded with chocolate. He and his mom ate it together, giggling. The therapist took their picture. He learned to snuggle and mold to his mother. Just before his fourth birthday James ran toward his mother, and he kept running into her sweeping embrace.

James began to come into his parents' bed when he had night terrors. They slipped James into his own sleeping bag next to their bed after he fell back to sleep. He began to associate his parents with comfort and safety. He climbed back into bed for a morning cuddle.

James stopped approaching strangers when Marlys used a "handholder."[1] He asked for it even at home when company came.

Marlys and James played an hour while his sister was in kin-

---

[1] The handholder is a product bought from baby or toddler sections of department stores. It is a six-foot spiral plastic cord between matching Velcro-fastening wristbands, which connects the parent and child.

dergarten. He loved to play horsy ride on his mother's knees. He had to watch her eyes to know when her knees would open and drop him. He also enjoyed a rousing game of hide and seek.

When James did refer to "truckers," the therapist told him that someone had taught him the wrong way. She told him that he had awesome parents, who could teach him the right way. Everyone seemed matter-of-fact in expecting him to learn. If he swore at parents, he had to pay them back with a job, which had to be done before dessert, books, or television. He opened his mouth to swear at his mom and dad one evening, paused, and instead asked what was for dessert.

James was completing Phase II. He was also developing a positive, secure attachment style with his parents. It still had some of the features of his former, disorganized attachment style. James showed exclusive attachment and was showing emotional attunement to parents. He would continue to learn more about a secure way of relating to parents as the years passed, but for now, he was ready for Phase III.

Marlys' and Luis' tasks in moving James through Phase II were

- giving James a "welcome, little one," in their eyes, words and gestures. James had never been truly welcomed in the world.
- using self-care so that they could keep nurturing James;
- providing kinesthetic attachment cueing for James, whose primary way of feeling close was a kinesthetic modality;
- finding breakthroughs with James, through which he tried closeness and found it positive instead of threatening;
- buffering James from overwhelming events, helping him rather than having him fight or dissociate.
- neutralizing the effectiveness of James' negative behaviors.
- helping James seek out their nurturance for excitement and attention;
- concentrating on play instead of control;
- accepting and promoting James' positive attachment to Luis first, and Marlys second;

- learning how to get close by both signaling for closeness and responding to signals for closeness.

James' tasks in this phase were

- regulating himself to a safe environment,
- accepting parental help for his fears,
- establishing positive attachment with both Luis and Marlys,
- inhibiting aggression,
- accepting praise.

In both vignettes the children were initially reluctant to accept a change in caregivers. The differences in the types of attachments that the children had previously formed showed in the degree of challenge that they posed to their parents. The children both attached, but the planned support for James was enhanced by necessity. The reactions that children have when they are moved in this phase are listed below. Several of the factors were demonstrated in the vignettes of Mai Yin and James.

Children's Reactions to Being Moved in Phase II

Children who have been moved from a caregiver to whom they were attached, even if the attachment was not secure, show the following reactions when moved in this phase:

- Children may bat at the new parent's face, arch their bodies when held, avert their eyes, or use full eye contact only while yelling.
- Children seem to be searching for the lost special someone.
- Their past developmental milestones may be lost. Children may look dazed, or in shock, with little personality.
- Children may sleep too much or too little.
- Children lose their ability to predict environment, which is a precursor of logical thought and cause and effect. In the changed environment they do not know how to signal their needs to their parents.
- Most foster children who are moved between families become ill—which gives the new parents a chance to prove their care while the

child is more dependent.

- Children are depressed, wandering from activity to activity, over-sleeping, and behaving irritably.
- Children over or under eat.
- Children look and act frantic. They cannot calm down.

Techniques that Promote Attachment during Phase II of Emotional Development

- Use the suggestions from Phase I. Children will typically regress developmentally with a move. Parents will need to move backwards with them and bring them forward again.
- The parent should hold the bottle, maintaining eye contact and using a comfortable feeding position. Although the child is able to hold the bottle, the parent can use this powerful cue for attachment. Even though the baby may have "moved on" to a cup, try the bottle again for its value in bonding. If they will not have it, try again in a couple of weeks after the move.
- Stroke the child's palms or the soles of her feet while talking to her or cuddling with her. Again, this is powerful in cueing the child for attachment.
- Insist on more and more eye contact the longer the child is in the home. Make certain that good things happen after eye contact most of the time—smiles, play, and snuggles.
- Take pictures of the child with his parent, showing high nurture and fun. Make a book of the pictures. Enlarge pictures for the walls.
- When children are close, reach out occasionally and stroke their cheeks. Cheeks are sensitive areas to cue for attachment.
- Carry this child a lot.
- Emphasize that parents always come back. Especially for the older child doing this phase, use words to talk about coming back.
- Keep children with the parents, using childcare minimally during this phase.

Children who have suffered neglect and abandonment tend to be vulnerable in this phase. Parents who must use childcare do best with a constant person coming into the home and making the care routine as short as possible. Education, or even the use of developmental preschool, is secondary to bonding.(This should not preclude getting specialty evaluations done and beginning occupational or speech therapy when this is indicated.) After children know who their special people are and are attached to parents, they can separate, knowing that their parent will come back.

Summary of Phase II

Children who have completed Phase II have developed an enduring template of how to relate in a family. They have learned to read the cues on their parents' faces as to the meaning of the world around them. They develop relationship skills to connect with hostile, safe, or indifferent parents, respectively. It does take a consistent parent figure to do the work of Phase II, which is forming an exclusive relationship with a parent. Fundamental beliefs about intimacy and self-acceptance have their roots formed in this phase.

Phase II Checklist for Emotional Tasks

The following is a checklist that helps parents know whether the child is mastering some of the emotional tasks of Phase II:

___The child clearly prefers the parent to comfort her when she is hurt or sick.

___The child does cute things in order to get attention from the parent.

___The child looks to the parent for reassurance in strange situations.

___The child likes to cuddle with the parent.

___The child smiles and laughs with the parent with full eye contact.

___The child spends a lot of time close to the parent.

___The child often protests the parent's departure.

Phase III—I Did It My Way!

Normal Achievements of Children in Phase III

"No! Mine!"

After a baby forms an exclusive bond to a parent, the work of the next phase is to develop the baby's own awareness of himself, or his autonomy. Babies who have had no extra challenges in their lives enter this phase about halfway through the second year of life. They complete the work of this phase about one year later.

In Phase III, children's joyous recognition that they can have a different idea than their parents' is summed in a single word, "No!" This can be amusing to parents, who carry on "discussions" like this:

"Jessee, do you want to go outside to swing on the swings?"

"No!" Jessee responds.

"O.K., let's get your shoes on. Do you want the blue shoes or your boots?"

"Boots!" says Jessee.

Children do push away in order to establish themselves as autonomous in this phase. However, typically they do not push far. They still want closeness, lap-sitting, singing games, and stories. They are continuing to learn more about their parents and themselves and are building relationships—not building a wall. For example, children who are coming into Phase III at a later age may argue over where to walk the dog. They still want their parents to come along.

A wise parent does not overly shame children who are in this phase, nor does he overreact. Parents can take interest in their children's choices as expressions of part of their child's identity. For example, a boy may want to wear a short sleeved shirt and no jacket in winter. A parent can reply, "Simon, I can hear that you are a tough and hardy kid. Of course, as a great parent, I must have you wear a coat. I could not live with myself if I did not care well for you. Thanks for sharing how rugged you are, though."

Children in this phase, who are also in the ages of between one-and-one-half and two-and one-half years old, complete the following tasks:

• They know their basic identity—name, age, boy, girl.

- They learn rules and need rituals.
- They love to repeat the family members' names like a litany. Family members are this child's religion. Some children do not make easy converts to their new families.
- They begin controlling their world through language.
- They know that some actions follow other actions. For example, that when Mom or Dad pick up their briefcases, they will walk out the door. Or, that when the phone rings, Mom will leave, freeing the child to pour out and dance in the Cheerios!

Tasks of the parents in Phase III include

- helping children to enjoy their own identity and mastery,
- setting consistent and safe limits,
- enjoying spending time with their children,
- teaching about the world in a manner that builds curiosity,
- helping children to continue their growth of attachment by building the relationship, (See attachment-producing tips later in this section.)
- continuing to help children to stretch their positive emotional states and calm down or move beyond their negative states,
- teaching children that they are good, and that they can get positive attention.

Children who are in this phase at an older chronological age will also crave some of this learning repeated in an age-appropriate manner. They like rituals, need rules and structure, and prefer to know what comes next. They need to know the key words to use in order to provide some control over their world. They crave knowing who their family members are and hearing their own names in the litany. When older children are adopted, for a time, parents will have to mention two families in the list of family members.

Children learn some basic limits during this phase. Gradually they come to resign themselves to putting limits on all of their wants. They love and want to please parents, which helps guide their actions. Equally important, parents provide behavioral limits that cause them to decide to follow basic instructions. In Phase II, no matter what age, they are learning to please the parent, and beginning to predict the parent's response. In Phase III, children continue building on this knowledge, learning that they feel uncomfortable when the parent is disappointed.

In some ways this phase resembles the identity work of the adolescent. The identity themes are not as developed in this phase as in adolescent emotional phases. Adolescents are getting ready to assert themselves as separate emotionally, so they can eventually leave home. These younger children are simply asserting themselves as separate.

When children are being moved in this phase, it is difficult for parents to determine whether children are reacting normally in Phase III or showing red flags of adjustment difficulties. A child can actually be locked in protest over the move and refusing to bond to the parents. It can be mistaken as, "Oh, she's independent. She's just two." Alternately, after being moved into a new home during this phase, some children are afraid to say, "No." Children can think that they lost a control battle with their parents, and were moved as a result.

Vignettes about Children in Phase III

In the next vignette, Mai Yin and Mary proceed into the next phase. Mai Yin's limits in childcare show up.

Mary was delighted that she was the only person Mai Yin wanted for the first several months. But by twenty months, after she had been with her mother for six months, Mai Yin was able to trust that her mom always came back, as evidenced by only a few tears when Mom left for an evening. This was more than timely. Mary, a single parent, was getting poorer by the day, having already extended her parenting leave. Mary went to work 32 hours per week, which was her plan.

Even after two weeks in which to adjust to day care, Mai Yin reacted poorly with crankiness, anger, and sleep disturbance. By the end of the workweek, Mary was vividly reminded of their first few days in China. Mai Yin had the same panicked look. Mary decided that 24 hours a week seemed to be their limit. She arranged to work the other eight hours from home. Slowly over the next year, she extended the week to 32 hours of childcare, and worked additional hours after Mai Yin slept.

Mai Yin regularly performed for her mother. She loved praise, like other children her age and stage. She insisted on certain items, which also was normal for her age and stage. She had to have her train plate and train spoon to eat. Although it could be irritating, Mary accepted this as part of Mai Yin's age.

When Mai Yin was negative, Mary was quite low key. She saved her big reactions for praiseworthy activities. Non-compliance was boring for Mai Yin. For example, Mary sat her facing the wall for the count of 30 when she kept stuffing the toilet. Mary stooped behind her, holding her in position. After the count, she turned Mai Yin back to her saying seriously, "When you put the shoes in the toilet, you will have to look at the wall. Mommy does not like you to put the shoes in the toilet." Mai Yin looked ashamed, but not too miserable. They went together and rescued the shoes from the toilet.

Mary noticed that Mai Yin was interested in using the potty. Mary did not hold Mai Yin's toileting back, but decided to wait until she said, "No!" less frequently. She could still get locked into anger and frustration when things were not her idea. Mary was having such a great time with her that she did not want to introduce the task of toileting until she matured. Mary thought that she had already accomplished a great deal in this phase by incorporating work and day care into their lives.

Mary noticed that Mai Yin was already developing an identity for herself as a "good girl." In fact she heard Mai Yin saying, "bad, bad girl" one day when applying toothpaste to the hairbrush. Mary was annoyed that someone had used such a phrase with Mai Yin. She never had. It developed that the day care provider had not either. She was able to form these constructs herself. Usually, Mai Yin thought of herself as good. She could not quite make the cognitive leap with Mary that she stayed good when she did naughty things. Mai Yin was on a normal track for Phase III. The only area of difficulty was day care, which Mary negotiated successfully.

Mary's Phase III tasks were

- supplying praise as Mai Yin moved into a phase in which she responded to positive reinforcement;
- giving Mai Yin a "good" self-identity;
- helping Mai Yin adjust to day care without triggering memories from her move in China;
- using high nurturance activities like play, singing, snuggling and stroking the soles of Mai Yin's feet while reading to her;
- avoiding control battles while setting basic limits;
- focusing on positive behavior;
- keeping the family financially solvent.

At the same time, Mai Yin's Phase III tasks were

- learning to respond to praise,
- learning to accept limits,
- continuing to enjoy nurture,
- making choices and learning about ways to master her world,
- knowing herself and her mother better,
- accepting day care routines.

Mai Yin continued through Phase III with a positive, secure attachment. Her emotional and chronological developmental ages were similar. Fortunately, her mother had financial resources to give Mai Yin what she needed.

Children who have a background with more maltreatment and failed bonding attempts can present with more challenges in this phase. Brady, in the next vignette, has the challenge of thinking of himself as "bad." Brady's story demonstrates more tasks to change the nature of his attachment, and his self-image.

Brady, who was six years old, heard his mother call him a great kid. To correct her mistake, he stared at her face while dotting grape juice on the tablecloth. Automatically, he left the table, quickly grabbing three muffins while heading for his room. He was glad to go there for time out. After all, he had just "won" and he had food to hoard. He could hear his mother saying some-thing. He and the cat perceived the content of his mother's speech with about the same degree of accuracy. It sounded like, "blah, blah, blah" to him. When would this woman ever learn? He was *not* a good kid. He was a fighter. When he got close in the last family, and he also said "No" a lot, they left. Brady really wanted to be in this family. He tested them with his defiance. Did they really want a son like him? These people were so stubborn! They missed that he was unstoppable!

Emotionally, he was years younger than children who have typically worked all the way through Phase III. He was working through Phase III—again. He had been with his birth family un-til he was two-and-one-half years old. After his father was incar-cerated, his mother became increasingly intolerant of Brady's oppositional behavior. His mother's initial delight in Brady's ex-clusive attachment to her changed as Brady began to assert him-self. Her parenting ineffectiveness soured into an expectation that Brady was a felon in the making, who would leave her like his dad had. She made many tearful threats to Brady about what would happen to him if he kept leaving the apartment when she was asleep. Gloomily, she decided to say goodbye to Brady before he could reject her. She asked for foster care for Brady, relinquishing her own parental rights after his father's were terminated.

Brady had arrived at his adoptive family at age five. They were doing a great job in helping him to regulate and helping him form a bond to them. He loved his mother and father. However, when he came through this third emotional phase again, exerting his independence, he played out the events in his first family. He ex-pected rejection again when he opposed.

Brady's mom decided that she would stop using time out and stop talking so much. After he acted out, she kept him with her, making him do the right thing two times, or doing a chore to make up for his inappropriate behavior. She made a big deal over the right behavior.

Brady's mom began to tell him stories about an imaginary puppy. This dog was delightful, but quite naughty. Imagining a parallel experience, Brady was told that the dog had not learned obedience. She framed the dog's learning as part of the job of the new owners. She never drew the connection, but Brady would ask if she thought the dog would learn. She told him that she was sure of it. She stressed how much the owners loved the puppy. "Like you love me, Momma?" Brady inserted. They drew pictures of the imaginary puppy and his bravery. While they were drawing together on big paper, Brady would breathe deeply and relax against his mother. She reached over, stroking his cheek. Their picture-drawing time was part of their daily ritual.

To Brady, his father seemed to be a sideline figure. He played with his dad, but his emotional intensity at this stage was directed to Mom. As a result, some days Dad took over the parenting as soon as he came home. They called it "passing the baton." His dad bluntly described their situation to their agency, "My job is to keep my wife sane. If I can do this, she will haul Brady through this testing period."

Each day by breakfast, when Brady staged his opening volley, he began to resist his mother's closeness. His mother decided to get a better start to the day. She rocked him in the morning just as he was opening his eyes. She traced his lips with her fingertips. He responded warmly. She also began to give him baths in the afternoons, which settled him. They swam almost every day. He had to hold onto her in the pool, which allowed lots of skin-to-skin contact. One day in the pool he said, "I am learning to be a great kid, Mom. I do lots of things your way and make you happy."

During Phase III Brady's parents' tasks were

- finding times and ways to nurture Brady that he would not resist,
- not giving up,
- working as a team so that the mother could have time to recoup,
- teaching him that he could learn about positive relationships,
- setting limits without getting mired in control battles,
- helping him to re-regulate himself so that he was wired for a safe environment and relationship, not an unsafe one,
- taking the power away from him when he was using it to sabotage his relationships,

- working creatively with him, touching his heart.

At this same time, Brady's tasks were

- learning to tolerate and enjoy praise,
- enjoying getting close to a reliable parent,
- allowing himself to hope for his future,
- changing his self-concept to a positive one,
- allowing parents to care for him.

Techniques and words that help produce Attachment in Phase III

- Freely use ideas from the earlier Phase I and II lists, incorporating bottle-feeding, rocking, foot-stroking, gazing, movement and play into the day's routine.
- Help children produce order through their choices. Commonly they need "the red cup and train plate" for eating, for example. Parents who are sensitive to their children's choices cause children to feel understood.
- Phase III children typically love praise. If a child sabotages praise directly, point out how strong they are in mastering an activity, rather than a direct reference to them as praiseworthy. Children will still take in the message of praise, without their defenses arising. The parents' positivism draws children closer.
- Children may have a "bad" self-image. Make the case, in overt ways if they will tolerate them, or subtle, unexpected ways, that they are wonderful. Internalized shame, which fuels the "I am bad" feeling, makes it difficult for children to attach. Parents make the case that they are accepting and children are acceptable.
- This child may have already learned that when attempting to attach, he or she was met with rejection, separation, or unpredictable responses. Parents help children find the courage to try again by telling their child plainly that they are great, safe parents. Friends can be coached to contribute comments like, "What a fantastic mom!" "What a good heart James has!"

- Many children at this stage begin toilet training. Children who are "young" emotionally may be very slow to do their business where and when requested. Do not make this a battle since it is not winnable. (Additionally, the toilet and its contents are an unpleasant control focus for parents and children.)

- Establish rituals for bedtime, meals, etc. that are predictable. If known, use rituals from in the past for a period of time.

- Keep the number of changes in the home to a minimum. For example, tell the family friend to come for her two-week visit next year, not this year.

- Build a positive reinforcement cycle. Many children get attention for negative behavior by this age. Keep excitement for when the child is doing well. Make non-compliance as boring as possible.

- Do not use consequences for misbehavior that include pain or isolation from the parent. Many children moving into a new home at this phase are not happy to be with parents following the move and are getting what they want when time-out is in their room. Physical discipline confirms that parents are a poor bet to trust, since they inflict pain.

- Maintain the child's favorite food in the daily diet. For deprived children, be clear that there is always food available. For example, keep out a fruit bowl.

- Spend time playing with the child. Many children have not learned how to play if they have come from deprived settings. Spend one-on-one time teaching them to play.

- Make a videotape of parents playing, eating and singing with their child. Share this television program with the child. Children who are afraid of parental interaction become de-sensitized through watching these videos.

- Play games like hide and seek. The excitement of the chase and the being "found" is delightful for children who are forming attachments.

Summary of Phase III Emotional Development

Children who finish Phase III have learned that they have family members whom they can trust. They are well-loved and understood by those family members in a positive, secure attachment. In less favorable attachment styles, there is less sensitivity in this understanding, but children usually know that they are loved—at least connected—at some level Children in Phase III with positive, secure attachments learn that their environment is not overwhelming or hostile as long as they have parents to help them. In insecure attachments even if the parent exposes the child to overwhelming events at times, children still find intermittent protection through their parents.

Finally, children are learning in a positive, secure attachment that compliance works rather well for them. Children in other attachment styles may have a higher conflict level with parents or become afraid to oppose parents through their own choices. In all attachment styles, some beginning compromise is made during this phase with children's autonomy and limits. Children will have developed the degree of emotional attunement possible given the quality of relationship with their caretaker. Their identity, separate from their parents, grows during this Phase.

Phase III Checklist for Emotional Tasks

___The child looks for the parent several times a day just to see what she is doing and to interact with him or her.

___The child calms down after a temper tantrum, and accepts naps or stopping an activity.

___The child likes the parent's praise.

___The child hugs the parent back, even when he did not initiate the hug.

___The child shows concern, but does not disintegrate, if the parent gets hurt or distressed.

___The child uses the parent to help calm down.

___The child does things that are cute or playful in order to get parental attention.

___The child acts guilty when parents show disapproval after he makes a mess, breaks items, or chases the family pet.

___The child stays within five feet of the parent for significant portions of the day.

Phase IV—Masters of the Universe

Normal Achievements of Children in Phase IV

In Phase IV, children are more outwardly focused. They take their previous learning about the nature of their world, and their parents and themselves, into a sheltered social context, like playgroups and preschool.

Children, who are on an emotional development curve with secure attachments, are developing trust in others and confidence in themselves. They believe that when people meet them, people will probably like them, just as they like themselves and their families like them. Children who have insecure attachments doubt that the people they meet will like them or be trustworthy, just as they doubt their own value or goodness, and their families' value and goodness.

In children who have had no extra challenges, this phase begins at about age two-and-one-half or three, and concludes about one year later, that is by age three-and-one-half to four years. Conscience development moves rapidly in this phase and age. The developmental sequence is as follows:

1. Children know the parents' rules, but cannot control their actions.
2. Children control their actions for short periods of time. They obey rules to please parents, as well as to avoid consequences. They feel appropriate but not overwhelming shame when faced with the disapproving parent.
3. They know the rules even when parents are not present. As they identify with the parent, they take on their values in a concrete fashion. "Mommy says not to hit," they might quote.

Some children may be getting to this phase for the first time at a later age. They may have reached this stage of development previously with other parent figures. Once they transfer attachment or form a new attachment, they will resume the work of this phase. Children who have never had a meaningful connection to a parent figure may still have a sense of right from wrong. Their mastery is limited to learning the avoidance of shaming and punishment by abiding by rules. In other words, they show a conditioned response instead of real conscience development.[2]

A child who is in this phase at the expected chronological age is a good candidate for toilet training. The opposition has ebbed from the earlier phase. When children are in this phase at an older age and have not mastered toilet training, it is a wonderful time for toilet training. Toileting can be presented as a mastery theme. Using the toilet like bigger people is appealing to children. Children tend to be inclined to social acceptance in this outwardly focused phase.

Phase IV is one in which children continue their growth in identity. They increase in trusting and sociability, liking themselves and learning to cooperate, or mistrusting and behaving warily, doubting themselves and hesitating about cooperation. They know their gender, and they have a sense about whether it is good or bad to be their gender. As in the previous phase, they have a sense of themselves as good or bad. Since they see themselves as the center of the world, they will believe themselves to be the cause of the things that occur in their lives.

During this phase, children continue to identify with parents. Importantly, they are learning to do things parents' ways, even when they do not feel like it. Parents are teaching cooperation, waiting, and acceptance of "no," helping ready their children to participate in the community.

Tasks of the parents in Phase IV include

- rewarding children's initiative;
- assisting children in increasing their mastery of the world around them by supplying children with facts, obtaining items for play, and providing opportunities to master tasks;
- teaching respect for others and themselves, by an emphasis on empathy and the interruption of negative acts;
- responding playfully to children;
- setting limits that are safe and consistent;
- differentiating clearly the roles of parents and children;

---

[2] Children over the age of eleven can determine right from wrong, in spite of lack of attachment. Certain institutional systems teach these values. The conscience development seems to be based on an attachment to the community, rather than family. The accountability is to the community.

- continuing to foster a positive self-image of children;
- teaching children that rules are fair;
- helping children to talk about their world;
- helping children to express angry feelings without hurting others, e.g., "Use your words!"

Some children are entering Phase IV later because they were delayed at earlier phases. With care, they continue on the curve of secure attachment, developing trust and self-confidence. The next vignette describes this process.

Vignettes about Phase IV Children

> John was born quite prematurely to a fourteen-year-old girl and her sixteen-year-old boyfriend. They requested foster care, due to John's complicated medical needs, their resources, and their ages. The baby was discharged from the hospital into a skilled foster home. The birthparents made an open adoption plan when John was a year old, whereupon John was immediately placed with little preparation into a foster-adopt home. John grieved his foster mother, did not transfer his attachment to his new parents, and began to lose weight. His new foster-adopt parents knew that John was not doing well in their home. Although it was painful, they shared the situation with the agency and with the birthparents.
>
> In cooperation with the agency, the birthmother requested that John move back to the foster home. After many visits, John was carefully moved into another adoptive home at two years of age. This little boy transferred his attachment, moved through the other phases, and entered Phase IV by five years of age. He is attached to his adoptive parents and has contact with his birthparents.

In the brief vignette above, John had challenges in the past, but entered Phase IV curious, trusting, imaginative, and wanting to go to preschool. He rode his bike with training wheels, eager to have his parents praise his exploits. He was learning not to hit or bite when angry. His parents had only typical parenting on their list of tasks:

- continuing to nurture John
- helping him to learn more about himself—building identity
- helping him with toilet training—which largely involved dad modeling the "bombs away" peeing method on toilet paper
- teaching John emotional calm-down and containment;
- feeding the roots of John's curiosity
- affirming John's gender identity as a boy.

How positive the above list seems! When children have mistrust in themselves and their world, they enter the phase with more negative beliefs. Phase IV children who move after maltreatment enter their families knowing how shamefully small they are in the world. If they have been hurt through abuse, they are anxious around adults. This can be masked by bravado, as they pretend that they are big and self-reliant. Alternately, they may withdraw. Either reaction makes bonding a challenge.

Up through the elementary years, children still believe in wishful thinking. During the ages of three through six children are most devoted to the belief in wishful thinking. If they were moved after wishing for a move, they will take responsibility for the move. They can begin to believe in their own omnipotence. Children who have been moved have sometimes perfected "the look." Children pair an especially malevolent face with the silent wish that their parents would go away forever. When they are subsequently moved to a new home, they believe that "the look" made people disappear from their lives. When enraged, they may try it on new parents, and then feel terrified later.

Children who have not attached do not feel any distress over parents' disapproval, or any pleasure in following the rules. They are motivated by behavioral consequences. This makes an extremely tough road for parents, who need to supervise and devise consequences all day, every day. When children move during this phase, attachment figures change as well as the rules. Both stymie conscience development.

The next vignette describes a child who is trying to do Phase IV work after maltreatment and several moves. Her keenly felt responsibility for her wishes and their results are apparent in her story. How that impedes her attachment, and ways to overcome that impediment, follow.

Noel was a charmer at the age of four. She was bright and unusually verbal. She was in a guardianship with her mother's godparents, Isaac and Yolanda, who initially kept Noel until the birthmother could take parenting classes and obtain suitable housing, when Noel was two-and-one-half. As the birthmother's situation deteriorated instead of improving, temporary care evolved into parenting.

Noel had spent days with her godparents since infancy. She seemed to think that she was just visiting until overnight visits with her birthmother stopped. Her easy transition stalled when Noel saw them as parents rather than godparents. With a jolt, they realized that the cute play, during which Noel took care of adults, was not play. It was Noel's reality. They also realized that Noel did not show any remorse about misbehavior. Noel seemed to spend her time thinking of ways to elude their supervision, rather than learning right from wrong. Noel described how helpful she had been to her birthmother, "I brought her drinks, turned on the television, and picked up the house. I took good care of her." Noel had already formed a relationship style of codependence—that is, taking care of someone else in order to get some of one's own needs met. Her mastery themes were not used for age-appropriate tasks, but used for a role reversal. Noel had transferred her exclusive attachment to her new parents, and had a sense of her own autonomy, based on mistrust of parents. She was oppositional, unless she was in control.

As Isaac and Yolanda acquainted Noel with normal expectations of children her age— bedtimes, mealtimes, and privacy— Noel became outraged. She had power when being treated like a peer, or playing mother. In her world, power was essential for safety. How dare they threaten her! She was her birthmother's best friend. She identified with her birthmother. She normally called Isaac "Dad," and enjoyed him. But when he set a limit, she was outraged. Angrily, she told him, "Go home! We are breaking up!" She did not understand roles.

Noel's insistence on control of her parents became extreme as she felt more pressure to trust them. She hit Yolanda—hard, in the face, and without remorse—almost weekly. She hid Isaac's blood pressure medication after listening in on a discussion of its importance to his health.

Finally, during one very difficult afternoon, Isaac and Yolanda disciplined Noel. Then Yolanda rocked her and gave her a bottle. Noel began to sob in her foster mother's lap, grieving like the child she was, "I loved her so much. I did such a good job. I did everything that she asked me!"

Yolanda said, "You did a wonderful job of loving her. It seems that you could not have tried harder." Noel nodded, too choked with tears to speak.

Yolanda continued, "It still did not work, though. Even when you did all those jobs for her, she still could not find a safe house for you or take care of you."

"I miss her a lot," Noel wailed.

"I know you do," Yolanda said. "I do, too. She is my godchild. I tried hard, too."

Isaac was blinking back tears. "I miss her, too." He paused and continued. "But now it's time for you to let yourself be a little girl, and to let us take care of you." He slid an arm around her and his wife. Noel hugged back hard.

Over the next months this type of conversation happened several times. Each time, she got the caring message that she was a child. She had tremendous doubt about herself as doing a good job loving her parent, and felt responsible for the move. Of course, she had been furious with her birthmother, and had wished that she would go away. That was also discussed in terms that every child feels like that, and even more so if they feel scared. Nicole received affirmation for her past efforts. She also got the message that it was time to change her efforts.

Parental rights were terminated, with adoption by Yolanda and Isaac in process. Noel would fall off in her progress, and seemed to be keeping her old skills in case she ever moved back with her birthmother. After Noel shared that her birthmother had told her on the phone that she would be coming for her soon, conversations that Noel had with her birthmother were monitored. Isaac and Yolanda asserted themselves as the permanent family. Noel had few setbacks.

Noel began to model after her mom. She cooperated with Isaac, instead of treating him like a boyfriend who needed to go home. At the hair salon, she asked, "May I have my hair treated like my Mom's?"

As parents, Yolanda and Isaac's tasks in this phase were

- helping Noel to model after them, and to accept the reality of the loss of her first parent;
- showing Noel sensitive care about her loss, so that she could grieve with them;
- limiting Noel in a manner that helped her learn new rules;
- helping Noel to use words to work through frustration and pain;
- providing closeness for Noel, as a trade for control;
- rebuilding Noel's sense of self, reducing shame for the loss of her birthmother;
- providing emotional attunement for Noel;
- helping Noel to make a differentiation between the past and present;
- teaching Noel how to cooperate without feeling as if she were losing.

Noel's tasks during this same time were

- mastering tasks for her developmental age, rather than caring for her birthmother;
- grieving her loss of her birthmother, and getting support for the grief;
- developing empathy for others based on the empathy shown to her;
- accepting her parents as her new models;
- letting go of the fantasy of herself as the master of the adults;
- believing that her adoptive parents were dependable.

Techniques, Words and Concepts that Promote Attachment in Phase IV

- Use the tips from the former phases freely. Children who enter Phase IV at age eleven are usually too old for bottle-feeding. Other techniques are appropriate, however.
- Allow this child to regress into more infantile stages when they are needy. (In reality, most adults regress when they need comfort and care.)
- Get cuddly bedclothes for the little person. Do not be afraid to rock the child to sleep. Reassure her that parents will be there in the morning.
- Encourage the child to come into the parents' room if afraid at night. Parents can use a sleeping bag beside their bed so that the child can come in for consolation, without their having to get up and put them back to bed. (Some parents choose a "family bed." This is usually not a good option for challenging children. This parenting is so difficult that parents should not sacrifice their own sleep or sexual intimacy on any regular basis.)
- Tell children the reasons for adoption or foster care that make sense. (This varies according to cognitive age, not just emotional age.) Children will make up their own reasons for adoption if they are not told concrete reasons that make sense to them. For example, telling children that the angels arranged the adoption is not helpful. Telling a child a truthful reason, like there was not enough food in their birthfamily, is helpful in starting a discussion. It leads to good questions.

Indicators of Disruptions in Phase IV Development, with Suggestions for Remediations

When children are moved during Phase IV, or have problems in Phase IV due to earlier moves, they may experience disruptions in development like those mentioned below, with suggestions for remediation.

- Children who have been severely neglected, especially those from institutions from Eastern Europe, need drastically reduced stimulation until they adjust to a normal environment. Just introduce a few toys at a time. Children should not have the run of the house. It is simply too much of a change. It is good nurturance to gradually build a tolerance to stimulation. Simplify the surroundings. In a simpler structure, parents need make and enforce only a few rules.

- Reassure the children that she is lovable. Chilren sometimes feel given away. In almost every case, due to the egocentrism of this age, they feel that they are responsible for the move.

- Maintain as much of children's identity as possible. If they bring their belongings with them, parents should keep them all. Even if some of the items look quite worn, they help them feel connected with their lives before their move to their family. Take pictures of children immediately, displaying those pictures.

- If children throw tantrums, hold the them close. Often children will break into crying and grieve while parents hold and comfort them.

- Children will often claim that they are quite hurt when their injury is minor. This gives them the opportunity to cry for a while, getting a cycle of comfort developed with their parents. It helps them to get sensitive care for their hearts, if parents kiss and hug, instead of dismissing the injury. There is an injury to the heart, but at times children can only express it through injuries to fingers and knees.

- Children will often be in a state of shock when they move. Help these children to move into a predictable schedule, full of nurture. Be prepared to explain the circumstances of the move over and over again. Keep as much of their former schedule as possible.

Summary of Phase IV Emotional Development

Children in Phase IV leave the phase with an ability to function outside of the care of their parents for periods of time. They develop social skills so that they can either cooperate with others or defend themselves against others during this phase. Conscience development moves quickly in this phase. Children master abilities at this phase, and feel good about what they master, or feel inadequate about what they master. Children who are safe and supported are poised at the brink of an outward look at their world. They are excited and enthusiastic about being with other children. It is a time that imagination, and imaginative play, begins. Children who are not feeling safe begin to feel pressure to cooperate and calm down at this phase. They begin to get societal messages that are less accepting. Phase IV children feel increasing confidence, or lack of confidence, about their gender and identity depending on their attachment styles and beliefs in the home.

Checklist for Phase IV Emotional Tasks

___The child wants cuddles and snuggles from parents, although he may sometimes be coy.

___The child wants parents for bedtime rituals.

___The child wants parents to see his accomplishments.

___The child checks on parents' whereabouts when he is doing something against the rules.

___The child competes for parents' positive attention and does not interrupt the attention when she gets it.

___The child gets parents' help in solving problems, preferring their help to a stranger's help.

___The child gives eye contact and responsive smiling to parents many times a day.

___The child imitates parents' activities and tries to stay physically close to them.

___The child mimics some mannerisms of the parent, and states their rules.

Phase V—Magical Child, Great Romantic

Normal Achievements in Phase V

Barring extra challenges, children enter Phase V at about three-and-one-half or four years of age, completing the phase at six or seven years of age. With several moves and losses, some children are making strong progress, yet moving into Phase V years later. Phase V children are great romantics. They continue in gender development, identity, curiosity, and imagination throughout this phase. In two-parent families, they tend to want to marry their opposite-sex parent. (The older child usually is savvy enough to keep this tidbit to himself, but will ask some cagey questions about Mom's or Dad's longevity.) Single parents can find that their children are inordinately interested in their romantic life or the absence of one.

Children in this phase are dogmatic and bossy. They tend to understand relationships only from their own points of view. They may have a hard time understanding why parents did not adopt their birthmother, too. They ask why they cannot sleep in your bed. They concede defeat in the last area of privilege only because parents are bigger, and big people get more of what they want!

Children of this age want friends. They enjoy group activities enormously. They are imaginative—to the extent that they get carried away by their fantasies at times. Some parents have had to interrupt a zealous child jumping over the stairs with a cape on—ready to fly. They like to wear costumes as they try on different personas. Sometimes they require others to call them by a particular name, i.e. Princess, Batman, Dolphin Girl. Parents remain emotional touchpoints for children in this phase, but they have their own plans for the day. They like to read the same story or watch the same movie repetitively, drawing from its images the imaginative themes for the day. They like collections of items, all just a little varied, as props for play. Competence is a huge emphasis at this phase. Children want to be competent in their world, so they acquire new skills daily. Children are driven to learn more. Children develop in their gender identity, usually liking to be their gender. Most children play with the children of the other gender freely.

Children go through a developmental window of speaking about their anger, not hitting when angry, by the middle of the phase. Without challenges, the end of the phase concludes roughly by the start of kindergarten. It is obviously beneficial for children to have learned not to hit by the time that they start school. The aggressiveness that results from maltreatment tends to stand out more by the end of Phase V.

During this phase children want to know why they are not with their birthparents. Some children are ready for a simple story, rather than one reason. While it is important to give truthful reasons, frame causes so children are not alarmed that the conditions will reoccur in their current family. Explanations need to be concrete. For example, "There was not enough food in your family in Russia. Your birthparents knew that there was food in the orphanage. That is why they left you in the market where you could be noticed and taken to the orphanage. They may have hoped that you would be adopted. They knew that you needed a family with enough food and love, just like other children. They wanted you to live, and to have a good life."

Drawing some simple pictures with verbal explanations helps children to sequence events in their lives. Children cognitively under the age of seven have trouble with sequencing, as do children with auditory processing problems. Often the lifebook has pictures that can be used to help children form a simple story line. Incorporate into their life history, if it is at all possible, the statements below, which come from Dr. Vera Fahlberg (1989):

A. Your birthmother (parents) loved you.

B. She (they) would have raised you if she (they) could.

C. She (they) could not raise you and made this choice for you.

These statements endow children with worth and give permission for children to love their current family. They set a framework for a discussion that includes some sad feelings as well as happy ones. Some children are only interested in birthmother. Older children, especially those who remember relationships with birthfathers, need to hear permission from both birthparents to move into loving relationships with their new families.

At this phase, a lifebook should be developed. It is important for children to believe that their parents know their histories and recognize their identities prior to coming to their families. A lifebook helps children to develop a life story, incorporating both the events and feelings of their lives. It also provides a tool through which the parent can talk with the child. A helpful and creative description of how to form a lifebook for young children who have had earlier caregivers or have been adopted internationally is contained in Mary Hopkins-Best's book, *Toddler Adoption: The Weaver's Craft* (2012).

Vignettes about Phase V Children

In Ani's vignette, the phase's accent on gender brings issues to a peak. Issues of control and anger continue to mar the relationship that Ani has with her mother. In contrast, her attachment style with her father is more trusting.

Ani, age six, was suspicious and nasty around her mother. She told everyone that she wished to be a boy, like her brother. Instead of enjoying an occasion to identify with her mother, she slit the skirts of the special dresses that she and her mother were to wear together. She showed remorse and apologized, but later got angry again for no reason. Ani spent time with her father, enjoying his camaraderie. She had decided to marry him, but had a hard time putting her dislike for being a female with this decision. They would eat at McDonalds's every day, she dreamed. Ani rarely played. She was aloof when her mother tried to spend time with her. Sometimes she would draw close, only to keep a space between herself and her mother again. Affection was on Ani's terms.

Ani and her mother went to therapy in order to improve their relationship. Ani decided to sit on her mother's lap, having surmised that this seemed to please the therapist. Maybe she would never have to come back to therapy! Her mother mouthed the words to the therapist, "She never sits on my lap at home."

Citing recent examples, the therapist questioned Ani's control and mistrust of her mother. Pressured, Ani blurted her evidence for mistrust, "But I remember when she left me. I remember when I was hungry and she did not come. You say that I have a great mom, but she left me!" In an effort to avoid painful events in her life, her parents had omitted any mention of the conditions in the Romanian orphanage in which she had lived. The picture in the lifebook showed castles for Romania.

As they reviewed her lifebook, her mother added a few pages. Those pages included pictures of the iron crib where Ani had spent months six through twenty-two of her life in Romania. As she examined the pictures and heard about the poverty in Romania, Ani said intensely, "Now I understand. Now I know what happened to me!" She turned to her mother and said, "I thought that you were lying to cover up for yourself. I thought that I cried so much that you gave up and left me."

Ani's struggle with the past made it hard for her to identify with her mother. She did not like girls or women much. She was ashamed of being a baby girl who was not worth good care, and angry with her mother for leaving her. Explanations that were realistic helped Ani to realize that neither of these judgments were necessary. Ani began to identify more with her mother after their frank conversations. She also became more confident with her peers.

She did feel sadness in knowing that her birthmother could not raise her, yet her sadness was secondary to her relief—she had not been left by her mother. Ani had merged her memories of her caregivers with her mother's identity. In the session, her mother leaned close to Ani, speaking from her core, "I have never, never left you. I never will."

Ani's goals in the family were to be fun to be with, and to stay close to her mother. Ani worked on her goals through rocking and reading, painting, and going for walks and talks with her mother. She arrested her indiscriminate friendliness. Formerly, she had seemed eager to go with friends. She often forgot to say goodbye to her mother. After she deepened her relationship with her mother, Ani became frightened at a girlfriend's sleepover, asking to go home. She cried when her mom picked her up at midnight. "I missed you." she said. "Now I know what that feeling is. It is *lonely*. I was *lonely* for you. I do not think that I am ready for sleepovers yet."

Ani had had an attachment with her mother coming into the phase. However, it was made secure in Phase V. The problems that Ani experienced in Phase IV with gender and identification with her mother were remedied by adoption explanations, attachment techniques, and enhanced security.

If children move to a new family during this phase, their loyalty to the former parent figure will need careful consideration. The romanticism of the phase flavors the way in which the lost parent is perceived. Jerome's story, which follows, illustrates this romantic loyalty, as well as its influence on gender and shame.

Jerome lived with his mom for the first five years of his life. He was her "little man." His parents had divorced when he was two years old. He could not remember when they all lived together. His father had disappeared from his life.

As his mother dated a new man, Jerome became jealous. The new man tried to make friends. Jerome preferred having Mom to himself—and the man scared him. One day the man hurt his bottom. Jerome hated him. The man threatened to hurt Jerome worse if he told. He also told Jerome that he would never see his mom again if he told.

Jerome's mom used the boyfriend for childcare, since he seemed so willing. Sometimes she said, "My big man and my little man," beaming at them both. Jerome felt angry, sick, and small at her words.

On a weekend trip to his grandparent's house, Jerome cried, saying that he did not want to go home. With caring support, Jerome finally told why. His grandmother called Children's Protective Services after a phone call to the mother resulted in her total disbelief. He went to his mother's half-sister's home the next day. By the first court hearing date Jerome's mother had married this boyfriend.

Jerome reflected that his mother's boyfriend's threats had come true. He never saw his mother again. He wondered whether the boyfriend was also right about hurting him for talking, this time worse. He wished that he were not a male. If he had not been, then he would not have been hurt, he thought. He romanticized his birth mother. He still expected her to appear and to whisk him away. He wished hard for this. He wished on evening stars and on his birthday candles.

Jerome's new mother had a voice and mannerisms similar to his birthmother's. Jerome found this reassuring. His parents worked hard in helping him to stabilize after the losses in his life. They used a low-key, but structured routine and stayed available emotionally.

They took him to a doctor, who assured him that every part of him, even his genitals, were normal. Jerome had worried that something had been left inside him, or that he was damaged in an area that he could not inspect. He had tried to look at his bottom, but his neck would not stretch that far. It was a relief to find that he was healed now.

Jerome began to recast his image of maleness through contact with his father. One night, he overheard his father telling his mother that he wished he could punch "that creep." Jerome realized that "that creep" meant the boyfriend. Jerome felt strangely relieved. Someone else was angry at the terrible insult done to Jerome. He did not feel so small knowing that his father, who was enormous, might hurt the abuser sometime in the future. He liked to watch his father eat, getting even larger. He knew that his dad could squish the abuser just by sitting on him. Jerome began to develop loyalty to his father. He often offered him seconds at the table.

Jerome entered therapy, exacting revenge on the predator during play therapy. Jerome sat with his mother during one session, in which he told the whole story. Her sensitive care caused him to cry about the abuse for the first time. He internalized her sorrow and care, replacing the insensitivity shown to him by the predator. "You were a wonderful boy," she said. "This should never have happened to you."

Jerome looked at the therapist, as if for a second opinion. The therapist added, "There is nothing about *you* that caused this abuse. Did you know that this man is on a list of people who should not be around children? This man has done this abuse to other girls and boys."

Jerome asked questions about abuse of both genders. He began to believe that his abuse did not stem from his maleness. Without comparing herself to the birthmother, Jerome's mother committed herself to protecting him. Later in the day, Jerome told his mother that when he grew up, he would take care of her, after Dad died of old age. He paused, adding charitably, "I will take care of Dad too, if he is still alive." His mother nodded her appreciation.

Jerome began to walk like his dad. His dad walked big, easy, and unafraid. Jerome felt those same feelings when walking like Dad. He pushed away from his mother a little, but not too far. He spent more time with his dad and began getting ready for the soccer and baseball seasons. Jerome stopped looking for "that bad guy" in the crowd.

Jerome enjoyed horseplay with his dad without becoming afraid or fighting him. He liked the way his dad smelled. He slept in his dad's t-shirts and felt safer. Jerome still worried about his birthmother's welfare. His mother heard his worries, and prayed with him for his birthmother during night prayers. One day after night prayers he said about his birthmother, "She was kind of weak. I mean, she kind of let me be in charge at home sometimes. I was way too young." Jerome's mother did not undo his progress by adding any comments. She nodded.

Jerome decided to become a policeman. He made a mental image of himself as strong, armed, and always right. In doing so, he was finishing the work of Phase V, with a restoration of his sex role development. His identification with his own sex was no longer frightening. He had resumed his romantic style of relationship with his adoptive mother, typical of Phase V. As he began moving out of the romantic stage, ready to model more after his father, he showed another sign of moving past Phase V. He was re-connecting with the activities typical of children in his phase.

Jerome's parents tasks in Phase V were

• helping Jerome to transfer his attachment to his parents;

- providing overt expressions of safety;
- finding and being active in Jerome's therapy;
- permitting Jerome's loyalty to his birthmother but not his fantasies of returning to her;
- helping Jerome to use his father and mother for protection;
- helping Jerome to refocus on the present, encouraging healthy activities that he could master.

At the same time, Jerome's tasks were:

- transferring his attachment to the adoptive parents;
- entering into a realistic understanding of his sex role, neither a "little man," nor a victim, but a boy, who deserved protection;
- establishing a close relationship with a same sex parent;
- trading his desire for a romantic relationship with his mom for a closer relationship with his dad;
- establishing a narrative, or story line, of his life that incorporated facts and feelings, so that knew what happened to him and what it meant;
- beginning to understand his birthmother's limitations;
- entering into age-appropriate activities, and becoming present-focused.

As the vignettes of Ani and Jerome show, children may be dominating or controlling when they interact with their parents. It helps the child move to a healthier attachment model if parents teach ways that "work for everybody." Parents practice and talk about "winning without anybody losing."

In discipline, parents do best in avoiding punitive situations that reinforce that the child only has the choice of being a victim. The hurt child can more readily shift to a positive attachment model once he understands that things have changed. Instead of two choices, hurting or getting hurt, there is a third choice of trusting and cooperating. Everybody gets treated with respect.

Children who have experienced loss and trauma have the task of reducing the intensity of their negative responses at this phase. Kids can enjoy the *Frog And Toad* (Lobel, 1979) books if they are close to the chronological age of this phase. They can be guided through a discussion of the differences between the *Frog And Toad* world and scary or anxious world that they remember from before placement. For children above the age of nine, The *Trumpet of the Swan* (White, 1970) gives the same set of contrasts right within the book. It has the added advantage of a swan, who overcomes physical disability challenges without internalizing shame.

Parents can help frightened children who are flooded with fear in this phase by using an imaginary remote control. Children need to fast forward through scary memories, so that they can enjoy their current, safe world. Children usually have glimpsed and then fast forwarded through scary previews. They have an understanding about how to do this. Primary grade children who are in Phase V describe that this technique works well for them. (This is described further in Chapter 10.) For example, parents might say to a child who becomes afraid when food is taken away, "Chad, I am your great mom. I am only putting away leftovers so that they do not go bad. Fast forward, Chad, to your safe life. There is lots of food here. Would you like an apple from the fruit bowl?"

Techniques, Concepts, and Words that Improve Attachment for the Phase V Child

- To deepen attachment, many parents continue to use attachment suggestions from a previous stage. They usually use the techniques for the earliest ages only intermittently. For example, a child who experiences loss reactions around anniversaries may do some bottle-feeding and rocking with the parent, as she says that she is feeling lonely. As she passes the anniversary, she may choose a snuggle time with a book, instead.

- Children in this phase may be assigned a goal of staying close to a parent when parents want to deepen attachment. Parents can practice at home with children the close and good feeling children get when they are getting hugs. Later, parents can reward children for working on "staying close," or "keeping the safe feeling at the grocery store." Kids can earn rewards, like going for ice cream after working hard on "being close" for two days, in addition to the intangible rewards of feeling secure.

- Sometimes children romanticize and dramatize the placement story and their birth parent unduly. Sometimes they think that the birth parent is perpetually crying. That the birthparent did grieve, but may be living a happy life, can be quite a revelation for this concrete-thinking child. Using a cartoon method, parents can draw the birthparent, moving them through frames. The current frame can have the birthparent's smiling face.

- Children feel freer to have a happy life if they do not feel that their birthparent is still crying for them unrelentingly. Often a birthparent's letters, or relative's reports, provide facts about the birthparent's life. "What do you think my birthmother is doing now?" A child asked in my office. "She is probably getting ready to go home," answered her father. "She works for a school, and it is almost 3:30." Children are self-centered at this age. They need a little help in knowing that birthparents are attending to different matters.

- Some children think that it might have been better for them had they been born of the opposite sex. For sexually abused children, this question is best handled in the context of the total treatment. For children whose placement was connected to their gender, it helps children to discuss how things might have been different had they been a different gender. Parents can talk about how, in this family or country, the parents like girls as well as boys, and do not consider them second best. Or, parents can say that in this country we have retirement money, so we do not have to depend on a son in our old age.

- At times, the record or interviews with past caregivers shows a clear gender bias. We can affirm the child's perception that clues from the history indicate that their foster mom *did* like girls better than boys, for example. She did not seem to know how to enjoy a little boy or girl. Parents can mention that they have always liked *both* boys and girls. Parents make this point gracefully when using the terms, "my daughter," or "my son," respectfully, when referring to their children.

- Wishful thinking and magical beliefs can be both wonderful and overwhelming at this phase. Older children often continue to engage in wishful thinking long after this phase should have concluded. They stay stuck in a belief in wishes and omens. Children can retain a belief that their wishing to change homes made it happen. The power of wishful thinking must be examined or tested to reduce its power, as in the paragraphs that follow.

- It is harmful for children to believe that they were responsible for making their birthparents leave. To set up a test, parents can use personal examples as a set-up for the discussion. For example, a parent could share that, as a child, they wished that the back seat of the car would disappear along with their sibling, so that they alone would remain in the front seat as the only child between their parents. After a dramatic pause, they point out that their brothers and sisters never disappeared, and that they are glad now. Parents easily go on to say that most kids wish sometimes for their parent to disappear, but wishing does not make it happen. That is not why they have a new family.

- Parents can further test magical powers together with their child. The parent can wish hard for a chair in the room to disappear. Nothing will happen. Then parents can have the child wish with all his or her might that the parent will disappear, or that a person appears. Nothing will happen. This tends to reassure kids, who are quite magical in their thinking but afraid to test their beliefs.

- Children at this phase may also feel that if they talk about someone, it might cause the person to reappear. For kids who are scared and angry with an abuser, parents can say, "I am mad at him for what he did to you!" Parents can demonstrate that the expression of ideas or feelings is not dangerous. This exercise helps children to feel freer in expressing their anger directly, i.e. "I am angry at the policeman for taking me away." Children can bring up topics for help in understanding them, when they are not afraid that by bringing up the topic, the event will happen again. Even children who are ten or eleven years old worry that the "bad guy" will feel their anger and come back to punish them. In cases of abuse by the birthparent, anger is often re-directed to adoptive or foster parents. As one Phase V child said, "I did not want to dump my mad on my birthmother, so I gave it to my mother. I am afraid of my birthmother."

- Honest discussion helps children to sort out with whom they are angry, and with whom they are not. In the process of discussing their feelings, sometimes kids will turn to a mom and dad and say,

"Sorry that I dumped my mad feelings on you!" It helps the attachment process if the child is not pushing the parent away with their angry feelings.

- Parents can supply children with a simple manila folder. On one side is a picture of the child sad, scared and/or mad, with the first big attachment disappointment. For example, the child with no parent and an overwhelmed sibling as their caretaker may be pictured on one side. On the other side of the folder, the child is snuggled in and content on the parent's lap, or in an embrace. When the child is having a hard time, he can go sit with the folder a while until he can think of the choice that fits the present, getting the feeling shift. One boy tells his mother, "I am going upstairs to get my folder from my drawer. I need to get my happy back!"

- Children of this phase have complex relationship problems to solve, but simple brain equipment. They do not have abstract ability. Adults sort through ideas and concepts, arranging them deftly, and still end up confused at times. Children are often bothered by an issue, without the ability to even bring up the topic. Sometimes children do not have the conceptual ability to even phrase a helpful question. Sometimes parents can tell a story about another child, with some of the same issues, and mention some problems in attachment that they overcame. Children will show the appropriate curiosity around their own issues, asking questions or asking for more information.

- Children in this phase should avoid new stresses to attachment. Most children of this phase with a history of attachment loss cannot tolerate the parent's absence for longer than five days. The attachment figure on whom the child most relies can be a father who works while the mother stays at home. Even with the mother at home, the child can go into anger and grief as the father travels.

Summary of Phase V Emotional Development

This romantic phase can be a delightful phase for parents, whether it occurs when a child is five or ten years old. Parents receive lovely notes, pictures, and hugs at this phase. Children's unaffected romanticism and love are treasures for parents. Children who are completing this phase successfully feel good about their gender. They have hope for the future, describing it in terms of their gender-role development. They tend to be increasingly competent with peers. As a result, they enter the community in peer activities with groups.

Children in this phase are believers in magic, becoming more interested in facts in the next phase. Their conscience development increases dramatically in this phase. Their sense of themselves as competent to do things and learn things continues to grow when they are successful in this phase. Alternately they enter the next phase feeling inept. Children with challenges leave the phase with poorly developed consciences, low self-confidence, and tenuous cooperation capabilities. Optimally their identification with parents, and their cooperation with parents, readies them for more time away from parents and home.

Checklist for Phase V Emotional Tasks

___The child seems generally interested in sharing her interests with the parent.

___The child likes to play with the parent.

___The child seems to like the parent.

___The child looks at the parent and smiles many times a day.

___The child hugs the parent and likes it when the parent hugs her.

___The child accepts discipline as fair after an initial protest or sulk.

___The child tries to please the parent much of the time and gets distressed when she fails.

___The child shows a full range of emotions.

___The child wants the parent when he gets sick or overwhelmed.

___The child does not show pleasure when parents get hurt, but shows distress and empathy.

___The child wants to grow up to be like the parent in some ways.

___The child is making friends and enjoying play with friends.

___The child continues to want to master new skills.

An Overview of the Ongoing Phases

The next phases of emotional development describe children's relationships to peers and communities, in addition to their relationships to their families. Because of the increasing complexity of the maturing personality, it is clearest to have specific information on select topic areas, rather than trying to convey those topics within a developmental phase discussion.

Parents are encouraged to keep in mind children's developmental tasks as outlined in the next two phases while they are reading the book chapters that specifically apply to topics. Within the chapters there is material describing the impact of issues like trauma and loss on developmental tasks. The examples include techniques useful for children in ongoing phases. While the focus of this book is on children, individuals who are interested in reading about attachment and adoption issues along the life cycle are encouraged to use the Resource List in the back of this book.

In parenting children who have had challenges in attachments, parents are continuing their work, deepening trust and love throughout ongoing phases. In spite of good gains, parents must be more careful than they would need to be if there had not been breaks in attachment.

Phase VI—Joining In and Finding My Place

Tasks of Phase VI Children

When there have not been other challenges, children enter Phase VI at the age of six or seven years. They continue in this phase through the age of eleven or twelve. The beginning of this phase is noticeable—children decide that they want to be like their peers. At age seven or eight they would rather be like others, than stand out with a unique feature. Children start this phase rigidly conforming, gradually becoming more flexible throughout the phase. They become interested in joining with other children in clubs, school, and imaginative group play. They want to be a competent member of a group. Teachers and coaches, their perceived guides in this process, often outrank parents in their authority.

For adopted and foster children, it is during this phase that they recognize that, against the standard set by their peers, their lives have been more difficult or complicated. Because of the pressure to conform, they will be unwilling to talk about this difference in public. But in the support of a caring home or therapy, they explore some of their feelings of loss about their birthparents and feelings of being dissimilar to their peers. This is essential homework, because by the next phase they will need to incorporate this work into their identities, and share who they are with peers.

Children put the "feelings components" of their life stories together during this phase. Often they get angry that they had no choice to prevent loss from occurring in their lives. Sheltered children can angrily demand that parents "fix it!"

A second grade boy, who was feeling sad about his birthmother, said to his parents, "Do you mean that I have this bad feeling in my life; and that you knew that I would have it someday; and that you did nothing to prevent it? You just let it happen! What kind of parents are you, anyway?" His anger was a response to loss. He did not feel that it was fair for him to have to cope with feelings of loss.

Of course, the type of parents he had were parents who were planning to support and strengthen him in order to process his loss. He continued in his identity formation. He later laughed about his initial indignation. A family inside joke was, "What kind of parents are you, anyway?"

The feelings and thoughts that are concrete in the beginning of this phase become layered and complex by the end of the phase. Children pick up the nuances of status, privilege, stigma, pain, helplessness, and exploitation throughout Phase VI. By the end of the phase, they understand losses in these layered terms. Parents will find that children not only grow in identity throughout this phase, but they understand the meaning of the identity of others.

> One girl said, "When they talk about drugs in my classes, they look down on people. I know they would look down on my birthmother and on me. I let one girl do a peer review of my autobiography. She did not know what to say. I felt sorry for her. Hey, I should have saved that sympathy for myself. Why should I feel sorry for her? I am the one who went through it."

This is a typical description from an eleven-year-old. During this phase, they are gathering information, but do not yet have it in a package that they dare present to their peers. They rely on trusted adults to process the most potent information with them.

Being competent and industrious are major tasks of this stage. Children who have learned to become passive in order to survive often need a push-start and a dose of reality to develop industry in this phase. "I'm not doing anything wrong," is a poor substitute for doing what is right in this phase and in the rest of life. The industry that is expected in this phase enables children to learn to read, to work on projects, and to develop individual competencies.

Phase VI has an emphasis on being able to take a place among peers and to become competent at school, sports, friendships and interests. Children who earlier learned to withdraw in order to cope with frustration need to relearn how to cope with frustration by working hard on both emotional and daily life tasks. Otherwise, they will develop a self-concept of inferiority (Erikson, 1968).

As this phase continues, children become more interested in facts. This is a good time in which to provide children with facts supporting their own identity formation. As part of this process, children like to learn facts about their birthparents. For example, how tall their birthfather was, whether the birthparents were married, and so forth. Facts about the child's ethnicity and adoption story are important in the child's development of identity. Because children yearn to be the same as others in important respects, it is helpful for children to find others who share similarities. Adoption groups and culture camps are wonderful examples of ways in which to meet this need.

Children who have had foster care moves and exposure to prenatal drug or alcohol use often want to meet other children who have gone through similar experiences. With some forethought, professionals can often help families meet other families who have compatible children. Children enjoy meeting someone likeable with a similar background. It helps them to accept that they are "good" people, in spite of having had a "bad" start in life.

As the hormones that cause sexual development also effect the brain, children begin to develop abstract thought. This happens towards the end of Phase VI, at age eleven or twelve. As in the other phases, the chronological age and emotional ages can vary widely. Children are ready to rework their adoption or foster story again as they develop more abstract thinking abilities. At this juncture, more of the "why" questions are ready to be asked. The significance of formerly known facts becomes important as children understand the meaning of the facts. Children will have new feelings about things that did not seem important at earlier phases.

One young girl said, "I know that they told me about this, but I really did not know what it meant until now." As the brain becomes more like an adult's brain, children mature in their capacity to place meanings and facts together in reference to their sense of self.

Girls do a form of "matching" during this stage. They practice an elaborate form of being in synchronicity with each other and of allowing the group to dictate what they should do and like. They form cliques from grades three through six. Good teachers break up and neutralize these cliques, but they are part of group education. Girls who cannot "match," i.e. conform and respond to gestures, intonation, and styles because of delayed social skills, become ostracized. Girls who will not conform to the group because they want to excel, or because they are taught to resist peer pressure, will be left out, but only erratically. The girls who cannot, as opposed to will not match are at risk. If they cannot make friends with other girls in this phase, they will look to boys in the next phase for peer acceptance. Without girl friends, research shows young girls to be at risk for premature sexual involvement. Parents are encouraged to use the techniques in Chapter 12 to help girls. Additionally, the Resource List has a reference on social skills.

As the phase draws to a close, children realize that parents have "feet of clay." They recognize that their parents are not the demigods that they had thought them to be. Parents of children who have had attachment problems dread this realization. However, only children with secure attachment have to de-idealize their parents as part of a normal developmental process. Parents of children who have ongoing attachment problems note that their children continue to maintain a higher opinion of them after their attachment work on trust. The parents simply keep following through on their attachment-producing techniques. (More information on this is contained in Chapter 9.)

At the end of the phase, children do have differences in the ways that their brains function. Emotional modulation becomes more difficult, and memory tends to be erratic as children's brains move into puberty. Often children late in this phase will need more sleep as they are growing. It frightens many early teens when they feel more out-of-control. Talking to them about the changes in their moods, not just their bodies, helps them to feel better, and helps parents to partner with them in making plans for things to go better,

Techniques, Words, and Concepts that Promote Attachment in Phase VI

As in the other phases, freely draw from the lists previously developed and try these additional new techniques:

- Spend time with children at this age. Look for activities to do with children that are exciting, have movement, are fun, and offer stimulation.
- Maintain rituals that are comforting. Continue with nightly routines, cuddle times, rocking, and shared events.
- Help children to find areas of interest and competence. Encourage those areas without taking them over.
- Spend time with this child, not just taking him places. For example, take him skiing, do not just put him on the ski bus.
- For children who are not getting competent messages from school, explore and expand on other areas of competence. Find out how the school gives rewards to a delayed student. Ask for this treatment.
- Keep the home pace slow enough to allow for discussions and nurturance.
- Help children to form friendships by sharing strategies for making friends and inviting friends over.
- Make certain that parents remain associated with food.

- Get children to school ten to fifteen minutes early. That is the time period in which many social groupings are formed for the day, including recess plans.
- Make valuing statements about children. Compliment their efforts as much or more than their achievements.
- When does the child feel closest to you? Do more of that.
- Do not discipline with a sense of futility. Insert optimism that children will learn and master.
- Get good therapy in this stage for children who have any maltreatment in their past. Ask to be included in the therapy.
- Help children to find out facts about birth relatives, including positive hereditary traits.

A Checklist for Phase VI Emotional Tasks

___The child uses the parent for comfort and help when she is are emotionally upset.

___The child says that he loves the parent even when he do es do not need something.

___The child shares things about himself with parents rather than being secretive.

___When the child is sick or hurt, he wants the parent close.

___The child feels remorse if something special of the parent's is ruined.

___The child is honest with the parent. (Children often have a lying lapse at about age eight years, and then start telling the truth again.)

___The child has a value system similar to the parents.

___The child thinks of the parent as strong and effective.

___The child uses parents to calm down when she is distressed.

___The child uses the parent's help in gaining knowledge about his world.

___The child tries to find the parents in the house, just to know their whereabouts.

___The child feels secure in parent's limits.

___The child has friends.

___The child has capabilities of which he is proud.

___The child shows appropriate grief over sad parts of his own life story.

___The child shows empathy towards others.

Phase VII—Knowing Myself and Sharing Myself

Phase VII usually takes place between ages twelve or thirteen and nineteen years of age. Sexual development and the drive to be with other teens cause teens to enter into emotional tasks of this phase, regardless of their success with the tasks in earlier phases. Often, gaps in development are not made up until sometime in adult years, if then.

Teens have the task of learning who they are, including a sense of their own competency, their sexuality, and acceptability to their peer group. The need for inclusion, and the need to extend oneself to others in a peer relationship is a major task of adolescence (Erikson, 1968). Teens need tremendous emotional support in order to do this work. At the same time they need space to be with their peers. Learning to share who they are in an increasingly authentic and emotionally secure manner continues throughout the adolescent years.

Teens push away from parents during the earliest part of this phase. They need to separate so that they can become "stand alone" personalities. In other words, they cannot tack on their parent's identity, coping styles, or strengths as they navigate their way through their peer group. They push away to explore ways in which they are different from and similar to their parents. Based on who they are, and their own perceptions of themselves and of the world, they develop a more complete way of coping and socializing. As they develop more comfort with themselves, their beliefs, and their styles, the conflict that is typical for about a year around age thirteen begins to diminish. Parents can enable this process by continuing to set limits, and by allowing enough space and emotional support to help teens to develop themselves. Recognizing ways in which teens are different from parents helps, rather than harms the process. Parents who savor watching their teen's unfolding personalities, and who do not express dismay that they are different from themselves, usually enjoy the teen years.

Some of the specific tasks during these years include

- developing, and feeling comfortable with who they are—identity,
- learning enough about themselves to select and work in a career or vocational track;
- becoming comfortable with ones own gender as a sexually mature person;
- developing close relationships with peers throughout the phase, and sharing personal information about oneself in the last part of the phase;
- sorting through similarities and dissimilarities with birth and adoptive or foster parents;
- integrating loss issues, and their meaning, into one's identity;
- developing strong peer relationships that sustain one's growth and development;
- developing individual competencies in skill areas;
- individualizing value systems;
- working through parental conflict in the early half of the phase, and maintaining strong family relationships in the later half of the phase;
- preparing to leave home without losing family connection;
- developing romantic relationships, by the end of the phase, that are respectful of self and others.

Teens who feel that they might have been to blame for childhood moves, sexual abuse, and maltreatment feel conflict when trying to share themselves with others. They are concerned that others will mirror shame back to them, rather than regard. In an optimal scenario, teens with difficult issues can learn emotionally healthy ways to share themselves with friends, using parents for advice and structure. Less optimally, teens can act out their unresolved issues of shame, exposing themselves recklessly to emotional and physical risk, and incurring further emotional damage.

Teens determine how they are the same as and different from two sets of parents: current foster or adoptive parents and birthparents The increased complexity of forming identity in the teen years by adoptees has been described and discussed by several researchers. The ability to speak openly with one's family about adoption issues has been linked with higher functioning in teens (Brodzinsky, Schechter, 1990).

Finding one's potential vocational or professional areas of interest and aptitude are important tasks in this phase. This tends to be particularly potent for people in terms of the manner in which they leave their families. If they are planning to go to community college, for example, and live at home, there is a proscribed route. If they plan to work in a family business or a community industry, there is another route. If they are planning to go away to college, there is another process. Some families have only one traditional way of leaving the family. To emancipate successfully the route needs to be defined clearly for teens, and to be something they can reasonably expect to accomplish, given their abilities. Some increased effort to find the best route for each child is preventative, especially if the teen is unlikely to leave the family and home for the first time in the manner that other family members will.

Later-placed adopted children often need several additional years on the timeline in order to complete their emotional and educational tasks before leaving home. Normalizing this reality throughout teen years helps teens to think not in terms of age, but in terms of the skill set that they will need in order to leave the home.

It is also helpful to stress the ways in which children will always have their family, pointing out how holidays are celebrated, and describing a family's ongoing help and contact. Histories of abandonment sometimes cause teens to experience vivid feelings of loss as they contemplate leaving home for the first time. Sometimes they want to leave prematurely, getting the loss over with. They miss receiving family support in dealing with finances, disappointing roommates, disheartening romances, illness, drunken behavior, defunct cars, and other late-teen calamities. Discussing the themes of loss and emancipation throughout the teen years gives teens time to predict and adjust to feelings of separation, rather than to react to them.

Teens finish Phase VII with an idealized view of what parents and the world should be like. Parents should be perfect. Of course, parents are imperfect, and this is a disappointment which helps them move out of the family home with less regret. By the end of the phase, teens are forming deep friendships with peers. They are learning the skills that will eventually help them to develop an exclusive, intimate, sexual, committed adult relationship.

Techniques, Words, and Concepts that Promote Identity and Attachment in Phase VII

- When teens begin to separate, parents can agree with the process. Words like "Of course you want to do that differently than I would, since you think about this differently," help to let the teen know that parents recognize him as separate.
- Parents can set up limits, while still sympathizing with the request. For example, a girl wanted to visit an out-of-state boyfriend. Her parents refused. "We cannot let you go, simply because we could never feel safe. But tell us about this great guy," they said.
- One teen said in front of his friends, "I know that my mother loves me. She always cooks for me." That was the priority for this mother in continuing a connection through adolescence.
- Use eye and physical contact. Even if teens seem to shrug parents off, do not stop. It continues to convey the consistent message.
- Respect the teen's tastes. Do not debate something that is a matter of taste. (The exception would be something disrespectful to others. For example, pornography on the wall is more than a matter of taste.)
- Compromise. Teens need to learn to negotiate. Make deals, be reasonable, and teach them the fine art of "win/win."
- Parents should apologize when they have a temper problem, renege on a commitment, etc. Usually by mid-teen years, teens will follow suit.
- Continue to keep night rituals. Some years teens will want them, some not. They are very reassuring throughout teen years.

- When teens want to talk, they want to talk right then. Keep some walk-in "office hours," for teens, making parent time easy to obtain.
- Find fun activities to do with teens, and do them.
- Keep all the birthday and holiday rituals. These tend to be very meaningful throughout teen years, even if they asked to be excused the year before!
- Buy thoughtful surprises for the teen, indicating an awareness of things that they find delightful. This can be a chocolate bar that is the teen's favorite, or an interesting book on a topic that the teen did not know the parent was aware of.
- Do not try to be "cool." Be parents—nurturing, kind, structured parents who give teens the confidence that they are still anchored.
- Supply teens with identity information that will help them with their difficult task of identity formation.
- Take them to a good therapist to sort through difficult identity issues and loss issues.
- Any teen with a history of maltreatment benefits coming into teen years with a relationship with a therapist who feels comfortable and safe to the teen.

Parents' Checklist for Stage VII Emotional Development

___The teen uses the parent for help when in an emergency.

___The teen says that they love the parent even when they do not need something. (Teens may miss a couple years of "I love you," and still be on-track.)

___The teen shares things about themselves with parents rather than being secretive. (Again, there are some lapses with teens, but they should not be entirely reclusive.)

___When the teen is sick or hurt, she wants the parent close.

___The teen feels remorseful if something special of the parent's is ruined.

___The teen is usually honest with the parent. (Teens may decline to discuss topics, and are cagey, but should not be dishonest. Intrusive parents may contribute to this problem.)

___The teen's value system is individualized from the parent's without being antisocial.

___The teen thinks of the parent as strong and effective, with no more than one year's lapse.

___The teen uses the parents or trustworthy peers to calm down when they are distressed.

___The teen uses the parent's help in gaining knowledge about their world.

___The teen finds the parent in the house, just to know their whereabouts.

___The teen feels secure within parent's limits.

Conclusion

Attachment is a relationship, when described in its simplest form. While this section deals with children's attachment and ways to nurture that attachment, the work is not over in childhood. People can strive, successfully, to love honestly, deeply, and with empathy throughout their lives. Most parents and professionals working in the area of attachment face their own gaps as they help children. Like the children they serve, they can choose patterns of mutual respect and love, promoting healthy relationships.

CHAPTER 9

The Shape of Progress

Both children and parents are so heartened by progress. More than one child has said to me, "My heart is getting better now. I used to be a broken-hearted girl, but I am not any more!" But what does progress look like? This chapter describes expected patterns of progress, as well as ways to sustain progress when it starts to slip.

What Does Progress Look Like — Cycles or Curves?

What does progress look like in children with attachment and neglect issues? Do the developmental achievements show steady growth? Does progress look like ten steps forward and six steps back, then fifteen steps forward and five steps back, then twenty steps forward and five steps back— defining cycles?

Progress in some children shows a smooth curve. They move through attachment stages like Sleeping Beauties, kissed awake by loving parents. Parents who are using the checklists from the previous chapter are reassured to find that their children are recovering in spite of a poor start. Their children may not be gaining against the developmental curve, and they show delay when measured against peers without deprivation, but they move along the curve without further lags. These children enjoy parents and rarely show problems with aggressive impulses, fear, or mistrust. These are the types of children who inspire caseworkers to advise, "All this child needs is a loving home." Parents who have such children often describe themselves as "lucky," or "blessed." They are right. With the use of high nurture techniques, some children do move along a smooth curve.

The shape of progress for children with more attachment breaks and trauma is seldom a steady slope after arriving in their families. The curve is interrupted by a series of backward loops or regressions, each indicating a loss of past emotional gains. Sometimes children regain their footing without assistance, moving out and past the regression into new gains. Parents assist so that children spend more time moving forward, and less time in the regressions, or downward loops of the cycle. When parents supply support, children lose less of their childhoods replaying the past.

Making and Maintaining Progress after a Difficult Start

Most parents are discouraged when their children regress. They wonder if all their hard won progress is gone forever. But regression is not abnormal. Instead it is the expected pattern of progress. In downturns, parents should concentrate on helping children regain closeness and connection. Parents can also help children to develop strategies to cope with trauma reminders and fears.

What causes the spiral to begin its loop backwards? Children hit trauma triggers—reminders of trauma that cause them to feel in danger again. Reminders, or triggers, cause their brains to begin responding similarly to the way that it did during the original trauma. This is not a volitional response. Children may encounter a reminder just as they are doing rather well. When they do, they quickly reach for old defenses like dissociation, fighting, or wetting. They do not have strategies to cope with the trauma reminder.

Another reason for regressing is that children fear that by trusting they will find themselves vulnerable. Children progress, showing cooperative behaviors and trusting for longer periods of time. Then, they realize that they are trusting, and that they have left the weaponry of resistance behind. They feel unsafe and exposed. Control behaviors increase. These children often bounce from numbness to fury. Sneaky behaviors or outright defiance crop up as children distance themselves from parents. They blame parents for the distance because children do not want to feel shame. Children's anger is also a signal to parents for help—"I am in trouble! Help me!"

If parents fall into the trap of using their emotions to get their children back in line, or trying a very different approach, children feel more apprehension. Having parents change approaches further threatens children who are afraid that they are trusting too much. It confirms that parents are unreliable. Parents, instead, can point out the they are not going to change, but that they are going to give the child more love and more structure until the child is acting more maturely again.

Parents often find it helpful to go back to the foundational levels of caring for their children, starting by increasing comforting rituals for their children. Most children described in this book experienced their worst losses around an absence of comfort. They do not seek out comfort automatically when overwhelmed and afraid. Building a comforting ritual with parents helps children to learn to get care when they are overwhelmed.

What does a comforting ritual look like? It is a cuddle time tailored to the taste of a child. Many children use a light blanket, pulling it over them as they sit on their parents' laps. Their shoulders are stroked, or their head is scratched, or their back is rubbed. Stories are told or created. It is quiet, soothing, and pleasant. Some children have never experienced a comforting time, so they have to have options demonstrated for them. "What feels best to you?" parents might ask. "Do you like having your back rubbed or your face stroked?" Five or six options for the snuggle time can be demonstrated and described. Children may then choose the things that make them feel comforted and loved for their own ritual.

Obviously, a goal is to help children to talk about their fears rather than to use personality traits meant to deal with an unsafe life. Another goal is helping children to recognize their traumatic triggers so that they can avoid the triggers. Therapists help in both of these goals, but parents must provide the safe, calm base and take over day-to-day strategies.

Differences between Regressions and Emerging Problems

The normal shape of progress for children with trauma and attachment issues is cyclical. Nonetheless, a vigilant attitude towards regressions is necessary. Parents should monitor for signs that herald serious mental illness. Getting the child in, or back in, for mental health counseling is necessary if children mention or play out that it would be better if they were dead.

One boy's parents called, saying that he had opened the car door threatening to drag his head on the pavement. Even though his mood shifted upward within a few minutes, and he insisted that it was an isolated impulse, the parents wisely acted on the sign. It turned out that he was seeing mental images of prostitution and domestic violence from the past. He could not stop the mental images and the horrible feelings that resulted. This is called "flooding." It makes traumatized people feel like they are back in the traumatic situation. Flooding from memories can stop a child's progress. This boy needed immediate help. This was not only a downward cycle, but a crisis in his post-traumatic stress disorder.

While a traumatic trigger can produce regression, it can also produce a crisis with danger to a child. Sometimes children do their trauma work in layers. A new layer will cause a child to get stuck and stay stuck until they are helped by treatment.

Children who have the onset of mood disorders may appear to be regressing. When people have had one episode of clinical depression, the Mayo Department of Psychiatry found that they have a 50 percent risk of reoccurrence. After a second episode, the risk is 90 percent (Sampson, 2001, p. 739). Parents will need to be attentive to recurrence.

When children are moving into depression, some of the signs are that they are irritable, they cannot concentrate, they are guilty, they are blaming, they feel hopeless, they get overwhelmed, they are easily frustrated, they are negative, they have sleeping irregularities, and they may have eating issues. If children say that they want to kill themselves, or that they wish they were dead, parents should make an immediate appointment for a mental health assessment. Some parents have said, "Oh, he says that all of the time to get attention." In turn, I have wondered what it takes to get the parents to attend!

When birth relatives have mood disorders or histories of medicating themselves with alcohol or drugs, parents should be especially careful in monitoring their children. One large study showed that over 50 percent of substance-abusing individuals had major psychopathology (Zeanah, 2000, p. 167). Most of the major mental illnesses have a genetic component.

Depressed children may need an antidepressant, as well as a course of counseling, in order to make progress. Because of the physiological changes that occur during depression, children can get "stuck" in depression if not helped professionally. Teens are at especially high-risk for suicide, no matter if they promise that they will never kill themselves. Parents may rely on their teen's good intentions upon making the promise, but parents should never trust their teen's depression. Even suicide contracts have been found to be ineffective.

Suicide remains the second most common cause of death for female teens around the world, tuberculosis being the top killer. It is the fourth most common cause of death for male teens, following traffic accidents, tuberculosis, and violence (Jamison, 1999, p. 49).

When children have upward mood shifts, acting expansively, talking about the future, and showing ample energy, parents sometimes breathe a sigh of relief, thinking that depression has passed. Actually, this may be the upswing of the manic part of manic-depressive illness. A good assessment by a child psychiatrist is important at this stage. Mood swings can seem to mimic the cycling that is normal for children with attachment and trauma. The difference is that the mood cycles get more extreme over time, not less extreme.

Professionals struggle with children's regressions as they watch for signs of disorders. I ask parents to have a good physical for a child to rule in or rule out the influence of other health factors. Over the years, children I have seen have been found to have had anemia, diabetes, mononucleosis, and sinus and ear infections which have contributed to their apparent regressions. Professionals may ask parents for permission to consult about their child, or ask for a co-therapist's opinion, just to be certain that they are not missing anything. Of course, sometimes a child is developing a mood disorder, simultaneous to having cycles from posttraumatic stress disorder and attachment issues. That reality necessitates a more comprehensive treatment plan. Sadly, parents do not have the luxury of allowing for one problem only in their child. Given the pressure on parents, it helps to "share the wealth" of the responsibility for the child's mental health with a therapist who knows the child.

Help for the Downturns

Supporting Children through Periods of Regression

When children move into regression, parents do not have to create new techniques to deal with their child. Parents can re-introduce some of the attachment-producing techniques that they have used in the past. For example, the parent "assigns" ten minutes of rocking, reading stories together, bottle-feeding, etc., in order to overcome emotional distance and increase the child's security.

One eight-year-old boy was remarkable in his inability to tolerate touch from his parents, except by his own infrequent initiation. The parents were encouraged to touch him a great deal more. As he weathered a particularly horrible stint of processing traumatic material from his past, he protested every "assignment" of physical affection—both at the beginning and at the end of the assignment! He invariably asked for more time at the end. He still showed difficult behaviors, but he and his parents felt remarkably better-connected. Their family self-esteem went up in spite of the difficult material that he was processing.

Some children who both avoid and want to talk about their painful topics do well with a limit on talking about these subjects every day. For example, the child whose brother recently became homeless may be told, "From 8:00 to 8:10 we will talk about your brother." This seems to give a child time to work on the issue, but helps him to contain the emotions during the day. The child is also less likely to flood with emotions, to go numb, or to begin decelerating into a downward cycle.

When a child is processing hard information, encourage ways for him to release tension. Parents can say, "You are dumping lots of energy into your body when you think of this problem. You can either choose a chore or choose biking for twenty minutes. That will get the energy out." (Other examples are running up and down the hill, running around the outside of the house ten times, etc.) Or, if it is later at night, offer a stationery bike or a bath versus washing the kitchen floor. This will, in the short-run, help the child to calm. Later, it builds positive behavior patterns for self-maintenance.

Parents know who in the community cares about their children. When the children are tired of trying and are feeling discouraged, those people can lend special support to the child.

One boy in my practice has six quality people besides his parents who are calling him or seeing him in person on a weekly basis during downturns. Three of the people are grandparents, one is a friend of the family, one is an aunt, and one is a co-worker of the parent. These people are saying very direct things about his value, future, and identity. This helps to take some pressure off the parents, and helps the child to get a sense of optimism and hope from a supportive community.

Another child who frequented his principal's office for discipline began to meet with the principal daily for fifteen minutes in order to go over his achievements and to talk. The principal was grateful to have a request made of him that was more positive. During their visits, as they got to know each other, the principal shared that he had been adopted. The boy felt that he fit better in school. The request of the principal was not made to "shape up" the boy at school, but to calm him. But it achieved a desirable "shape up" effect.

Some children benefit from an extra hour of sleep when they are going through regressions. Often they need more rest time to help them to cope better. After finding that an earlier bedtime works over a few cycles, children will often volunteer that they need an earlier bedtime when they are going through hard times.

Some parents know to provide extra support during anniversaries of difficult events. There is a high likelihood of a downturn during those times. They arrange automatically for a therapy session during that time.

For example, a boy who was moved into foster care in July, and who lost a father in August, had a bad stretch to get through in the summer for several years. He had been seriously depressed. His parents and I made a plan for him. During the summer his parents arranged for additional therapy sessions, avoided out-of-town trips, allowed extra sleep, served great food, promoted exercise, arranged family-only camping trips, and scheduled lots of snuggle time. Eventually, he needed fewer props, but he knows how to get extra emotional and physical support for that time of year should he need it for the future.

He called me last August just to check in by phone. "I'm handling it, Deborah," he said. Then he yelled to his mother while holding the phone out, "Mom, what else am I having trouble with that I should talk to Deborah about?" This teen had learned to get parental support and to depend on others appropriately. His functioning was, and is, very high with that support.

An especially fun exercise during downturns is to find out what children find to be delightful and to do more of it. The lists of what kids want more of in their lives can be enjoyable to generate. First parents need to get agreement that children actually will allow those good things into their lives. Without agreement, some children will sabotage the plans, since they do not think that they deserve good things. Parents and children make plans for more good stuff in their day. Every day a plan is drawn up to add a few extras from the list.

This is a good technique, long-term, to help children to learn how to use fun and pleasure to help offset hard times. One child said to me, "It's hard not to go back to unhappy, when you have been unhappy all your life." Kids need to learn how to move past a depressive lifestyle. Having fun, and fun with your family, boosts self-esteem.

Occasionally, I give kids days off. If a child seems to be losing ground at school, return him home for a few days or even a week or two to recoup. He rests from so much outside contact, and gets recharged to cope with the world in a constructive way again. Parents usually only use a few days a year, so school progress is not much affected. For the occasional child who is out ten days in a year, the problems are serious enough that school achievement is secondary to health. In these cases the school is the communication loop with parents and therapist. Working parents have used sick days to stay out with their child. Some parents have asked a grandparent or relative to come in while they work. Often the regression has so worn the parent down, that a two-day break is a welcome respite for both of them to sleep in and recharge. Using these breaks has helped keep kids from ruining the gains that they have made in the school and community over a series of months. While these breaks need to be used judiciously, they have helped children to keep friendships and reputations that would otherwise be at risk.

Motivating Children to Move through Regression

Some children who have been through a great deal of suffering develop pride in resisting their parents' help. If they are doing well, they think that their parents are winning. They would rather deprive themselves of privileges than let their parents help them. They become masters of regression. Children who have had trauma and extreme neglect seem to replay these situations, to their own detriment. Parents feel heartbroken.

> One mother said, "the biggest obstacle for my daughter is her tendency to control and fight. She spends at least half of her tutoring time fighting with the tutor. She is a gifted athlete, but she won't get into her uniform until we are late. She criticizes me as a form of humor." The mother and father wore worried and overworked expressions. The girl looked both ashamed and victorious.

In a situation like this, keep the nurture going. However, children need to focus on the problems, not outwitting parents. The child in the example above did not work on her problems. Her parents were working too much. The next time that the girl insulted the tutor, the mother made a written note of it. When allowance time came, the girl had no allowance. It had gone for combat pay for the tutor.

To deal with her daughter's tardiness, the parent set the timer, warning her daughter that they had ten minutes before leaving, ample time to dress. When the timer went off, the mother got into the driver's seat, looked into the empty back seat, and then came back in the house. She announced that they were late, and that she would not be driving. The mother went on to lock herself in her room, turning up her favorite music to drown out her daughter's protests. This parent made a point of making herself happy. The parent began assigning jobs for nasty comments. Until the jobs were done, life was quite restricted. Her daughter was told that she was loved. She also heard that she could make herself less miserable. (This technique is described in Chapter 10.)

> Later the girl told me, "I feel bad when I treat my mother that way, but another part of me likes to hurt her. I want to make someone else feel as bad as I feel sometimes. When I know that I will be the one to pay if I hurt her, it helps me to do the right thing. Then I think that I am a better daughter." The girl added

with irritation, "I did not like when you gave me your *Most Miserable Kid of the Week Award,* Deborah! I tried hard to do better, because I just hated when I got that award. I am glad that I only got it once. I was so mad at you. You told me later that you did that because you cared about me. I was suicidal, but pretending that I was fine. I really didn't like myself, and thought that I could never change. So why talk to you and just embarrass myself? You knew that I was miserable, and you made me stop pretending."

Obviously, this is a girl who has now benefited from therapy and some insight. When children are stuck in a cycle, they may be fighting, but they feel a shamed hopelessness about their situation. Motivating them to try something positive helps them to "turn things around" towards upward growth.

When children are regressed, their parents may want to non-punitively "time-in" children with parents. For example, parents will say, "Sally, it seems like you are having a hard time remembering how to be a family girl. You will need to stay in the same room as I am in for the next hour." This does not give the child the distance that the misbehavior has aimed to earn. Instead the child is given closeness, even if under protest.

Summary

When children are regressing, increase nurture. Usually the fighting or distancing is caused by fear. Parents can help the agitated child to slow down, accept comfort, talk about feelings, or improve his physical state. Gradually, children learn to seek out parents when they are hurting.

Parents do best if they can sidestep control battles, making the battle boring and non-productive for the child. Parents can align with children, saying things like, "Sometimes everybody feels like putting their mad onto other people. Of course, it would not be right to teach you that you can dump on me. That's why you had to clean the toilets for calling me those potty names. I love how clean they turned out to be. Thank you! But I can help you with your scared and mad. While you cleaned the toilets, it gave me a chance to think. I was noticing that you got these big feelings after that phone call from your brother. Maybe we can figure out together what happened. After we snuggle a while, we can talk about it."

In the examples above, parents stayed focused on ways to help their child. They did not allow the control issue to be the major point. They dealt with the misbehavior as a side issue, still aligning with their child. They did not insist that they solve their child's problem. Otherwise, by refusing to work on the problem, the child would have won a victory at his own expense. Instead, these parents provided nurture, motivation, strategies, and safety.

CHAPTER 10

Relaxing the Grip of Anxiety and Control

A controlling child makes certain that nothing in the household goes simply unless it is in the direction that he chooses. Parents may talk about the rights of others, taking turns, or their own tiredness, but such talk is in vain. Why does their child need to be calling the shots all of the time? An anxious child shows a pattern of desperate neediness in relating to her parents. Talking does not seem to get into the core of anxious children. This chapter focuses on ways to calm anxiety and reduce control by helping children to become emotionally sturdier. It gives parents ways to bring balance into the family without further destabilizing their children.

What Contributes to High Anxiety and Control?

Children who have high anxiety tend to use controlling behaviors as a way to lessen out-of-control feelings. Since they are poor at calming themselves, they try to control the people and things around them. Readers may notice that this seems to be the human condition. Most people will react in a controlling way when anxious. There is pressure to curb this, since others do not like being controlled. The following vignette about Kaylene illustrates a pattern that evolves in anxious children.

Kaylene had never been so happy in all her life. She and her mother were dancing with scarves. Kaylene, at age five, could easily transform her rhinestone tiara into the real thing! She loved her mother so much! Her mother, the Queen! Giggling, Kaylene danced on. Her mother, laughing said, "Kaylene, time to brush teeth and start for bed." And Kaylene danced on.

"Kaylene, we can always play more tomorrow. Now teeth." Her mother showed lots of her own teeth in a determinedly cheerful smile.

Kaylene lost her power of hearing and danced on. "I just have to do this last dance thing! Why do you have to spoil every thing! Now we have to start all over again," Kaylene insisted.

"Actually, Kaylene, it is time for brushing. You can either start up the stairs by the time I count to three, or I will put up the scarves and tiara until you can obey better." Kaylene's mother had good parenting skills. Her limit was clear. She was not yelling—at least not yet and not tonight.

Kaylene shifted to the real battle. "Then I get to sleep with you. It's only fair since you have ruined my play. I was going to do a special dance for you, and now you have ruined it." Kaylene moved into full assault. "You will have to carry me upstairs if you want me there. You are so mean. I hate you. You are a bad mommy. You hate me. You throw my heart in the trash. Why didn't you just leave me in China?" Kaylene was weeping now. At this stage in her meltdown the most extended bedtime would never have calmed her. "You leave me, just leave me alone, leave me like you always do. I want my momma." Kaylene was incoherent in her demands.

Her mother tried reassurance, "I'm here for you. It's just bedtime, that's all," her mother continued. After Kaylene's last horrible comment it seemed that bedtime was not really the issue.

Any separation from her mother seemed to be an issue. Kaylene had never seemed to really calm with her mother gone, whether for bedtime or daycare. She did all right in daycare, but she seemed emotionally muted. In this current nighttime drama, she was suffering. Her mother saw her act out the drama of her early abandonment every night. It was both heart-wrenching and a royal pain for the mother.

Kaylene's mother had checked with other parents who had gone to China in her group. One of the parents said that their neurologist had mentioned the possibility that her daughter's anxiety was due to the deprivation in the orphanage in the first six months. It had been so cold in the winter that the babies had quilts tied across their lined up cribs so that they stayed warm. They were only picked up on a schedule, due to the demands of so many babies and the difficulty of keeping the quilts in place.

When Kaylene's mother checked a book on emotional development, she did note that anxiety and frustration were supposed to have beginning development in ages three through six months. Kaylene had been adopted at about a year and a half. She was about two or three months old when she was brought to the orphanage. Was she remembering being abandoned? Was it the deprivation? Was her reaction due to having no special someone for so long? It was hard to figure out.

The mother fantasized about having someone come to take over for about a week so that she could have a few days to herself without having to feel Kaylene's daily anxiety. As a single parent, there was little relief in sight. She would not have traded Kaylene for the world. Yet, this separation and anxiety thing was hard on both of them.

The vignette above describes the difficulty in ever defining the one variable that might account for prolonged separation anxiety. It seems that once some children get frustrated or anxious, they recall other overwhelming, anxious feelings. Within two minutes, their anxiety escalates from zero to one hundred miles per hour. The comfort introduced by parents does not become part of a new template for some children. Instead, they feel hopelessness and mistrust of their parents every time they separate from parents. Some special techniques to help these children are described throughout the rest of the chapter.

The Over-stimulated Brain

Anxious children like Kaylene do not get labeled as "attachment-disordered." Parents do mention that they have "issues." It is hard for these children to trust parents' enduring love. Parents and children give and receive love, but even this relatively easy situation can push parents' resources to the maximum. Some children who start out anxious become more controlling over time. The process can deteriorate with age, rather than improve. (See Chapter 3 for a discussion on Insecure, Anxiously Ambivalent Attachment). Parents are looking for ways to help their children to calm down.

The words that people say to themselves to talk themselves through difficult situations are referred to as "self talk." This resembles the encouraging or comforting talk that people have heard from their parents as children. It sounds like, "You are doing great," or "Keep on going," or "Remember why you came," or "You will be fine, just get started." People elaborate on the framework that their parents laid. This self-talk is enormously helpful for most people in helping them to reduce anxiety. However, it tends to fail people, the more anxious they get. The work of Bessell van der Kolk, M.D. explains why this is so.

The parts of the brain that are linguistic, organizational, and thoughtful are parts of the brain that people shift away from during very emotionally intense states, or when they are accessing traumatic memories (Van der kolk, 1994.) Unless they have rehearsed it often and have used it before, they are overwhelmed with anxiety, children in highly anxious states can no longer access self-talk, In my experience with children under the age of eight, there is usually less than two minutes of available time before children have flooded with anxiety and have started into their ranting, anxious behaviors. As children get older, they tend to gain only a couple more minutes. The suggestions, exercises, and aids in this chapter help children before they melt down.

Auditory processing is the process of understanding, ordering, and deriving meaning from language. It is compromised when children are highly stressed or highly anxious. Children who have a constant high state of arousal can become over-stimulated by a small stressor. As parents try to put it into a sequence, or context, children hear the mention of the event, and move into an over-stimulated state. Even though their parents are attempting to help children to sequence events through talking, relying on auditory processing, many highly anxious children lose the sequencing when they hear the part about bedtime or parents leaving. They cannot regain the sequence to comprehend the part about parents returning.

The Experience-Dependent Brain

Maturation of the brain, including its pathways for emotion and emotional regulation, is "experience dependent." That is, social interaction directly influences the way that the central nervous system develops (Sroufe, 1995, pp.11-51). The brain's early map for emotions influences how children react emotionally later in childhood. Children who have experienced deprivation early in life tend to have brains that do not regulate emotions well. They over-react and under-react in a way that is adaptive to their old environment. When they are nurturing, comforting, and positively stimulating, parents give children experiences that form a new perceptual map.

By three months of age, babies have the capacity for showing excitement, distress, and delight. By six months, babies have the capacity for the development of excitement, delight, distress, fear, disgust, and anger. While infants cannot be considered as having these states yet fully developed as emotions, they have begun to build the physiological branches that will develop into emotions. By twelve months, the capacity for delight, elation, affection, excitement, distress, fear, disgust, and anger is in place. By eighteen months, even further branching in the brain occurs, with jealousy, affection for adults, affection for children, excitement, delight, elation, distress, fear, disgust, and anger states all possible. By this point, the states are considered emotions. (Sroufe, 1995, p.59-64).

Experiences develop both the emotional state, as well as the beginning modulation of the emotional state. Emotional states can develop later than the early windows, but most children have a harder time sustaining positive states after over-development in states of fear, disgust, distress (wariness), and anger.

Even if children have no memory of deprivation or abuse, experience impacts emotional development in the brain. After reading this, parents might say, "Then what's the use? Why even try?" Humans are adaptable, changing and reaching goals throughout their lives. It is a misuse of information to limit children. The information is helpful as an explanation. When parents have a "why" for the harder road that they are walking with their child, it helps them to make peace with the rugged terrain.

Parenting Attitudes that Assist Children's Stability

Parents are the pacesetters and emotional touchpoints in the home. If children do not have good emotional regulation, it does not make sense to give them the freedom to set the emotional tone for the home. Like music that has the accent on the first beat, parents accent the beginning of emotional interactions. They set the pacing, not the child.

Some parents become so wary of children's outbursts, that they nervously observe their child, making constant adjustment to keep children from blowing up. Instead, parents should be constantly directing the child back to the parent as a person of security, calm, and joy. Parents can cue children to calm down by taking a few deep breaths themselves, and then smiling. Parents can model having a good time. When parents look nervous and harried, it only causes children to remain wary. Parents need to do some of their own work, taking responsibility for having a positive life and attitude.

Children often are afraid that they are too hard for parents to handle. Parents who can project a calm assurance that children are not too much for them help their children to feel secure. Children may lean on or fight such a strong parent, but they do feel that the parent has the power to protect or stop them.

If children are truly too hard for parents, additional help can be sought so that the parent can handle the child. One child began to bully his parent every Sunday night. For several weeks, his uncle arrived late Sunday afternoon to provide reinforcement for his parent. Another child spent two weeks in a psychiatric treatment facility, returning home after he accepted help for self-mutilating behavior. The point is not that parents can single-handedly cope with everything that their child can dish out. Instead, it is that parents can muster the resources necessary to help their child. I say to children that I want them to get the help to change and grow in their home." However, if that does not work, I am willing to get help out-of-home for them. That way, I can give them the best opportunity to return to live in their families.

Techniques and Nurturing to Instill Calm

Some of the following suggestions can help anxious children who use control to feel more comfortable. These suggestions are not a substitute for therapy, but work nicely with therapy in helping a child to feel better.

Exercises Parents Can Use with Anxious Children

Play out the Positive Ending

Children who are pessimistic and fearful can be invited to tell how they wish that a certain event would go. Ask them to act out that preferred ending. Role playing the positive ending gives children control. It also helps to curb the further development of a pessimistic, paranoid way of thinking. For example, one child played out going roller-skating with her brother, rather than brooding on a possibility that she would never see him again. They had been adopted by different families. Within two months she had invited him to go roller-skating and had accomplished that wished-for activity. This worked better than reassurances. She has since tried this in other areas of her life, like a successful first day of school.

Pictographs or Flannelgraphs

Young children with anxiety often respond well to visual sequences of events. Small pictures of daily events may be drawn out on felt, and arranged on a larger piece of felt. Children and parents can arrange the felt pictures in an order of events, displaying what will happen for that day or the next day. Children who seem to expect abandonment can see that in the morning Mom is there, or see and talk about what it feels like when Mom picks them up at day care. A difficulty common with younger, anxious children is that they tend to stop processing information when they come to the part of a daily sequencing that involves separation. This visual aid helps them to get to the other side of the sequence in which there is reunion. This is a good aid for children with permanent auditory processing problems or emotionally produced auditory processing problems.

Brain Shift

This technique helps parents catch children who are starting to lose it, or melt down. Parents ask children questions that require them to use a different part of the brain. Swanson and Thompson describe this technique by having parents ask a child, "Are you too hot? Here, let me feel your forehead. I think that you are too hot." This will give the parent a moment to also calm a child. Another question is, "Can you smell that? I think that I smell french fries." As children shift away from the emotional centers of the brain to test this, parents have a chance to steer their child (Swanson, Thompson, 1997). If used in time, this technique helps children to stop processing highly stressful information.

Asking children if they are hungry, or if they need a drink of water serves the same function. Or, ask children if they need to go to the bathroom. Afterwards, parents might re-start the conversation saying, "We need to practice the 'Mom comes back feeling' before we do anything else." (If children do not need the bathroom, drinks, or food, parents might want to use the bathroom, get a drink, take off a sweater, etc.)

Another diverting tactic is the interesting subject. Most of us, including children, can be engaged by particular absorbing conversational topics. Typical lead questions might be, "Well, how about those Yankees?" Or, "Which rookie card do you think is the best?" Leading a child into these topics leads her out of an anxious or angry response. Over time, children often learn how to do this type of activity for themselves, because brain development is experience-dependent.

Deep Breathing

First show children how to produce anxiety in themselves. Ask them to take many shallow breaths so that they are panting. They will have some of the same feeling that they have with anxiety. Then, show them how to fill up their bellies (diaphragms) with air. Have them blow out the scared feeling first, being careful to blow all of the air out. Next have them breathe in and hold the air. Then blow all of the way out again, and breathe in again. It is important that they are really filling their lungs, and slowing down their breathing. Children like being capable of stopping an anxious response. They also begin to recognize when their shoulders are up, and they are taking shallow little breaths. With non-verbal cues from parents, who gently push shoulders down, rub their backs, and take deep breaths with them, children can correct their breathing and take control of their anxiety. In time, they can do this for themselves.

Many children are so anxious, that when asked to take a deep breath, they cannot get a deep breath in unless they blow out first. I work with children until they can get a "jelly belly" (a soft, relaxed tummy). It works well for some older children to have a timer on their watches which is set to go off on the hour. The timer reminds them to do diaphragmatic breathing throughout the day. This helps anxious children feel much better. With hyper-arousal reduced, they melt down less frequently.

Showing the Correct Amount of Emotion for the Event

When children are showing a great amount of emotion in proportion to an event, work on what the normal amount of emotion might be. Guess aloud how much feeling generated by something else might have been hooked onto this event. Using outstretched hands, parents can show how much emotion usually is attributed to a prior event and how much to the current event. Then, ask if children can bring their feelings down by thinking of the current event and the old event separately. Parents can talk about the current event and follow-up by supplying a strategy to cope or reassurances. They can talk, in turn, about the old event, following up with strategies for coping, or offering some comfort. At that point, children can show the amount of emotion again by holding their hands apart to indicate the size of the feeling. They are surprised and pleased that the feelings have gotten so small. They grin and giggle at their success, which is quite endearing to parents.

Fast Forward

Most children are able to understand the concept of the remote control with a fast forward button. They know that when certain obnoxious scenes come on the screen, that hitting a button moves them to more pleasant scenes in the program. When children get stuck in an anxious or overwhelming place and begin to respond to it, tell them to fast forward. A little boy who was ruminating and getting anxious over his sister's hospitalization was told to fast forward to the part about her getting out of the hospital. He was told to go look at her in the living room. She had been well for months.

Gear Shift

Describe the concept of shifting gears. Then, talk about how certain gears would not work in a neighborhood. High gear is for on the freeway. Talk about what gears work in the morning, getting ready for school. Which gear is for soccer? Talk or role-play about how to shift back down after an exciting event, using slower breathing, calm music, soothing self-talk, etc. Children can practice shifting gears, becoming proficient in moving between arousal states in order to meet the needs of the occasion. Then, parents can suggest things like, "Please shift to second, Sergei, we are entering the grocery store now." Or, "Go ahead and shift it to overdrive, Sergei. It's free time in the pool." Give rewards to children who are gaining proficiency in sifting gears. One boy was able to go see the monster truck show when he could shift down reliably.

Overexposure

Sometimes it works well to keep exposing children to an anxiety-producing event until they become de-sensitized. In doing this it is important to make certain that the child is not being re-traumatized. De-sensitizing is used when possible so that life is not so restricted. As an example, a child who will not permit her mother to go the mailbox while watching her out the window might have to watch her make ten trips within one half hour. If the child was still cranky, clingy, and anxious, the mom could do another ten trips in the afternoon. We would persist until the girl no longer showed an anxious response to the mailbox run.

Aides for Hyper-aroused Children

Carrying Pictures

Have the child get the wonderful feeling of how much they love their parent or parents, and then take a picture of them expressing that feeling. Label the picture. For example, "Andrei loving his mother." Parents can laminate the pictures and hang them on yarn around their small children's necks. The pictures go with children to day care or preschool. When they get tense, they can look at the pictures, and say, "Mom will come back. She loves me." Children often generate the comforting feelings and produce the resultant calm-down once they see the picture. Older children can carry their pictures in their pockets. Sometimes it only takes patting their pockets for them to become more relaxed.

Time-Out from Stimulus

Some children's senses become overloaded. They have too much information coming in and they become tense. These children will release their overload through periodic blow-ups. To help such a child, parents might time their longest time of compliance, and then give them breaks before they blow up. If handled without criticism, this usually goes well. For example, parents can say, "Wow, Jon, what great attitude over the last hour. I would like to give you a 15-minute break in which you can do what you want in your room. We will do that so you can keep up this great morning. Super job!"

Use of Hoods and Sunglasses

When children become easily over-stimulated and anxious, using the hoods on their sweatshirts or shirts can help. Children can learn to put their hoods up for a while when beginning to feel over-stimulated. Sunglasses can have the same buffering effect for over-stimulated children.

Using Odors and Fragrances

Smell is so primitive that it works well to change a mood or to calm a person down. Parents can put a drop of their shampoo or perfume on their children's wrists when they are going to be separated for a while.

Then, when children get anxious, they can smell their wrists, calming down when they associate that fragrance with the calming influence of their parents. Parents can let children sleep in their shirts or nightgowns, especially if these are ones that parents have worn and not laundered. It helps children to calm at bedtime. Parents can also let children use parents' unlaundered pillowcases on their own pillows, with the same effect. One little boy said, "It's just like Momma is there with me in bed, except she's not there, but my mind says she's there." Such is the logic of children, which makes this kind of strategy effective much of the time!

Pictures by the Bed

Put pictures of children with their parents right by the bed. It is surprising to me how many children, beset by bad dreams involving abandonment, tell me that they checked the picture, rolled over, and went back to sleep instead of heading for the parent's room.

The Grabber

Children who are afraid of being taken in the night sometimes need a method of protection. Parental reassurances can fall short. Children who are terribly anxious are afraid that they will become so fearful that they will be unable to shout or speak. While they are working on getting their voice back in therapy, a device for the short-term helps. A common novelty item in children's play stores is a claw-like device that has a handle with a spring in it. When children pull the handle, the device makes a startling, raspy noise while the claw grabs. The "grabber" is under the bed of many children. It helps them to feel safer. Logistically, there are flaws in this arrangement as a practical deterrent to the criminal element. However, it works for children's anxieties rather well. If parents are unable to find a grabber, improvise with barbecue tongs.

Options from the list above allow children to feel more comfortable, lessening the need for so much control. Sometimes, children like the power that they have had in being in charge of the family. Even though controlling behaviors may have begun as a response to anxiety, they have been sustained because they gave freedom from rules, chores, and authority. Some of the things that help controlling kids are listed below.

Techniques that Help with Control Battles

Jobs

Children who are causing extra work for others because of their disagreeable and controlling behavior may be given jobs to do. This labor pays back the family for the extra effort the child is requiring. The assigned job must be done before the "next good thing." Basically, the good things in life are the privileges that are part of family life: books, desserts, television, toys, etc. Until the job is done, none of those things are available to a child. If the child resists and delays, they wait, with the parents enforcing the "no good things" rule in a firm, matter-of-fact manner.

If James, for example, were to call his sister a "poopy head," then James would get the responsibility to do restitution by making his sister's bed before the next good thing. Retreating into his room in order to play in his room would not be an option for James. If James chose to wait, he would need to do so where he could be observed. After a few hours of boredom, even children who proclaimed, "Never!" will usually grumble their way off to do the job. Cheeriness is not a requirement for completing the job.

Fines

Some children who seem to be natural bean counters respond well to fines. If Annie were to hit her mother, it might be a $5.00 fine. Annie's mother would collect the money and spend it ostentatiously upon herself. If Annie were to raise her hand to threaten her mother, the fine would also be enforced. Children can also be fined on behalf of others. A girl who intimidated her sister by bumping into her was fined for each bump. The practice stopped immediately. The girl admitted that she did it to let her sister know that she was in charge. She agreed that the fines were fair. (This section refers to the younger child when discussing hitting. Physical abuse or threats by older children are not addressed in this section.)

Worker Status

Worker status is simply an extension of the "jobs" concept as described earlier. It is used when children are regressing, using a pattern of non-stop opposition to parents. I refer to children who are being blatantly disrespectful to parents as not acting like "family boys" or "family girls." They get to be on "worker status" until they get the concept of taking on the responsibilities of being in a family. While on worker status, they have no privileges. For example, six-year-old Shelley was placed on worker status because she was oppositional to the parent. Shelley needed to vacuum two rooms correctly. If she behaved agreeably and cooperatively, at the end of her task, she could ask to go back on "family girl" status. If she were still surly, the parents would keep giving her chances to work until she could act like a family girl. (There is a limit to this intervention. Children are not to be on "worker status" overnight. Consequence differently if opposition is not resolved by the end of the day. It is not to go on for a series of days.) Interestingly, children have often told me that this was one of the most effective pieces in helping them turn things around. The work helps them to do restitution, as well as calms them, and gives incentive to make changes.

Time In

Children who are having a hard time benefit from a non-punitive "time in" with a parent. Parents can say, "Jim, you seem to be having a rocky morning after yesterday's visitation. I would like you to stay in the same room as I am until you seem like you are feeling better. Right now you have a big 'no' coming out of you. You will be with me until that gets smaller."

Over the Lap

While this is inappropriate for older children, when young children destroy things, try to hurt others, or run away when upset, I suggest that parents place them tummy side down over the parent's lap. This position is safe for a young child, and gives good protection from being hurt. Parents should be certain that they do not hurt the child. Put a pillow between the parent's legs and the child's tummy for the thin child. The child's head hangs down from one end of the lap, and the child's legs dangle from the other side of the parent's lap. It is fairly easily to hold the child's legs with one arm and the child's hands with the other arm.

When the child calms down, turn him over in your lap and talk. If he begins a fight again, turn him back over. He needs to control himself for about thirty seconds without yelling or fighting in order to be let go. While the child still may be angry, the goal is just to get him to control anger well enough not to fight. Parents tell their children something like this at the end. "Susan, good choice not to fight your parents. You will have five minutes to continue your calm down. Then, you will need to sweep the front porch. That was the job that you were doing before your hissy fit. You will need to sweep the back porch as well, in order to pay me for the time that I just spent in helping you with your hissy fit."

Children who rage over the lap beyond fifteen minutes will need professional help, which includes consultation about being safe in the home.

Give Alternatives that Include Calm-down

Parent says, "Sean, you have a few minutes to calm down with your blanket. Then, you will go outside to start cleaning up after the dog. Think about some ways that you could do this dog job without getting even more jobs as a consequence. Right now though, you can relax and calm down."

Practice Compliance

Children can be given five-minute sessions in which they do things that their parents ask them to do. This time is structured, fun, and filled with praise. It resembles the "Simon Says" game. Children do what parents say, and get lots of attention. This game starts to redefine what it means when parents are in charge. Instead of feeling like they are losing, children find that it feels silly, non-threatening, and fun. This starts to redefine control.

A rule-of-thumb for control battles is that when parents start yelling, children have won. When children become controlling, it is helpful to reflect on what parents and children would be doing if they were not in a control battle at that moment. Often, children would be separating from parents. Giving more support and structure usually are keys to success in helping children to overcome control battles.

Trust in parents is not improved when all of children's efforts are going into control. Because of this, the more children try to control, the more parents should be talking about why it is hard for the child to trust.

When parents argue with children over a control issue, they are moving onto children's turf, at children's timing, for a fight—a poor strategy for parents. They are not working on trust and compliance.

The consequences for control battles should be a lot of boring trouble for children. It helps the whole family when children are not given the power to begin control battles. As much as possible, parents should make certain that healthy family patterns dominate and that control battles become side issues.

CHAPTER 11

The Fairness Factor

This chapter focuses on brothers and sisters and mothers and fathers. Parents want their families to revolve around positive relationships and shared values. If children coming into the family have special needs, it is important to make certain that, beyond an expected and necessary initial adjustment period, the family as a whole is not propelled into a long-term pattern that makes its focus one member's special needs. Beginning with a story describing a family's successful movement through an adjustment period and into very healthy functioning, this chapter goes on to provide concepts and techniques useful in guiding other families along similar paths.

Re-balancing the Family after a Placement

Jim is a boy born to capable, resourceful parents. He has a one-year-older sister, Megan, and a three-years-younger brother, Joe, both of whom were adopted at birth. Jim was a pre-teen at the beginning of the two years that this account chronicles. This is Jim's account of his new sister, Lili, who joined their family through adoption, and the changes in the family as a result of her adoption. Jim's story illustrates the pressures that siblings feel and the healthy ways that parents work to rebalance their family. The vignette is told from Jim's, rather than Lili's or the parents' perspectives, to emphasize the development of other people in the family. The sections in the remainder of the chapter refer back to some of the examples in the vignette.

Jim had grown four inches in the last year. At age eleven, he was not at the most upbeat stage in his life. He had figured out that his parents were not all that bright. His mother said that he was going through a normal stage of "de-idealizing his parent." That typified her weirdness. Nobody in his school talked like that. The biggest evidence of their failing was in the arrival of his five-year-old "new sister." They had blown it big time. During the family meeting before Lili came, Mom and Dad described her "special needs." Even his brother got it!

"Mom, Dad, you've brought home a bad girl!" Joey had exclaimed. His parents explained things so that Joey started looking happy!

As his parents kept talking, Jim sat in a state of shock. When he tuned back in they were describing possible sexual acting out and hitting. Jim just knew that *he* would never baby-sit. He was amazed when Megan, his sister, said to their parents, "Sure, I can watch her after school on Tuesdays and Wednesdays while you run the boys to baseball and trumpet. I don't have as much homework those nights."

Nothing in Jim wanted to help in any way. He felt ashamed of himself and mad at his parents that they had made him feel so selfish. It was just that nobody in his class would ever understand if they heard about Lili. Jim felt crushed by the impending burden of this sister. He blurted, "You don't realize how much it took out of me to help Joey to turn out O.K. This time, it's just impossible!"

Mom and Dad stared at him when he said this. Megan was so annoying! She laughed and then went to her room. He heard the door close. He had no allies to change his parents' minds.

Lili moved in gradually over the next few weeks. Jim found himself rounded up for a session of family therapy. He didn't see why he had to go since Joey was the one complaining. Lili had been "accidentally" hurting Joey. Jim was curious about that, because Lili actually seemed to like Joey best. The therapist taught Joey how to put his hand out against Lili's forehead and command, "Back off, Lili!" Lili also had to ask before she touched any of the kids. On the way home in the car, Lili asked Joey if she could hit him.

"No!" said Joey, with his rehearsed, commanding voice. Jim relaxed. The session with that therapist was funny. Getting out of the car, Lili climbed over Joey, digging a knee into his stomach. Joey told Mom. Lili had to go to bed fifteen minutes early. Dad spent those fifteen minutes throwing balls to Joey. It seemed fair to Jim.

Later that night, Mom and Dad came into Jim's room. Mom said, "Whether Lili turns out O.K. is an adult problem. It's not your job. When we adopted Joey, he was a baby. It was easier." Mom said that Jim had to concentrate on baseball, school, and his life. They would be the ones to help Lili. The therapist had asked him in the session what he did not want to have changed in his life. He hadn't known then. He to think about it. Jim had his list now:

"I don't want to be late for baseball practices anymore," he said. "Lili gets into my room, too, and breaks little things. I know it's her! Also, Dad and I haven't gone to the batting range, and I'm like number eight in the batting order now! It's really embarrassing. Last year I was number three! I'm afraid to have my friends over, too. She is always following me." Jim started to cry with big, gulping sounds. He leaned into Mom and Dad and choked out, "I'm afraid that you'll think I'm mean and selfish, and that you won't love me!"

Mom said, "Jim, everybody in the family has needs, not just Lili. We care about you as much as we ever did. We didn't know what it would be like to parent Lili. No one really knew her. Now we are making adjustments in our family so that things can go better for everybody." Dad squeezed Jim, and Mom stroked his hair. Jim cried for a while and his parents stayed right there. He felt a burden move off him—like he could depend on his parents again.

The next day, Lili sneaked in his room again. When he told Mom, Lili had to do his job. He and Megan watched out the window from behind the curtains while Lili swept the front porch and the walk. She howled and threw the broom. Mom just kept reading the paper and sitting on the porch swing. She said, "You can come in the house for dinner when your job's done." Finally, Lili picked up the broom and got started.

When the pizza arrived with Dad, Lili swept into high gear. Mom said, "Great, Lili. Wow. Good choice to get your dinner with the family!"

Before he started his homework, Lili came to see him with Dad.

"Sorry," she said.

"Sorry, for what?" Dad said. "I will believe you're sorry when you look into Jim's eyes and tell him what you are sorry for."

Taking a big breath and looking at her shoes, she started, "Sorry..." She stopped, looked into Jim's face and tried again. "Sorry, Jim, for coming into your room and taking your markers." A look of real regret came over her face.

"I forgive you," Jim said. He did.

Mom told Megan that she was not going to baby-sit on Friday nights any more. Jim realized that Megan had also made a list of what she needed. It took a month, but when his friends began to come over again, Mom taught Lili to let them alone. She put a "hand holder," which Jim thought looked like a leash, on Lili's wrist to keep her close. Lili got the idea that she could not take over the guests. This was such a relief to Jim.

He had never been able to bring it up to Mom and Dad, but he asked Megan, "What do I do if she pulls down her pants or something when my friends are over?"

Megan did not laugh. "That's a parent problem. When my friends are over, Mom or Dad will keep Lili close. Mom told me that I shouldn't have to think about any weird stuff that Lili learned somewhere else. It's not her fault that she learned it, but Mom and Dad handle any gross stuff. We don't have to think about it. She's getting better, anyhow. She hasn't tried to do anything like that since right after she came."

When Jim was twelve, he wrote his autobiography for school. He wrote that he had two sisters and a brother. He picked out a picture of his family that looked pretty good. Lili was cute now. He wasn't sure when she got cute. She was glued to his parents these days. Jim played on the trampoline with her sometimes. She'd laugh and laugh and laugh when he jumped beside her. When he needed to be picked up at school, Mom and Lili didn't embarrass him now. But he didn't risk talking much! They could really embarrass him in front of his friends!

He noticed that Mom and Dad did not let Megan make excuses for Lili. Megan sometimes tried to save Lili if she got in trouble. "Megan, her life is just plain going to be harder for several years," Dad finally said. "Megan, stop stepping in. She needs to learn the rules like everybody else. When she goes to school next year, there won't be anybody there to save her. Besides, weren't you and Mom supposed to go shopping tonight? Get your homework done so that you're ready."

That got Megan's attention. "Can we pick up Rachel, too?"

Joey still liked to sit and read stories with Lili and Dad. Joey acted like a baby sometimes when Lili was sitting on Mom's lap. Jim thought that was why Mom started to take Joey out for breakfast. Sometimes she played chase with Joey and Lili yelling, "Where is my giant, old baby?" For some reason, Joey really got a kick out of that. Mom would act all shocked when she "found" Joey and claimed that he had grown since that morning.

Joey still sat on Mom's and Dad's laps. He looked huge, but he wasn't ready to give it up. When Jim said, "Isn't he kind of big?" Mom and Dad reminded Jim that he had sat in laps until he was ten. Sometimes Joey acted like a little kid, even though he was not the youngest. Jim realized that Mom and Dad had let him do the same until he moved on by himself. Jim knew that he had turned out well, so he decided that Joey would turn out well.

It was almost two years before Lili started crying over missing her birthparents and a foster mother. She got really sad, and she cried two or three times a week. Jim felt awful when Lili was crying. He had grown up knowing that Megan and Joey missed their birthparents at certain stages. He got the same feeling that he had

had for Megan and Joey. He wished that he could make their sadness go away! He remembered how mad Joey was when he was seven. He had been really mad that Mom and Dad couldn't fix his feelings. Joey had yelled! "Why wasn't I given a choice?" Joey had ranted.

"You couldn't talk," Dad said.

Megan was starting to go places with guys now. Once Jim asked Mom if she was afraid that Megan would have a baby too young, like her birthmother. "No," Mom said. "Megan's a good decision-maker. She's been making good decisions and not many mistakes for a long time." That was true. Except for being oversensitive and too bossy, Megan was almost perfect!

Lili started school the next year. She was seven now. Mom had home-schooled her for kindergarten. Jim walked her down to the playground every day for a week before she started. Jim told her how to act so that other kids would like her. Lili listened hard, slid a hand in his, and whispered, "What about bad guys at school?"

"Lili, don't worry," he said. "Stay by the swings and away from the big kids. They play flyers-up over there." He pointed far from the elementary buildings. "Megan, Joey, and I all went to this school and nothing bad ever happened to us." That reassured Lili. She was not very big for her age. She looked and acted more like six than seven.

Jim had brought up Lili's size and maturity to Dad as a concern. Dad thought like Jim did, "Lili missed a lot. That's why we're putting her into first grade, not second."

"Just checking," Jim said, and took off. Lili seemed like she was going to do O.K. Jim had to make a couple phone calls to see who else had lunch period with him in eighth grade.

The vignette above was written from a sibling perspective. Jim, at age eleven, had not been able to stretch much. He had had a full plate simply because of normal developmental pressures. His parents had known that he should be continuing through his developmental stage, rather than attending to Lili's needs. Including Jim in "understanding the implications of sexual abuse" would make Jim face issues that were overwhelming for him, since some of his own sexual identity was just emerging.

As an eleven-year-old, he had just discovered that his parents were imperfect. As he adjusted to the concept of flawed parents who still maintained safety, structure, and nurture, Jim had more capacity to accept Lili. Jim did not pay much attention to the needs of his parents, which is typical for an eleven-to-thirteen-year-old in a well-functioning family. However, he was attuned to issues around his own image and identity and around fairness.

He began to show love for Lili after he was doing well himself. Steadying Jim in his own growth eventually paid off in a good relationship between Jim and Lili. Additionally, restoring fairness to the family with appropriate consequences helped Jim to resist resentment. In this vignette, Jim also noticed the characteristics and development of his siblings, not just of Lili. This is typical in family descriptions from siblings, when parents have been successful in neither scapegoating nor spoiling a special needs child.

After a lecture in which I presented on the needs of the brothers and sisters, an adoption professional approached me saying, "I was raised with a special needs adoptive brother and sister. All I ever heard was how to understand them, and what they were feeling and thinking. I was hurt a lot and depressed a lot. This is the first time I have heard someone talk about considering the needs of the brothers and sisters who do *not* have special needs."

Zeal to help a child with a poor start can result in overemphasizing the needs of one child. This can lead to a sick pattern, putting the well-being of the family at the mercy of the progress, or lack of progress, of this one family member. That reduces the power of any of the other family members to make plans for themselves for a good life. The other children may then carry that pattern into adult relationships, helping someone else in the hope that, if they meet someone else's needs, they might get their own needs met. This is otherwise known as a co-dependent relationship, which is not a compliment. It is also a poor strategy for happiness.

A better family deal sounds like, "We think that you are one of those kids who can make it in life. We will all be sad if you do not. We will help you in essential and reasonable ways: love, correction, education, spiritual guidance etc. However, we will go on to have good and meaningful lives, whether you do or do not succeed." This puts the onus for success on the person who makes the choices, not on other family members. It is "fair" in that the same deal is made for every family member. Granted, some people will have to work harder than others do. I like to concede that right from the beginning.

Assessing and Meeting the Needs of Siblings

When adding a new family member, it is healthy to identify both where each other child is developmentally and what each needs to stay on track developmentally.

Before or shortly after placement, parents can ask children what they need most from the parents or from the environment. After some thought, children can usually give some good suggestions about what they need. Even if parents cannot exactly meet those needs, they can counteroffer with something that will feel close to the same.

> One boy, whose parents were adopting a large sibling group, asked for Friday night to play games with his parents and friends. The younger children went to bed and teen friends arrived for a great time. "Game night" was a success for several years.

Knowing two or three main developmental tasks for each child's age helps parents to focus on progress through that stage. Keeping the daily schedule reliable also helps tremendously. Jim's story describes his distress about getting to baseball late. Rather than weighing Lili's tremendous needs against promptness to sports, parents recognized that this was distressing to a normal eleven-year-old.

Parents may be willing to take on challenges that other parents may not. However, it is important to keep challenges to their children within the normal range for typically developing children. During a crisis, this is impossible. Getting back to normal pacing and normal schedule after a crisis is imperative. Often parents need to get more resources and spend resources differently, in order to return to normalcy.

Ways to Talk to Siblings about Roles and Fairness

Sometimes a child will attempt to be the rescuer of a newly placed child. For example, in this chapter's vignette, Megan began to champion Lili. When this develops, it divides the family, with two against one factions. Pointing out why the rescuing will not help long-term helps nip this behavior. Then, it works nicely to point out what the child should be working on or enjoying instead.

This does not mean that siblings never make a healthy contribution. Vera Fahlberg, M.D. has described how helpful brothers and sisters can be to a newly placed child in describing what *really* happens in the home Children who cannot trust parents yet may check with children in the family to verify the parents' information (Fahlberg, 1989). An example of this from my own practice is in the example below:

> Sergei, age 8, was new to the home. Coming from an alcoholic family and an institution in Eastern Europe, Sergei was not at all sure that he could count on adults. His older brother Andrei, placed three years earlier from a similar background, told him what the parents were like. "They are a great mom and dad, Sergei!" Andrei was credible to Sergei, and this made his decision to trust much easier.

Performance Anxiety in Older Children

Sometimes a brother or sister has high emotional intelligence. Often these children are more aware of a sibling's needs, and feel pressure to help. Parents want to have some help, but still keep a sibling relatively free of the pressure for outcome.

A ten-year-old girl's family includes an older sister in guardianship with her family, her mother and father, and twin brothers adopted at age four. She made a board game for her brothers, labeled with areas titled, such as "Beach of Sassy Boys," "Marsh of Meltdowns," "Forest of Trust," "Family Boy Cove." She developed the game to encourage them on the right path, which, in the game, literally leads to parents. She also wrote tips for other siblings in her position.

TIPS FOR EVERYDAY LIFE WITH SIBLINGS

By Cass

Spend time with them. I've found that younger kids are usually "awed" by older kids. I used to think my older sister was perfect. (She's pretty close.) And now I can see my brothers really do look up to me. Wow!

Spend time with your mom, dad, and most importantly, yourself. You'll need time alone. Maybe in your room, with a sign up, saying, "Do not disturb," or something. If you share a room, ask to go the library. Draw in the sunshine. (It *is* kinda fun to read, too.)

If your brothers/sisters are getting on your nerves, tell them! Don't let the annoying things build up until you feel like you're going to explode! Just don't be too rude.

Don't be afraid to tell your parents about things that your siblings do to bug you. It's not tattle-tailing!(sic) It's telling them how you feel so they can make changes accordingly.

Cass has helpful concern for her brothers which is balanced by healthy self-interest. She has good self-esteem as a sister, without taking over responsibilities of her parents.

Experienced parents know that once the family pattern gets set, the first child helps to socialize the next child. Older children often tell me that they are working quite hard in helping the younger children to succeed. Older children are instructed by parents not to be bossy but are told to help—an inherent contradiction!

With later-placed children entering the family, parents should be up-front with the oldest children in taking some of the pressure off them. They may suffer some performance anxiety if their sibling is complicated. The developmental levels, emotional needs, and the temperament of children determine the extent of successful playing together, babysitting, room sharing, etc.

Children who have been adopted from institutions internationally often have a dominance that they have learned in the institution. Brothers and sisters can be bowled over as the child establishes a dominating position in the family. One boy described the hugs of his sister, who was half his size, as "choking, tight hugs…She looks like she's hugging me, but she really wants to choke me!" he said.

Forming good boundaries with clear consequences for boundary violations is essential from the beginning of placement.

One mother said sourly, "He stepped on my foot every day for four years. I thought he had poor coordination. I felt sorry for him and taught his sister to feel sorry for him. All the time he was laughing at us. Now I know that he liked to hurt. It was his way of taking charge of us every morning. When I told him that he had a job for every time he 'accidentally' tripped on someone, it stopped."

Teaching other children in the family ways to defend the space around them can be a necessity. When there is a dominance issue in a child's placement, other children must learn the "stop sign." They put their hands in front of them with their palm out. This is their personal space. The palm out is their stop sign. If a child gets too close, they can say, with stop sign out, "Back off!" Of course, the newly adopted child can use the same stop sign. It gives her a way to assure her own personal space without using domination.

Other boundaries that children must be taught to observe carefully include

- staying out of other family member's rooms or possessions,
- not talking over others,
- not interrupting personal conversations,
- not eavesdropping on personal conversations,
- not dominating company,
- and not insisting on a disproportionate amount of the parents' attention.

To improve boundaries, parents can rehearse with children as a means of improving outcome. For example, a parent might say, "Tomorrow we will be watching your sister's piano recital. Why don't we make a plan so that you can do well, even if you get jealous?" Parents can use a system of tools drawn from the previous chapter—fines, jobs, restrictions, encouragement, and practice of appropriate responses— in order to keep things fair in the family. They should be certain to include fairness to themselves as part of their system.

Traumatic Information—Preventing Toxic Reactions in Other Children

Children who have been traumatized will regularly bring trauma themes into their play. When a traumatized child is placed, play between brothers and sisters must be supervised. The rule of thumb is that the non-traumatized child teaches the other sibling how to play under adult supervision.

An eight-year-old and her six-year-old sister talked about this. I told the eight-year-old that her sister had never learned to play. The eight-year-old wanted her sister to learn to play very badly. The six-year-old, who agreed that she played in the teasing, provocative manner that she had been taught previously, agreed that her sister would be in charge of the play themes and rules for the next six months. They reported back that it had worked well!

One seven-year old became ashen and began to stutter within a half-hour of play with her eleven-year old, newly placed sister. The traumatized sister was playing out the death of a mother doll, with the girl doll becoming lost. While there was no nastiness meant on the part of the older child, this theme was an indoctrination into hopelessness for the younger sister.

I tell kids that they need to get a parent if certain themes like death, nudity, and tragic accidents come up in the play. Or, if one of the kids gets a scary feeling, even if they do not know why, they need to get an adult.

One child suggested, "Let's play that the boy gets his head cracked open with a stick, and that his brains spill out, and his eyes roll back. Then I will be the woman who says, 'If you do not close your eyes, the witch will eat your orphan eyes.' Then they take the boy away and we do not watch. The boy never comes back. We see the blood on the floor. They can never get the mark off." The child's parents knew that she was playing oddly with her sisters, but had no idea of the horror until they supervised.

Another boy was playing out the knifing that he and his brother had both seen during a drug dispute. It included spasmodic movements after the knifing. In neither of these cases did the children disclose the incidents to the parents first. Instead they brought them into traumatic play to the detriment of siblings.

Children should not hear, see, or watch the narrative of their siblings' trauma stories. It is simply too heavy a burden for young shoulders. Parents should explain this to children in the family, telling them that there will be things that they will not know.

One woman said, "What do I tell my sixth grader when she asks why her sister gets so afraid at night?" Incredibly, this mother thought that every question deserved a full answer. Telling children that their brother or sister was hurt, that the sibling is safe now, that adults will help the sibling heal, and that telling the sibling's story would hurt their own development gives all of the essential pieces.

Not Scapegoating or Spoiling

There is a natural tendency for parents to want to make up to a child for their difficult beginnings. Spoiling children with lack of structure and low expectations merely moves children from one unhealthy end of the continuum—neglect— to the other—overindulgence. Children feel better about themselves when they are contributing to their families and when they are learning to be considerate of others. When paired with nurture, structure prevents overindulgence and keeps things civil and pleasant. Use structure.

Sometimes parents have grown up within a "scapegoating" family system in which one person is the cause of everything that feels wrong in the family. Parents who were themselves the children of alcoholic parents are especially vulnerable to blaming all of the family woes on the newly adopted child. Since the child may be difficult, it is easy to feel resentment that life has gotten so tough. It is a short distance from there to resenting the child, and an even shorter distance to scapegoating the child.

Increased pressure from adding a family member will intensify pre-existing difficulties in a family. Parents who had a difficult marriage talked about this.

> "It is easy to say that our son is to blame. We refuse to scape-goat him. This is our marriage, and it has always been rough. Both of us are oversensitive, selfish, stubborn, and we love each other too much to quit. The pressures that he brought did not help things, but our marriage problems predated him."

Warned about the tendency to scapegoat, these parents made a point of staying honest. They entered marriage counseling, making only mediocre progress, which was their pre-existing pattern.

Parents who scapegoat often take the child's latest misadventure as the theme for the day. Or, they make certain that the child is somehow causative for the drama in their lives. Typically, these parents are spending a lot of attention on the child, but it is not constructive attention. For example, they will complain about the child, but miss his counseling appointments. Or they take a child who has never been able to sit longer than twenty minutes to his sister's high school graduation. Shaming is the daily plight of this child, who provides the service of making his family appear noble and martyred.

Scapegoating families tend to cling to diagnoses given to their children. When their child has resolved from a clinically significant diagnosis, they act disappointed. These families have a struggle to face—change themselves or provide a continuing pathological pressure on their child.

Siblings placed together

There are times when brothers and sisters placed together will be extremely stressful for parents. When children have been traumatized, sexually abused, abandoned, and drug-affected, often caseworkers do not want to deliver another loss by separating brothers and sisters. However, the children can continue to trigger each other's traumatic reminders, pass on mean behaviors, sexually act out with each other, disrupt the beginnings of positive attachment to parents, and wear out parents.

> One little girl would erode her sister's beginning sense of safety by whispering at breakfast time, "Let's hide and play that our birthmom's boyfriend is coming to kidnap us." The sister, who had been sexually abused by him, was not able to calm down until dinner!

The more damage that children in a sibling group have sustained, the less likely that one family will be able to meet all of their needs. This is especially true if these children have already undergone a disruption.

Dr. Elinor Ames and her colleagues have done some extraordinary work in researching the development of children adopted from orphanages in Romania. Among her noteworthy contributions, she noted the extreme stress on mothers who adopt more than one Romanian child at a time (Ames, 1996.) But, this high stress on parents who have adopted more than one sibling from Romania has nothing to do with a particular country. The high stress that I see in parents who have adopted siblings from the worst orphanages is similar to the strain that I see in parents who have fostered or adopted siblings in the United States when the siblings have shared deprivation, moves in foster care, and trauma.

If the histories of the children show relatively mild to moderate problems, parents can be more optimistic about placement together. However, when the histories show severe problems, it is important to be realistic about how much energy each child will absorb. For children entering the home together with several severe issues, it can be quite difficult to interrupt some negative behavior patterns and introduce safety.

Sometimes siblings have eroticized, chaotic behavior patterns that make parental intervention extremely challenging. Siblings often know each other's trauma triggers, and can intentionally trigger trauma memories. Or, if one child begins to make progress, a sibling may interrupt the progress because of unresolved loyalty issues.

One child planned to whisper to her brother, "Just remember, parents can be mean. These are not really your parents. Your real parents will be back." Her motive, which she revealed to me, was to have someone do worse than she was doing in the family. She had noticed his progress and knew that her comment would upset him, since he had been terribly abused in his birthfamily. Fortunately, she told me her plan before she used it on him.

While the bond between the siblings is important, it has to be secondary to each child's opportunity to feel safe, to heal, and to become part of the adopted family. That being said, there are some ways to help siblings placed together.

At six years old, Tom had a history of being scared silent during victimization. He was being hurt by his eight-year-old sister, Sheri. They had been adopted together after a history of violence. When he found out that his sister would need to make his bed and do his chores when she hurt him, he began to tell on her. Tom would sit on his mother's lap and read a story while Sheri made his bed. This was helpful for both children. Tom experienced his parent's protection, and Sheri stopped dominating Tom. Without Tom to dominate, Sheri's loneliness moved her to respond to her parents.

Fighting and arguing are normal problems for children placed together. Typically, no one has socialized the children before, and the children are emotionally less modulated for reasons described in earlier chapters. It helps to have children have to earn time to play together. Parents must stop them while things are still going well. After a break, children have to convince the parents to give them more time. For example, if they play well together an average of fifteen minutes before one of the children hurts the other, the timer is set for ten minutes, with the children reporting at the ring to negotiate for more time. The next allotment of time might be another ten minutes. Children learn to get breaks while things are still going well.

It is important to be clear with each child that his primary task in the family is to learn to trust the parents. Make a point to have separation between the children, so that the parent has time to form an attachment with each child. Sometimes a childcare arrangement has to be made giving parents the freedom to do this. One parent sent her sons to developmental preschool and kindergarten respectively, just to give herself individual time with each child. She continued to work as an accountant part-time, but moved her work hours to 2:30-6:30, the time of day she did not enjoy with either boy.

It is helpful to try to understand what role each child played in a family prior to placement.

After Amy and her sisters came to the family, their foster-adopt parents noticed that Amy was resented and scapegoated by her siblings. The siblings blamed her for reporting the stepfather's abuse to a caseworker, which resulted in foster care placement. It became clear that Amy had been the family scapegoat even prior to that incident. Her birthmother either ignored or blamed Amy. The foster-adopt parents were emotionally abusing Amy within a few months after placement. The children had all kept the same dance, and soon the parents were dancing along. While the old roles did not excuse the emotionally abusive behavior, they were a critical factor in the home.

It took a move, putting Amy into a separate home, before Amy began to believe that she had worth. In the next home, the parent was prepared. She talked to Amy very directly about her provocative behaviors that invited abuse. Amy had to sit with option cards until she chose another option. Each card had an idea, with a corresponding picture, giving Amy choices. The choices were simple, and they included

- Ask for a hug and attention.
- Tell mom that you miss your birthfamily.
- Ask for something to do when bored.
- Play a game.
- Take a walk.
- Figure out with Mom why you feel so bad.

Amy would sit on a step, watching her mother work in the kitchen or her desk for a while. Finally, Amy would pick a card. After a while, she would stop herself in the midst of misbehavior as her mother moved towards the cards. "Whoops, whoops, I can change it around!" She would say.

When children enter families together, the older child often retains the role of parent. During the initial adjustment into the family, it is important that parents describe parent responsibilities quite concretely—they will discipline, plan meals, put children to bed, and so forth. If the oldest child is willing to make an age-appropriate contribution, use that contribution. One boy was a stellar kitchen organizer. He supervised the kitchen clean-up after each meal. He also knew that the youngest never slept without the pacifier—with the *blue* button. This was invaluable information that only a stubborn parent would refuse!

After placement, when children comprehend their parent's role, it is time to talk in more depth about responsibilities of the oldest child. With support, children will talk about their struggles to take care of the younger children, and how hard it has been. It helps to have them tell about their major achievements. Parents can tell them, "Good job!" After this support, parents can help them to get in touch with how much they missed themselves when they had to function as a parent. Parents can say that they do not want to have them miss out any more. Reviewing the child's role as parent can be poignant.

> One girl said, "I think I saved my sister from getting hurt."
> She started to cry and said, "But I'm not sure. I was only eight. I
> took her upstairs to the neighbor before I went to school. Some-
> times Mom had her before I got home."

The pressure that some of the children have lived with has been incredible. In giving recognition of how difficult their load has been, parents help lead children to relinquish it. In some cases I have sat with parents, honestly telling older children that I do not know if their brother or sister would have made it without them. I thank them for their hard work. However, I let them know that it would be a shame if they missed the rest of their own childhoods.

List what the older child could be doing if he were not still trying to parent. Parents can ask for agreement that good parents are now available for the younger siblings, and that this child can go back to enjoying some activities that she missed. Ask them to think of something that they would like to receive as a special award for a job well done. Examples I've heard from other children are a camera, a twelve-speed bike, a basketball hoop, and a cat. There is a private ceremony, with or without siblings depending on preferences, during which they receive their gift. Parents recognize their sacrifices for the other children. The child hears that the burdens of parenting will be passing to parents. Then the older child uses the gift, enjoying life age-appropriately.

Parents' Self-Care

Readjusting to Reality

What happens when the family finds itself in one of the most challenging parenting situations?

"We thought that our adjustment to parenting would take about a month! Then, we would be back to normal. That was three years ago. We can't even remember what normal used to be!" The man who was speaking was laughing, but he and his wife were choosing laughing over crying.

Another man described that he just could not accept that their family had changed much. His best friend said, "Well, I am just going to call you Victoria Falls. That's the source of denial. And only your friend will tell you that!"

A step towards adjustment is recognizing that the family has changed in a permanent way. This is a preliminary in building self-care for the family.

If the parents have been too taxed to clean and organize in the home for a year, that is the new reality. If parents are lonely and have not had time for friends after six months of placement, that is the new reality. If the parents have not been able to depend on neighborhood babysitters for six months, that is the new reality. If the children are not getting to school on time, are missing appointments and sports practices, and look unwashed after three months of placement, that is the new reality. The list could go on, but it is useless to think that things will switch back.

Parents should take stock of the state of the household, fearlessly and without guilt. They can write up and post a written list of household problems, needs, with ideas for resources. Then they can make realistic plans for reallocation of resources. (Sometimes the reallocation needs to be from State coffers into family resources.) Tackling the issues one-by-one helps parents to figure out strategies for managing the problems. If they cannot come up with a way to solve the problem, they can keep asking in the foster care or adoption communities for advice or help.

A major adjustment for families is the level of sophistication and the expense of resources necessary to keep the family in balance. Parents are surprised at the long-term nature of resource gathering for complicated children. There is such a desire for parents to see children moved out of foster care and institutions, that whether parents have resources available for the children that they are adopting can be overlooked, particularly by the parents themselves. Dr. Dana Johnson summarizes his views eloquently,

"Nothing would please me more than to have all insti-tutionalized children find permanent homes. However, nothing would make me feel worse than having a family adopt a child they were un-prepared to parent." (Johnson, 1997).

Parents can reapproach their adoption or foster care agency for post-placement services. Many times there are written materials, grant-sponsored programs, videotapes, and mentoring programs existent within the agency, or available by referral. If there are not, ask the agency for the name of their licensing agent. That individual will often know where such support is available in the community. Get on the internet, looking at some of the resources listed on the resource list in this book. Libraries and bookstores are able to order books listed in the resource section.

Families are finding that they are getting funding from a variety of sources. One typical family has counseling covered through their insurance for family counseling, and counseling funded by a federally funded adoption support program for their child. They receive respite care funded through the Division of Developmental Disabilities. They pay privately for Sibshop, a well-loved program for the siblings of their special needs children. Since the Sibshop is through a non-profit organization, it is particularly affordable. Their school district pays for tutoring. After they specifically requested a review, they received an adoption subsidy available to older children through their state. The cost of braces was partially reimbursed by the adoption support system, as well. The combination of resources and financial relief allowed the parents to enjoy some outings, plan a simple family vacation, and get some household help. They said, "Without this help, we would not have made it as an emotionally intact family. We would not have disrupted, but we would not have been the unit that we are today."

Parents with the most challenging children need support. If the parents get too tired to provide nurture, children cannot do well. Parents have to go through a mental shift, recognizing that supporting people with special needs is a priority in society. It is appropriate and necessary to get support for the family when members have special needs.

Parent Self-Care Tools

Parents often implement a program of self-care when they are already weary. Because of burnout, they sometimes gripe, "Why bother. It probably will not do any good anyway." This grouchy reaction is normal. But, most people can try anything for two or three weeks—even their own self-care. Parents cannot feel much worse than they already do, if they are burned out. The suggestions that come next have been parent favorites.

Fifty Pleasures

When parents have begun to be too worn out, it is often because they have spent so much time doing tasks that they have deleted the fun or enjoyable things in their life. I like to see parents make a list of fifty items that give them pleasure. These are individual lists. The list might include going to a movie, putting bubbles in the bath, getting a latte, painting toe nails, sleeping in Saturday morning, arranging flowers, making love, poking in a hardware store, looking at photo albums, and so forth. Every week, the person must attain fifty check marks on the list. Using the same item more than once is permitted. Sometimes life has stopped being pleasurable because all of the fun and pleasurable items have been dropped. This exercise helps to get the "to do" list redefined so that pleasure rises dramatically.

Support Group

Many parents say that their greatest source of help comes from getting together with some other people who are doing similar parenting. Some specialized support groups are listed in the Appendix Resource List. Finding parents who have children with similar challenges, which require similar parenting approaches, makes a big difference in feeling understood and in battling isolation. Often agencies are able to refer parents to other parents who adopted or fostered within the same time frame. Some mentoring projects match newer parents to those who are a little further along. These connections are invaluable in normalizing the specific challenges that parents have to face.

Sleep

Getting enough sleep is one of the easiest and most effective choices that parents can make for themselves. Lack of sleep makes parents want to hide from difficult children, causing more of a wincing reaction than an "I am available for bonding" reaction to their children. Sleep is critical to success (Thomas, 1998). Parents should routinely get a full eight hours of sleep, unless their sleep needs have always been much less. While this goes against the grain of society, specialized parenting is almost impossible to do with inadequate sleep. Parents who say that it is impossible, try it, saying, "I get so much more done now that I am not tired. I used to be so inefficient before. I never realized that the hour and a half a day when I watched television to keep myself awake, did paperwork, and cleaned at night, was so inefficient. I can get that done in about 20 minutes when I am not tired. And, I do not miss the show."

Pleasurable Hobbies

Parents should maintain some hobby or develop some interest that has special value just to them. It should not be involved with their child's success or lack of success. It must be a pleasant escape that satisfies the parent and continues to build her identity. A parent with a difficult child put in a garden with scent appeal. Another parent began quilting. Yet another began kickboxing. The appeal of the hobby should be that it feeds the creativity of the participant. It removes the parent from constantly fulfilling a role. Instead she is simply indulging herself, which is part of good self-care.

Margins of Time and Energy

Parents do best with high-stress children if they allow themselves margins of time to work within. Because parents need to supply extra energy with little warning, they need to rework schedules, putting in extra minutes and extra space for attention demands. Being able to represent this without guilt is a healthy mental attitude. One parent described it in a matter-of-fact way, "I told my neighbor that I could not pick up their daughter from her job on the way home from the kids' school. It would put pressure on me to make that stop, since I could only succeed if everything went perfectly. I wouldn't be a good friend to myself if I placed that burden on myself."

Quiet Time to Process

When parents have new and difficult events in their lives, lots of information has to be processed. The old ways by which they defined their lives, safety, and roles will need alteration. Most people need to do some re-tooling of their mental apparatus in order to fit the new circumstances of their lives. They need quiet time in which to do this thinking.

Paradoxically, almost all anxious children are noisy. It is critical for parents, especially stay-at-home parents, to have an hour a day of simple quiet at their disposal. Working parents should take their lunch breaks for themselves, not for all of their phone calls and errands. This time should be time to play or quiet time to process information. Stay-at-home parents should also take time to themselves. One woman walks her dog or plays with him on the porch. In the evenings one couple takes turns reading and sitting in the hot tub. Another couple discusses a good book nightly.

Thinking of Sports, Beauty, Goodness, and Loveliness

When parents are bonding to children and care about their pain, loss, and fear, they can get entwined with these emotions. To keep a balance, and to keep from becoming overwhelmed by despair over the nature of life, spend a lot of time in a healthy and positive environment. Having flowers in the house, going to football games, eating great deli food, visiting an art show, meeting spiritual needs and watching classic movies with happy endings are all examples of protecting positivism and goodness in life.

Re-setting Your Body Rhythm

When people spend time with an intense child, sometimes their body pacing starts getting set to their child's. When people spend time in nature, or sit in a hot tub, or take walks, their bodies have a chance to regain their natural rhythms. Taking short breaks during the day will also accomplish this slow-down. I am a great believer in "coffee breaks" for stay-at-home parents. Listening to music that is set at a tempo of 40-60 beats per minute will help parents to regulate themselves. Some parents use music set to nature themes for themselves and their children.

Respite Care

Unconsciously listening for a child's distress keeps parents at high-alert readiness. Leaving a child under the age of four with a respite provider during the first weeks of placement is not suggested. But parents find that they can have a respite provider come into the home. After a few times, the parent can begin to leave. Gradually, even with young children, the respite care can move to the respite provider's home. Older, English-speaking children can have respite care described and implemented right from the beginning.

While it helps the bonding to keep children with their parents, this must be balanced by the need for worn-out parents to get a break. Sometimes grandparents or other relatives will make a commitment for once a week. Parents are encouraged to take their relatives up on these offers. If parents are acting as respite for each other, the family system is in a deficit position. New energy is needed for energy-draining children. Do not simply cycle childcare tasks between the same tired people. Import energy to meet the needs of the family.

Healthy Families—The Accent on the Positive

Healthy families master the knack of keeping the accent on the positive. Although the family alters after a challenging placement, they work through grief, re-balance, add resources, and find new ways to make life good. Their identity is not wrapped around a child's trauma or limitations. Instead, they find ways to accommodate special needs, without the special needs becoming the focal point of life.

Having Fun—Again

Having fun is one of the ways that families build their self-esteem. Planning for fun is a way to value members of the family. In talking about their best life memories, most people will talk about their family vacations, and the fun times that they had.

Sometimes families have to alter the old ways of having fun in order to have fun in a new way. As families accept this, they can get creative.

One family always had a goal of attending Space Camp when their children were at a certain age. When it was time to enroll, the family realized that one daughter was not up to the experience. They traveled to visit friends who knew their daughter, allowed her to feel comfortable with them again, then left her with their friends while the rest of the family went to Space Camp, picking her up again for the next two weeks of vacation. Everyone had a great time. Their daughter accepted that she would be too frightened to enjoy Space Camp, and thought that the solution was fair.

Another family ran a large boat for recreation. When they could no longer travel due to a member's medical condition, they outfitted their home with state-of-the-art video systems, which were fun for all family members. They recognized that what they most enjoyed about the boating was the intimacy of having fun with just the family, with the excuse of being unavailable because they were gone on the boat. Their home became a fun place in which they purposefully made themselves unavailable for days at a time. The one person who missed the aesthetics of the water made frequent, short trips to the shore.

Some families reserve an hour, three days a week, for games. Another family has pajama days. No one gets dressed, ensuring that no outside-the-home business gets done. They buy in deli food or make pancakes and play board and video games all day. There is a ban on work of any kind. The telephone is not answered. This indulgence causes the family to feel special and privileged. The cost is negligible.

Families can improvise, because only the family knows what works well for them. The emphasis is not so much on going out to be entertained, but on loosening up at home to have fun together. Some people move the furniture, playing soccer in the game room in the winter. Or they will play flashlight tag in the evenings. Other families play card games, especially games like Old Maid that require guile and cunning. Having fun together removes family members from the danger zone of taking themselves too seriously.

CHAPTER 12

 # Building Emotional Intelligence

E motional intelligence includes key elements: emotional awareness— knowing how our emotions affect our behavior; self-assessment— knowing personal strengths and weaknesses including learning from experience; and self-confidence—being confident about capabilities, values and goals (Goleman, 1998). Infants are learning the language of emotions and the fundamentals of self-control while held, soothed, and talked to by their caregivers in the first year of life. This intense start on emotional development gives a base upon which to accumulate information about understanding social situations, one's desired place in the social context, and getting to that position in an approved fashion. Children with high emotional intelligence not only understand the social contexts in their lives, but manage their own emotions to reach realistic goals in these contexts. They pay close attention to the emotional signals of others, which are often given through body stance, eye contact, and voice tones.

Children who have templates that are faulty often misinterpret the social contexts in which they circulate. Children may have had caregivers who avoided eye contact and conveyed little about feelings due to depression or the demands of institutional life. They may have had loud or emotionally self-absorbed caregivers. New parents must take on a series of tasks in creating new definitions for feelings, the faces that match the feelings, the body stances that are appropriate in a social context, and the social gestures that convey friendship. There are often fundamental problems for these children regarding self-awareness and accurate assessment of self and others. This chapter describes age-appropriate methods to help non-infants learn the lessons missed in infancy. Some basics like eye contact, body proximity, responsive smiling, understanding others' faces, and respectful voice control are laid out in techniques, giving parents options for work in the home with their child.

Rebuilding Emotional Awareness

Skill in building and retaining healthy friendships is highly correlated with future happiness in life—much more so than are academic skills. All of the children I work with want friends. They want others to play with them. Close relationships with friends and family make them feel valued. But building trusting relationships with parents, making friends, acting with sensitivity towards others, and "reading" a group's emotional tone are all affected by one's ability to understand and act on emotional information.

Because of past disappointments, children can be so afraid of what they want, that they may give confusing signals to parents and friends. Or, children may have some neurological problem or deprivation experiences that lead them to either withdraw, or to use an overbearing, intense relational style. Some children who have been abused will inflict some pain on others occasionally to "show who's boss." Their pairing of pain and closeness seems acceptable to them—and to no one else.

Children with whom I work regularly include negative behaviors with their positive signals for friendship. They tend to be ashamed when directly challenged about these behaviors. However, their self-awareness is not developed to the extent that they reflect on their behaviors, with plans for change, unless assisted. The suggestions in this chapter are specifically geared for children who do not naturally learn how to make friends, describing ways that parents can help their children to perceive emotional information and to develop social skills, or "friendship skills." The chapter is undergirded with parent techniques that challenge behaviors so that friendship skills are not paired with friendship-defeating behaviors. Parents create better social awareness so that children feel assured when they enter social situations.

Why Some At-Risk Children Miss Emotional Signals

When infants show beginning feelings, their parents mirror facial expressions and use words, exaggerating children's feelings just a little. Parents take the baby's initial signal, interpret it, exaggerate it, and send it back, guiding the baby to know what facial expression goes with what feeling. Parents also mix in nonverbal information, including sounds with empathic intonation.

As babies learn how facial expressions and feelings correspond, they are able to "read" their parent's feelings as well. By ten months it is a safe bet that the well-cared-for baby will cry if his parent cries. A parent who is frightened will frighten the baby. A happy parent elicits a toothy grin from his baby, who waves arms, legs, and vocalizes.

Through mirroring, parents teach babies what their facial expressions look like, and how they are perceived. Not only do children learn to match their facial expressions with the feelings inside of them, but they learn to modulate the expression, based on the information that the parent gives them by way of response. For example, a child who is scared by a jack-in-the-box might have a parent who mirrors the scared expression, but who then alters theirs to happy interest saying, "You are all right. See, it is a toy." The baby or toddler will be watching the parent's facial expression much more than the jack-in-the-box in order to determine the degree of fear to show. In typical infants, in the tenth month the child most looks to the parent's face for emotional information (Call, Galenson, Tyson, 1983, pp.19-26). Babies will alter their own emotional responses to fit the expression on the parent's face.

Children who missed these learning windows lack the ability to read cues for comprehending the meaning of their own and others' facial expressions. They miss the meaning of expressions that help keep them in synchronicity with others. There is some research underway investigating whether the brain damage from serious early deprivation can affect this ability to "read' others' faces and body language. Certainly, with serious deprivation, the neurological development that was desirable did not occur. Sometimes children with Fetal Alcohol Syndrome can read expressions, but they do not know how to respond to or use the information that they have received, or they cannot distinguish between a playful, teasing expression and a serious one.

Another complication for children occurs when they have been with an unstable caregiver. Parents work with their own emotional states in order to respond and mirror back information to babies and children. Drug and alcohol affected parents teach children a bizarre connection between feelings and facial expressions. Anxious parents mirror distress and do not teach modulation. Children who are learning about feelings and facial expressions are supported or limited by parental abilities.

It is important to the development of self and relationships to know how one is feeling and match that with a consonant facial expression. The last half of this chapter describes some of the work that can be done to help children with this part of identity formation.

Why Some At-Risk Children Ignore Emotional Signals

Some at-risk children ignore emotional signals because, as described in the section above, they are true to the original emotional map taught to them. Children whose parents turn their faces away from inquiring glances teach children to ignore emotional information—or certain kinds of emotional information.

> At a home visit, I saw a little girl crying after a night of domestic violence. Her mother numbly combed her hair and said, "You are ugly when you cry." When the child pointed to the broken window in the kitchen, she was ignored.

Some children with ADHD ignore emotional signals because they cannot interrupt their activity easily. When others let them proceed, they learn that it pays off.

A boy in respite with me ran, dripping wet, from the locker room to the pool. He gleefully passed the boy who was walking according to the pool rules.

"Sam," I said, "go back to the locker room and walk out."

"Why?" he said. "My mother just makes me stop running and walk the rest of the way." Sam's eyes were darting to his friend. He knew that he could still beat his friend to the pool.

"Do you still run?" I asked.

"Yes," he said. "Until she tells me to stop."

"That is why you have to go back and start again," I said. By this time I was at his side ready to escort him back to the locker room, a necessary action because of his ADHD. I sympathized with his mother, knowing that this boy exploited her weariness. This boy ignored the warning look that I first gave him, ignored the warning look from his friend, and focused on the elation of "me, first." Sam did not anticipate that his "I beat!" would irritate his friend or the lifeguard.

Taking children backwards, and requiring them to deal with other people's emotional messages helps to teach children the social ramifications of their behaviors. In this case, Sam and I talked through the probable feelings of his friend if he beat him to the pool by breaking a rule. We also looked at the lifeguard, guessing his response. It only took a few sentences. Once stopped, Sam looked at the expressions on his friend's and on the lifeguard's faces. The latter was standing, not sitting, on his perch, prepared to swoop on Sam.

This type of day-in and day-out work with ADHD children helps lessen their disrespectful actions against others. It is best done in an active, instructional manner that ends with children doing things the right way.

Sam did *not* run to the locker room after the swim. He looked towards me, watching for my smile of appreciation for his compliance. Sam's ADHD is such that he will still have many more instances of ignoring others. However, it helps to decrease the impact of ADHD by training children to observe emotional signals. A steady percentage of children with ADHD go on to develop a pattern of disregard for the rights or property of others. Slowing children to pick up emotional information helps to curb the drift towards disrespect.

Children with Fetal Alcohol Syndrome or Alcohol-Related Neurodevelopmental Disorder miss or ignore emotional signals because of brain damage. Sometimes they know that something is wrong with a person. However, they are not able to translate that into, "I should stop what I am doing, because I am distressing that person." Or, even more confusing, some days they can get it and some days they do not. They can perceive the signal, but sometimes cannot get the meaning out of the emotional information.

A boy with FAS felt very sad when his sister described how she felt about his getting into her room and going through her belongings. However, he continued to do the behavior that caused her distress. In fact, he used tools to take her locks off and let himself in. The sad feeling was not present when he was breaking in. It was present later. Also, there was a poor connection between what he knew and felt, and what he did and felt. The boy could not learn from talking about the situation in another location. He had to be put in the physical location, i.e. outside the door, in order to make the connection between his sister's feelings and entering his sister's door. The template that formed was successful. He memorized how to act. Later, when asked what he was thinking of, he said, "My brother's door." He did not generalize the information to the next door—and he loved to go through doors. Templates for emotional sensitivity and performance had to be memorized for brother's and parents' doors.

Children with ADHD and FAS hit or push impulsively. If they have other complicating issues, they want to hurt. They ignore emotional signals because they do not care. This is due to a lack of empathy. They do not feel the hurt in others that would stop them from hurtful behavior. When children have both ADHD or FAS and a background of maltreatment, which is a common combination, usually the hitting and hurting of others is a combination of "I cannot stop hitting" and "I like to hurt others like I was hurt."

Matching Facial Expressions to Inside Feelings

Why Some At-Risk Children Give Misleading Signals

Children have a "freeze" capacity that is designed to help them in danger. They still their bodies and wait until danger is past. Sometimes a blank look or even a bright smile accompanies this "freeze." It is adaptive for children to have neutral or even positive expressions when in hostile surroundings. It helps them so that they do not attract negative, and potentially dangerous, attention.

When children move into nurturing homes, they still encounter situations that confuse or overwhelm them. They use the same bland look or smile. It misleads parents and teachers.

Lisa had a big tantrum at home after school. In figuring out what happened, Lisa's mother drew the school and Lisa coming out of school. "What kind of face should I draw on you, Lisa?" her mother asked. After thinking, Lisa took the pencil and drew a very sad face. Lisa said that she had had a substitute who did not know that she stays in at the lunch recess. Lisa goes to the library after lunch, a place in which she can calm down and get a break from over-stimulation. Lisa went outside, had no one to play with, got scared, and wet her pants a little.

At this, Lisa's mom said, "Honey, I wish that you had told me."

Lisa said, "Why didn't you know when I came out of the school?"

Lisa's mom drew the face that Lisa had showed to her. The face had a stretched smile, not the sad face Lisa drew. Lisa's mom said, "Of course I care that you had a bad day, Lisa. Come over and get a hug now so that you feel better."

After the hug, Lisa practiced expressions in the mirror, so that her inside feelings matched her face. Lisa needed to signal her feelings so that her mother could meet her needs.

Sometimes a therapist is needed as a coach in order to do the above exercise. However, many parents can either do it by themselves, or do it with another adult acting as a coach.

The goal is to help children to portray, through a facial expression, accurate information. They can see for themselves what expression they actually have in the mirror. They then have the chance to both change it and to get praise for allowing their parents to know them better.

Facial Expressions That Manipulate

Children who had early deprivation often give intense stares, effective in getting basic care needs met from neglectful parents or busy orphanage workers. Children carry these expressions into the adoptive or foster home. The expressions start out as a survival means. They continue because the child believes that the parents are not trustworthy, because it is habit, or because it is a powerful means of control.

When expressions are too intense because of habit, children are legitimately confused by the response that they are getting. Teachers or parents may rush over to find out why a child needs attention, when the calamity is only "I have a question." With some frank talking, and some sessions in the mirror, many children will tone down their expressions. They want to fit in more than they want to get attention.

The intense expressions are a form of manipulation for children who are signaling either to be "saved" from untrustworthy parents or from unfair consequences.

One boy was asked to complete a writing exercise, which was at his grade level, at my office. His parents went to lunch. He was aware that they were coming back. He typically hazed his parents by stretching out his assignments for hours with parents or siblings meting out answers for him.

Seated away from the waiting room and up the hall, he turned towards the waiting room, even extending an imploring arm, as he fixed a soulful and tortured gaze on all newcomers to the waiting room. He completed his assignment in fifteen minutes after he was removed to the backyard, but not before howling for about ten minutes. He yelled over another therapist who came out, did not save him, and told him to cut it out. Then I went out, suggesting less noise and more work. He closed his mouth abruptly. "It works other places, though," he said. "I do not like to do writing assignments." He explained to me later that he liked to get others' help. Staring at people or loud wailing usually worked for him.

This boy was not being traumatized by his homework. He had simply learned to use a very powerful combination of signals for things he did not care to do. While he had learned the signals to get care during his years in a chaotic and neglectful home, he used them when he did not get his way. Mirror work was not necessary for this boy. Consequences worked nicely. There also was a "heads-up" call to the teaching staff.

When children are using manipulative facial expressions, parents lose patience. The expressions are unnatural, confusing, and distancing. Parents sometimes recoil at the primitive nature of the expressions, but expect modulation within a short time. When children are ill inclined towards modulation, parents may feel disgusted and angry at times. One parent said, "She's been here four years! When is she going to get it! I will take care of her without those looks!"

It helps children if parents identify the looks that are being used to control adults. Take videotapes or pictures of children, reflecting both the facial expressions that are appropriate and inappropriate. Parents can show the tapes to children. Children tend to be ashamed of the times in which they are controlling. Parents should not use the tapes to overly shame their children, but to give them information with a request for change. When doing the exercises in therapy, I say to children, "I would be doing the same thing if I had to live in an orphanage, had a very depressed first mom," and so forth. However, that does not mean that the child should continue as if poor conditions are still present. When children are using appropriate facial expressions, parents should be certain to take great pictures, putting some on the refrigerator.

Children tend to use intense looks with guests or out in public. When they do, parents can say to their children, "Drop the gaze. This is not a 911 moment."

Complicity from friends also works well.

For the child balking at schoolwork and beseeching Mr. Nevil with his eyes, the parent can say "Mr. Nevil, do you think that John needs to be rescued from third grade, his mother, and teacher?"

Mr. Nevil should respond with dramatic flair, "Nice try, John. But I passed third grade. It is your turn. You are lucky to have such a fine mother." With some indignant rearranging of himself, John will get back to work.

Role-playing situations work well for many parents. After deprivation or prenatal exposure to substance, many children have verbal instruction as their weakest learning area, but many have role playing as their strongest.

For example, her parents have told Sarah that she is to role-play asking if she can go to her friend's to play. Sarah can practice the expression and then use it in asking her mother's permission. In the role-play, Sarah asks politely, "May I go to my friend's?" with correct expression.

The parent can then compliment Sarah.

Then, the parent can pretend to be Sarah, and Sarah, Mom. Mom will ask if she can go to Janelle's home the way Sarah does it She holds her body tight, her mouth is formed into a tight rectangle. Many teeth are showing, but little smiling is happening. She holds her breath at the end of the question, letting everyone know that lots of air is available for loud arguing.

Sarah starts to laugh, and does not know whether to say "Yes" or "No" to Mom. She usually breaks out of role, saying, "Stop that. I do not look like that, do I?"

Mom helps out by saying, "Sarah, tell me to ask the way that you showed me first, so that you can say, 'Yes' to the question, instead of 'No' to the look."

Sarah gives the instruction, and gives "Mom" permission.

After a few role plays like the above, children "get it" when parents say, "Bring it down, Sarah, so this good Mom can say, 'Yes' to your question, not 'No' to the way that you are asking." A hand signal for bringing down emotional intensity is helpful so that parents can prompt their children out in public without embarrassing them.

Eye Contact

An earlier section discussed children who give intense gazes at the wrong time. On the other end of the spectrum, and often in the same child, there is lack of normal eye contact. Children are missing the positive facial reactions from their parents when they avert their eyes. Parents should ask children for eye contact so that they can give them smiles, or positive emotional information. Children are missing parents' nods of encouragement, tilted heads of appreciation, and mouthed words like "Nice job."

Children who did not get eye contact early in life have neither the habit nor the neurological tolerance for steady eye contact. But it can be developed later. If it is not naturally appearing, parents are free to intervene.

One experienced adoptive mother worried about her boy's complete lack of eye contact. I suggested a few things, but the idea that she liked best was the chocolate kiss idea. When her boy approached her, with gaze, they both ate a chocolate kiss. He sucked on his, which only stayed melting on his lips while he looked in his mother's eyes. His gaze tolerance skyrocketed! He sustained gaze after the exercise concluded. Mother became sweet to him. His brown eyes were chocolate to her. She still sneaks chocolates to him.

Sometimes I tell children that they are letting their parents' smiles fall right on the floor. It is surprising and sad to see how many smiles children miss. Sometimes, I ask them not to look at parents, and to tell me what they think that they will see. Sadly, children will say, "That she will be mad at me. I do not know why!" This opens the opportunity to talk about how things have changed. Parents can tell their children that they deserve as many smiles as other children do. If children say that they do not need the parents' smiles, it is a sign that they have given up on the need for approval. Parents can say, "I need to give you 'I love you' messages from my eyes. It is in my 'good parent' rules."

Reward children when they make eye contact throughout the day. The rewards do not have to be constant, but steady. A smile, touch, joke, piece of gum, or small privilege helps to give the message that eye contact with the parent is safe, and deepening the relationship is pleasant.

Warning Looks—Using Brakes and Steering Correctly

There are times that children do need to see warning looks from parents. A common example that I see with worn-out parents is demonstrated by Molly.

Molly leans into her mother, her elbow digging hard into Mom's thigh. She waves a picture two inches from Mom's eye, threatening immediate corneal damage. Blinking and wincing, Mom rearranges her body quickly to reduce pain and regain some space. She gamely attempts to finish her sentence, to regain her train of thought. She gives Molly a warning look at , who smiles intensely at me, with no expression change after a quick scan of the parent.

Parents should stop children who are practicing this type of insensitivity. They can say things like, "You need to move three feet away from me until I have time to teach you how to sit beside me. I will let you know when I have time." When parents have time, part of the instruction is that children tell them what motivated the behavior. Examples that I have heard from children are "I don't like waiting while she talks," or "I do not want her to talk about me in front of other people," or "I never noticed her face before."

Maltreated children often bring up that former caregivers always ignored them. Parents can ask how they felt when people did not notice the look on their faces or look at their sad eyes. Parents ask them if they want to do it like the people who hurt them, or if they want to look at the eyes of family members, and become sensitive in the family way. Children almost always choose the latter.

When looks trigger abuse memories, children see warning looks and move into a frantic state. Music and Physical Education classes, in particular, are often understaffed for children who need high structure and help with transitions. As these teachers give some warning looks, children can become further stressed, moving into high motor activity. In order to de-sensitize abused children to warning looks, parents and children can practice at home. Children can learn to respond to "warning looks" that signal "shape up," not hostility. Working in front of a big mirror together, parents and children not only identify the looks, but play out being teachers or authority figures. It helps to de-sensitize children so that they can understand the need to put on the brakes with a particular behavior.

When encountering angry children or volatile situations, often children who have problems reading warning signals do not move away. They get close to it rather than steering away. Parents should role-play situations, so that children can practice seeing expressions, interpreting expressions, and moving away.

A girl approached her brother during his temper tantrums. In the former home, she helped him when he was being beaten. In their new home, she still approached him even though he was not being hurt. As a result, she was regularly kicked and hit. She also got too close to other distressed children in her preschool.

Steering away from angry children was one of the lessons that she practiced with her parents. She practiced seeing the expression, interpreting it, and then moving to another part of the room. During the role-play, her brother volunteered that he wanted her away from him when he got angry. "I calm down better without you," he said.

Children with ADHD and PTSD are particularly prone to movement towards dangerous situations. Role-playing gives them practice moving away from dangerous situations and helps them to form new motor (physical movement) patterns of moving away.

Understanding Body Language

Inappropriate and Appropriate Use of Body Stance and Space

Some children do not have the concept of where their own body is in relation to other people. The paradox is that children who shrink from physical contact are often crowding others' space or digging into parents' ribs on the same day that they avoid touch. It is the same problem, but with different manifestations. These children are limited by a combination of lack of information about their bodies and problems tolerating physical touch.

Parents can experiment with how much physical pressure is comfortable for their children and for themselves. This is a fun exercise. For example, parents can get and give just the right type of touch on arms, backs, heads and areas that are appropriate. Children feel competent when parents go "Ahhh…just right!" Children tend to be more serious, but often are coaxed into some humor or giggling. Parents usually cheat, and end up tickling a little. Parents can say that it is a shame that children did not get a chance to learn cuddly touch and snuggling before, but there is no reason that they can not learn it now.

During close body contact, children who have been hurt by adults often feel more comfortable if another person is there as a witness. Sometimes it is helpful to have another family member or a friend there to cheer on a parent and child, taking pictures. (If there is any hint that the children may have been used in pornography, omit the camera!)

Practices like these are also done for sexually abused children. Just because they have had the wrong type of physical closeness does not mean that they need to miss out on the right kind of closeness. Obviously, parents avoid traumatic reminders, so children are actually comforted and nurtured, rather than re-sensitized to trauma. For example, for a child who had been sexually abused in the evening in a bedroom, snuggle times might be in the morning in the living room.

Children often need to be taught how they are perceived by others. Children whose body stance is to have elbows out, fists tight, and spread legs are showing that they are ready to defend themselves. Some children stand this way and then wonder why they have no friends. They also wonder why they seem to attract fights. This type of negative or threatening physical posture, as well as postures for friendship, should be modeled to children.

When children intentionally pose in such a manner in order to intimidate other children, especially traumatized siblings, the behavior must be given a consequence. Some children have to lie on their backs for a minute or two right where they are in the house until they are able to stop this fighting mode. As they lie there, they usually feel sorry for themselves. Parents can mention that this is the same helpless feeling that they gave to their sibling. Parents can conclude with, "You do not like this, and neither does your sister. You may not scare others on purpose in this safe home. I keep it safe for you and safe for your sister. Are you ready to be part of the team?" If the child nods and says, "Yes," the parent hugs the child saying, "Let's get on with our morning." The sibling is addressed then. "Do you need to get back at your brother, or has your parent taken care of it?" Almost always, the sibling agrees that the parent has taken care of it. They also get a hug. If they do not agree, parents can anticipate complicating factors like other provocations that have been missed.

Some children need some work on knowing how much space to put between themselves and others, depending on their relationships. Drawing circles on the floor helps them to learn the amount of space that is comfortable for close family, for casual friends, and for withdrawal. They can practice moving within circles to convey social information. Intimate space is within eighteen inches. Lowered voice tones are used in that space. This space is only for the closest family member. Children who move inside of an eighteen-inch circle, especially face on, are unnerving to other children unless they are family members coming for a hug or whisper. Personal space is between eighteen inches and four feet. That is the space that shows children that friends or family want to speak, play, or eat together. The space between four and twelve feet is the space for social occasions. (Duke, Nowicki, Martin, p.162-164). Moving within a six foot circle shows that children are becoming interested in friendship. When they are moving outside of a twelve-foot circle, they are indicating a withdrawal from social involvement. Children who come for affection need to be within four feet of their parent.

Children need to learn that touch of others is only permitted on the outside of other children's arms, shoulders, or back, except by parents. Parents can touch tummies and playfully swat rears. Children who grab other children on their inner arms, thighs, or necks will only be tolerated if they are boys roughhousing—and that only briefly. Girls will not tolerate such touch except during dramas or plays or in emergencies in which they are grabbed to safety.

Working with circles on the floor gives children a way to crack the code of body placement. When children have FAS or ARND, role-play specific situations. Children are aided by footprints, which can be cut out of a vinyl bathmat or non-skid rug pad. The "feet" show children where they should stand correctly spaced apart from the "feet" of where others should stand. Examples of places for the "feet" include by the front door, outside of a shared bathroom, at the top of stairs, by the car in the garage. Children can put their feet on top of the footprints to learn spacing. Other family members assist by using the corresponding sets of footprints. (The footprints are also helpful when toilet training little boys, or when teaching children to wash hands at the sink without water splashes.)

When children are speaking with others, face-to-face, "55 percent of the emotional meaning is expressed through facial, postural, and gestural means, and 38 percent of the emotional meaning is transmitted through tone of voice. Only 7 percent of emotional meaning is actually expressed with words." (Duke, Nowicki, Martin, p. 7). Practicing nonverbal signals gives children competency in conveying their desires for friends and inclusion.

Replacing Shame-Based Perceptions with Accurate Perceptions

Children who have been humiliated through neglect and abuse often believe that everyone knows about it. They think that there is evidence of abuse, so visible that others know their shame, and can refer to it at any time. Some of the defensive posturing that children assume is due to this belief.

One girl said to me, "Of course there is something wrong with me! After getting dumped by my birthparents for five years, having one adoptive family change their mind, and getting left out at school every day it has to be me, not them!" Her defense was to act as snotty and rejecting as possible. She stayed outside of social space for games, but claimed that she was rejected.

Only after introducing documentation about her birth situation, and filming and viewing her own rejecting behavior, was she ready to risk a try at making friends. She found that with just a few alterations, she was included. She practiced responsive smiling, with eye contact, every morning before school. Her transformation was sudden and surprising to her. Previously, by believing that she was and would be rejected, she did not have to learn anything, risk anything, or develop character. She hated freely. She told me that she had always wanted friends. "Nobody told me how to do it," she said. "Now I know."

Another girl showed me a face of plaintive sadness, sure to attract a friend at recess, she thought. Her idea was to induce sympathy in others, who would feel sorry for an "orphan," so that they would include her. After looking at some videotaping of herself at the recess, she laughed at her own dramatic efforts and agreed that she needed to change strategies. Her peers in the second grade just looked confused by her. After some coaching, she tried new strategies with success. "Anyway," she said, "when I looked at that tape, I saw that I look like the other kids. All that I had to do is look friendly."

Parents can assure children that their histories are not apparent to other children. Some children are still withdrawn from grief and trauma. After they have attachment to their parents and grief and trauma work has shown progress, shaming is reduced. That is often a great time in which to encourage children to try friendship skills. Smiling at other children, with eye contact, is often the first thing that I encourage children to try. Children are elated when they discover that there is nothing innately wrong with them—that they can make a friend even if for only one recess. Parents can easily have children practice smiles with eye contact at home. Older cousins or teen babysitters are often good bets for children needing to rehearse friendship skills with others.

Having a friendly, but not submissive, body stance can be practiced. Children who walk in a friendly manner look approachable to other children. Children can have parents videotape them or they can role-play. Children seem to love having parents mimic some of the extremes of the two postures of dominating stance and submissive stance. Children like to "help" parents to correct their stances.

Children and parents also role-play other normal social interactions from home or school—asking instead of grabbing, giving in to another person's idea, standing up for his own idea, taking turns, giving space for others to talk, and so forth. In the resource section is a reference for *Teaching Your Child the Language of Social Success* (Duke, Nowicki, Martin). This book concentrates on non-verbal communication and has a wealth of ideas for instructing children in friendship skills at home and school.

CHAPTER 13

Forming a Team of Support

When it becomes clear that their children face attachment challenges, parents often feel discouraged that the tasks before them are so complicated and require far more sophistication or energy than they can supply over the long haul. This chapter suggests using a team concept for working successfully with children with special needs The team approach requires commitment from people besides the parents. This chapter offers suggestions for who to approach about becoming part of the team and what and how to share with each team member. Parents can use these ideas as a springboard to decide what they need for success in their own situations. Vignettes in this chapter demonstrate ways in which parents solve problems of community misperception, turning awkward situations into affirmations for parents and their families.

Explaining to Friends and Family

After parents have read some of the information in the preceding pages, they are usually excited about all the exercises that they can do to help their children. But, where to get the energy or time to do the techniques can seem daunting. One man said, "Hey, we got Jason in this shape. He was on fire when we met him! We know that we need all the help that we can get!" Other people, who may have a kinship placement, who are step-parenting, or who are birthparents in recovery, may have a much harder time accepting the concept of the need for a team. But the bare fact is that in order to successfully meet the needs of their kids, parents with challenging children will need to abandon the model of attempting to meet all of children's needs within the immediate family. The family simply lacks the expanse of resources and the margins of energy necessary to meet the needs of complicated children. While it takes some humility in every situation to accept help, it is in the best interests of a child to grow up in a family that is happy, not one that is constantly under stress from excessive demands.

After thinking very carefully about who should be included, parents should ask both professionals and friends to be part of their family's team. The commitment should be discussed with great care with each potential team member in terms of what the parents have in mind and what the limitations are around each team member's support and participation.

One family with a combination of typical and challenging children put together an expansive circle of support: They asked close friends if they would consider serving as extra, geographically near-by grandparents to their child. They asked a friend who was a "power shopper" if she would help them with clothes shopping. Another friend made a point of inviting the stay-at-home mother to go to a getaway weekend at least every three months. An aunt and uncle babysat once a week for a date night. A therapeutic respite provider made a commitment to help the family for the next several years. A teacher agreed to track their child's progress not just in her class, but throughout the rest of their elementary years, coming to school conferences and providing continuity in the education of the educators. A friend of the father's had breakfast with him once a week. Their therapist agreed to keep space for them, so that they could come back in for therapy at critical stages. In addition to this committed team, the parents also used childcare, sports camps, and tutoring to help their children. The family regularly looked like they were having a good time, even if one member happened to be having an off day.

Families facing atypical issues have a tendency to become more isolated, with fewer friends and a decreased support system if they are trying to meet the needs of a challenging child alone. Research has shown that families who have a member who becomes medically fragile will systematically lose connections over time unless they are active in preventing this process. When families are fostering and adopting challenging children, the same process begins to occur. The main reason for this loss of connection is that the family energy is depleted by the additional tasks that they have. It takes a series of decisions to prevent this drift. Forming a team helps to keep connections, get help with tasks, and enhance the support system.

Describing Attachment-Oriented Parenting

Parents vary in how much they want to share with others about their parenting. Most families tell close friends and relatives why they are parenting differently. In many cases it will also be necessary to share this information with a child's day-care providers and/or schoolteachers as well. There is a knack to telling the truth, but in a general way. Here is an example of appropriate sharing with a good friend, a relative, or a classroom teacher or daily care provider who has been recruited to the family's team.

"Our daughter is still learning the meaning of a family. She does best and is happiest when she is getting the amount of structure that she needs. That is why she is trying to get into your lap and treat you like her new mommy. If she had developed a relationship with you over the last several years, the lap sitting would be fine. But she has never even met you before! As it is, she is still choosing to get close to people she just met, but afraid to get close to her family. That is why we cannot allow her to sit on your lap yet. She needs to learn that family members are safe to love and love deeply. Otherwise, she will continue believing that people are replaceable; nobody is really worth caring for deeply.

"Since she has only been in our family for six months, and she was immature emotionally before she came, she needs the rules and supervision of about a four-year-old. It would not be fair to treat her like a seven-year-old, since she fails with the responsibilities of that age. That is why I keep her so close, give her so much structure, and have her check back in with me. As she matures, she will need less structure. I will be more than pleased to reduce the structure then, since it is a lot of work."

If those close to the family ask why parents do not demonstrate love by "giving her a day off," or "letting her do what she wants for a change," parents can respond to the kindness behind the request, without agreeing with the request. Parents should agree that it is sad to have to provide so much structure. It is sad that children have not had the kind of life that would permit such a possibility. Parents can say, "It would be denial to pretend that it would work. Of course, we have tried it, as have others. It is always hard to confront the evidence of pain in a child's life. If we pretend that things are normal, we are not helping her to succeed. You should know that the type of parenting that we are doing does cause the most rapid emotional growth in children. It is hard, but I think that she is worth the effort!"

Note that the parents are not demeaning or labeling their children in these explanations. They are respectful, but honest.

These types of personal descriptions are only for individuals that parents want or need to go to the emotional expense to inform. They are for people who are close to the family or will be closely involved in the child's daily life.

Do not give out information about sexual abuse, physical abuse, and extreme neglect except when it is necessary to a child's care plan and safety. When you do share, be certain that the team member with whom you are sharing understands the importance of maintaining the family's and the child's confidentiality. While parents may feel inclined to share that information with a very trusted confidante, children do not want the world to know about their issues as they get older. Share wisely.

A father shared his daughter's history of sexual abuse with his best friend. Unfortunately, the father did not think to make clear how very private he considered this information to be. The friend shared it with his son, for reasons that are unknown. Some years later, the son and daughter ended up in the same middle school. This boy told their peers, with a dismissive gesture towards her, "She's s.a.—You know, sexual abused." This girl had no idea how many faculty members knew her story, since the "best friend" was a teacher at the school. The betrayal was acutely felt. The girl, who had resolved her abuse issues beautifully, had boundaries superior to the father's friend! Even if parents think it is obvious, be certain to demand confidentially from a trusted friend!

Anticipate the day when a thirteen-year-old will ask how well their privacy was respected.

Supportive grandparents, who provided loving respite, received information from the parents about boundaries. They visited my office with their granddaughter in order to get tips on care for a child with extreme trauma. They had observed specifics about their granddaughter's sexual abuse due to the horrific night terrors that she had at their home. They had learned to respond to questions regarding abuse from curious relatives, "We do not know details, do not need to know details, and would never guess. We do not feel comfortable discussing our granddaughter's business any further."

Some people do not "get it" when attachment issues are explained to them. When children with attachment problems show classic symptoms of indiscriminate friendliness, no concerns appear in the person's mind. They seem to get stuck in the illusion, "This child loves me. He could not really have a problem if he thinks that I am so special!" This is not mature adult thinking.

Some people persist in encouraging a child's intimate shows of affection by saying, "But I do not understand." Believe them. Parents can respond with, "We are sorry that you do not understand. We hope that you can follow our wishes with our children, though, since we will miss seeing you if you cannot support us. What we are working on with Jason is complicated to explain. However, it is serious. He may not develop close relationships or a healthy conscience if we are not able to help him."

Not "getting" attachment does not free a person from the need to support the parents' wishes. If people cannot act supportively, the total family is best supported by less contact until the child is better attached.

If casual friends ask questions, you may or may not want to spend time educating them about attachment issues. Parents are under no obligation to educate casual acquaintances when their own emotions are entangled with the information. It can be very painful and draining to talk about the attachment issues and a child's special needs. Parents can say, "You know, it takes a lot out of me to talk about this. Maybe sometime in the future there will be a better time to talk about it." You can substitute *place* for the word *time* for people who want to discuss this personal issue in an inappropriate setting. Or, parents can say, "There are several good books on the subject. You may want to try your library or the Internet under the topic *attachment.*"

Setting Boundaries

Team members need to learn that until children are well-attached to their parents, big hugs, lap-sitting, long gazes, and being carried are intimate expressions of love reserved for members of the nuclear family—with the possible exception of grandparents. Children may have learned a survival tactic of getting attention and approval from anyone. Continuing this practice does not help them to feel safe or protected by the parents in the family.

Team members must also know that in the beginning attachment period with the child, the parents should be the ones feeding the child or giving food to the child. (Again, grandparents are possible exceptions.) After some attachment has formed, parents can ease off this exclusivity. Tell friends that this early attachment work parallels the arrangement parents have with infants—the parents do the feeding.

Parents should definitely be the ones giving sweets. In the first months of infancy, the taste buds experience almost everything as sweet. Children with deprivation in their backgrounds will often crave sweets, yearning for this early connection between parent and sweetness. Do not give this tool away. Parents should be the source of sweets until attachment is well-established.

Ask team members to drop eye contact if a child is gazing intensely. This gaze is often meant to exert control over others. If after two seconds of gaze, the friends avert their eyes and continue to do this every time the child starts to "lock on" with his tractor beam gaze, the child will give this game up. When the gaze fails, the child may try a new strategy. For example, during a bonding and attachment assessment, when I would not return intense gaze, a girl spit at me. On another occasion a boy attempted to pinch me when I kept dropping his gaze every two seconds. He succeeded in pinching the adoption worker who came in the room to observe.

A common behavior among attachment-disordered children is ignoring parents while asking adults in the presence of the parents for help. Ask friends and family and other team members to redirect the child to you for "help" that he may need. For example, "Ann, your mother can help you to wind up that toy."

When a child runs up to a friend, prior to having formed an exclusive attachment to you, it helps parents to have words to use.

For example, Ann climbs into the lap of a stranger, Mrs. Smith, even after repeated instructions about exclusivity. The parents can say, "Ann, you need to practice being part of our family, not looking for a new family. Mrs. Smith knows that you do not know her, and that you need to stay closer to your mother! Thanks for your support, Mrs. Smith," Mom continues as she retrieves Ann briskly. "Ann, let's start all over again so that you get this right."

Guide Ann through the steps of entering the room correctly with a polite greeting to Mrs. Smith followed by no physical contact. Mom says, "Great job, Ann."

If friends or acquaintances seem to want to help with diagnosing, do not appear receptive. Let them know that your child has been diagnosed, that you have professional support and advice, and that you are following a regimen known to be the most successful for the most children.

Parents complain that sometimes, with no encouragement, individuals will launch into a story that reminds them of the family's situation. People are entertained and fascinated by tales. Some of the stories have dreadful and unrelated outcomes. There are books and movies available for the purpose of entertaining others. Feel free to put your child off limits when it comes to being the subject of tales for others.

After hearing these unnecessary sad stories, mood is affected. Parents should watch and protect their mood gauges carefully! Parents can protect themselves from frustration by disengaging from these episodes, quickly excusing themselves to make a phone call, find the restroom, or check on something. It is certainly more appropriate to find an excuse than to fume about insensitivity later. Some people are drawn to special needs like a magnet, yet they have nothing positive to offer. Avoid these people.

Some people are supportive, but require an update upon each meeting. One family handles this in an efficient manner. They send out a monthly update on one of their children's progress to several personal friends, who pray for this child, as well as to other key team members. Then, when they encounter the friends with the whole family, they do not have to concentrate on giving an update. The friends can enjoy the adults and other siblings.

Spend time with people who seem to enjoy the potential of the whole family. Part of boundary setting is making certain that there are quality people included in the family circle of friends. Do include people who like family members, without feeling that they have to alter anybody. Some people have the capacity to see emerging character qualities in children and how these qualities might develop into careers or good characters. They still are reality-based, but seem to recognize strengths before they are fully present. They are wonderful friends. Spend time with people who help dream for a good future for all of the members of the family.

Asking for Affirmation of Using Specialized Parenting

Perfect the art of affirming yourself in the home and in public. In two-parent families, one parent can stand supportively behind the other, simply nodding support. It affects the whole family positively. Or, the parent who is observing can call out, "Super parenting."

A single parent can say, "Wow, I think that I just had a great parenting success there. I need to write it down. I want to remember it!" One single parent called one of her list of five supportive friends every evening. They had taken the time to learn about specialized parenting, with its high nurture and high structure demands. They listened and cheered for her as she told them about her day.

Some children count on the parent's embarrassment. The child will begin to act in some outrageous fashion, which draws attention as parents attempt to stop the child's misadventure. Parents can affirm themselves, and restore structure in the public setting.

Looking again at Ann, whom we met earlier, this time as she is climbing into the lap of a man whom she met thirty seconds ago. Her parent can say, "Lucky for you, Ann, that you have a mom who cares enough to teach you to be a family girl."

As the man mumbles something about it really being all right, the parent should continue, "Ann may guess that I am too embarrassed to talk about this in public. Luckily for Ann, I know how important it is for her to practice safety. Ann, you will try coming into the room again, this time in the family girl way." Exit with the child, rehearsing the preferred behavior, which is a polite nod to the total stranger. If Ann tantrums, wait through the tantrum before reintroducing her into the room. If she cannot handle the room without practicing poor behavior, she may not be ready for public settings yet.

One child intentionally humiliated her mother out in public. She would make comments about the size of her mother's rear end as she reached for items in the grocery store. The mother commented loudly, "I wonder what would motivate you to say such a rude thing? I am a great mother! I am wondering why you say such a mean thing to your mother?" The girl was appalled that her mother turned the attention back to her. She attempted to quiet her mother, never attempting the nasty game again. The parent affirmed herself, and additionally showed that she was not absorbing shame any longer.

Another child screamed so others could hear her, but not see her, "You are hurting me, my arm, my arm! Stop, please, Mom." The parent would not be doing anything but saying "No" to her child. The parent was afraid to travel or take the child in public.

Her strategy changed. She went on a trip, checked into the hotel, and called the front desk. "My child has temper tantrums," she explained. "If she starts screaming because she cannot go into the pool or have candy from the machine, your staff might worry since she screams that I am hurting her. You are free to use your passkey to walk in and check on us. That way, you do not have to call Children's Protective Services to check things out. They are busy with real safety issues, and they should not have to waste their time."

This child was mortified, but conceded that she had coerced her mother for two years in public situations. After one testing, during which a hotel manager made an appearance, she stopped. The hotel manager's comment to the mother was, "Good luck. I think that she's found her match in you."

When parents wonder if their children are really changing, it helps to look back over time. Often they have made fantastic strides with specialized parenting, but remain focused on how much more there is to do. Team members, who are slightly more distanced from the children than are their parents, may be especially helpful in this regard. Ask them to be alert for signs of progress and point out examples from time-to-time.

Then, stop to recognize goals. Parents who teach children not to bite should celebrate for their children. They should also celebrate the success of their parenting. Parents may enjoy keeping a great parenting achievements journal with the best successes. Or, in the example of licking the biting problems, parents could celebrate with cupcakes for the family and a movie for the successful adult. Parenting is filled with a series of projects. Acknowledge their achievement.

Tips for Teachers

Parents should feel free to share the following sections with their child's school.

Teachers must be aware that parents who are describing a combination of attachment, trauma, and neglect issues will be trying to alert them so that they can be prepared. Teachers who heed the parents can position themselves to be helpful to a child. The intensity of the parents can be easily misperceived. Teachers may feel an inappropriate need to assure parents that their child will do fine. This dismissive approach by teachers is anything but reassuring. Rather, such messages tell parents that a potential crucial ally in the helping team for their child is unprepared for their child.

> In one case, I called a teacher in May, since a student was entering her kindergarten class in the fall. The child had made wonderful gains with her attachment and trauma, but needed specific help. A simple plan for safety was developed and implemented. The girl did well with few accommodations. Unfortunately, when this teacher went out on maternity leave, the new teacher had three days of problems climaxing in having a chair heaved at him when he was not looking. The new teacher had discontinued the agreed upon plan unilaterally, as being unnecessary.

Children dealing with a combination of attachment and trauma issues need to have parents and teachers who are working together. Teachers must pay attention to the lessons that the parents have learned over time. Children deserve to have prepared staff when they enter the classroom. "Waiting to see if there are problems" never works as well as does good pro-active communication intended to prevent problems. Long before children get to the point where they are throwing chairs, they have been feeling more and more frightened and out-of-control. This is too taxing for children. Certainly no additional educational time was gained for any member of the kindergarten class described above.

Teachers who can affirm the parenting in the home, taking time to understand it, help children to feel that they really are in a world in which adults can be trusted and are unified. Educators will usually find themselves more successful because of the enhanced safety that the child feels.

Just as friends and family members may not understand high structure and high nurture parenting and may need specific information to help them understand why this rather rigid approach is in a child's best interests, so will teachers. Typically teachers are no better informed about either general adoption issues or attachment issues than is any member of the general public. When they see high structure, it is easy for them to assume that parents do not love their child. The important people in children's lives need to learn that parents are loving and are providing the structure that is appropriate for an emotionally younger or more emotionally fragile child. It is tempting for education professionals without prior experience with children with attachment challenges to believe that if the parents simply relaxed, then there would not be a problem. Parents know that this is wishful thinking; teachers need to learn that too. Help teachers learn that it is because parents are aware and responsive to problems that they are so structured. Teach them that successful parents have seen how much better their child performs with high structure, so work hard in providing the structure. Encourage them to ask what other approaches parents have tried that were not successful.

When dealing with the school, parents need to tell school personnel that they want to hear some positives, and not just negatives. Parents want a chance to rejoice in their child's achievements, put a great picture on the refrigerator, and share in their child's successes. Even if there are challenges, parents want some of the tangibles that help plot success for themselves and their child.

Solving School Problems at School

While parents want teachers to form a good team, teachers must recognize that parents are working hard at home. Coach teachers to inform parents about the child's problem, and the school's intervention, but be firm in requesting that they not tell about the problem and then expect parents to solve the problem that evening from home. For example, a teacher should not send a warning slip home to the parent concerning the game ball that the child threw on the school roof during the first recess. That issue should be taken care of with a consequence that immediately follows the incident. The parents certainly can be apprised of teacher's actions. However, it is much more effective if the child has immediate consequences. Help teachers, as part of the child's team, to learn the value to the child of being "caught" following rules. Ask teachers to send home a note to parents, with statements like, "Today I 'caught' Tim waiting in line politely."

Teachers will need to learn that warnings are not helpful for the children described in this book. Telling parents that the school "warned" their child, tells the parents that the child's behavior resulted in indecision on the part of the school. Children who have had a variety of caregivers in orphanages or foster homes have learned that it can work to their advantage to "wait out" the caregiver. They wait until the time passes and the problem disappears with the caregiver. Children need experience both in solving problems and in having consistent rules. This is why, for these children, warnings are not helpful. Learning that every time that they ignore a rule there will be a consequence helps children to form clear expectations. Helping children to find two or three solutions to the type of problems that tempt them to break rules will help them to learn to solve problems. Teachers should learn to be sure to remind children of some of their possible solutions prior to the time they need to make a good choice. Teachers can inquire curiously as to which solution a child will pick. Children can feel power and approval when they can choose good solutions.

The wise educator will request information from the parents as to what part of the school day might need structure, and some successful tactics from home that can be extrapolated to school.

Many children described in this book have had prenatal exposure to toxins, including alcohol and/or a background of severe deprivation. Teachers need to learn that these experiences compromise judgement. They will need to be clear about rules and specific about where and when the rules apply. Steady, but upbeat, reinforcement of rules helps children to make good choices. Long discussions about whether children really *meant* to hit another child, or to write on someone's project, etc. only teach children skills to debate their responsibility for actions. It is a better message to children to say that they may *never* hit or destroy someone's property as a choice.

The fact is that children are motivated to have friends. What they *mean* to do is to have friends. Teachers can help them to learn respectful behavior so that friendships can develop.

Shame and Control

It may be difficult for teachers to form a bond with the children about whom we are speaking. Instead of trying to do things the teacher's way, some of the children try to control teachers. It is easy to get into a control battle. Teachers need to be prepared for this and to learn that it works best to give commands to children that can be backed up, giving the commands while children are within arm's reach. The teacher should gently help children get to where they need to go, without disrupting the class. If children need a lot of help, teachers and parents should ask for an aide until children begin to get into a routine in the classroom.

Teachers should consult with parents about the emotional age of the child. If the child is emotionally a few years younger than her peers, teachers may determine that the child is doing her best. Or, they might ask if there are ADHD or FAS issues with this child. Recognition that a child is working her hardest takes the emotional charge out of most situations.

It is especially important that teachers know not to shame children in front of classmates as a form of control. This will only further damage their ability to make friends. Children will believe that they are in an insensitive environment again. Teachers should not use the corner, turn the desk, build a box, etc. Doing so unintentionally educates the student and the rest of the class that he is potently different. Teachers should keep this child in the front and center of the class in a calm, structured classroom. If this is not working, then a conference to determine how best to calm and focus the child should be convened. Some children need a much smaller, specialized classroom setting.

Teachers may also find it helpful to use a sensory modality other than simply the auditory modality in order to give directions. Children with the challenges mentioned above often have auditory processing problems. Instructions should be written on the board for such children. Younger children do well with pictures of steps contained in the activity. (Some of these pictures are in the teacher's instruction manual for visual teachers who need visual clues!)

It is very important that teachers be encouraged to keep their positive comments to negative comments in a 7:1 ratio. If these seem to be impossible ideals, then requesting an instructional aide is in the child's best interests.

Gotcha!

Some of the children who were in orphanages have a teasing, oppositional manner that has been part of a "get the orphanage worker back" game. These children need some descriptions of how the congregate school setting is different from the congregate orphanage setting. Some children who were in situations of maltreatment learned this thinly-veiled aggressiveness as well. Some specific social cueing, which should include a description of the teacher, her role, and how she will relate to the student, helps enormously in preventing this teasing behavior from starting. I like to have the child meet the teacher a few days before the first day of school so that the child can practice how to enter the classroom and relate to the teacher. I also like the child to hear and then role-play how she can get positive attention from the teacher. These early meetings provide an opportunity for practicing some compliance with the teacher and establishing an acceptable behavior pattern before other children are around. Typically, the child brings a gift to the classroom and teacher on this early visit, which starts things off in a positive way.

Fear

More than anything, the children described in this book tend to be fearful after having problems with attachment, neglect and loss. This can be masked behind bravado or dissociation. The child who is very frightened, even if she is using defenses, cannot learn very well. Bruce Perry's work on trauma has demonstrated the difference in brains that are being wired for danger, rather than for typical learning. Very high stress levels actually begin a process of brain damage. I like to work on making the child feel as comfortable and connected as possible. For example, allowing the child to wear a hooded sweatshirt in school often gives him the option of covering his head when he is feeling overwhelmed. Assemblies that feature disaster practice are often ones that should be missed by traumatized children.

Parent aides in the classroom are often quite frightening to traumatized children, as are substitutes. Unless the parent aide is to be a steady part of the classroom, children are better off staying closer to the teacher. Some children do better staying home on the days that substitutes are taking the classroom. Commonly I hear that the child never said anything in the way of complaint. Because linguistic ability is compromised when children are frightened, children will not be likely to tell their teacher that they are frightened at the time. Instead, they tend to dissociate or to become out-of-control behaviorally.

Maintaining a structured, but safe and nurturing, connection with children is essential to their learning when they have marked, underlying fear.

One master teacher worked beautifully with a difficult, severely abused child. He referred to him in the classroom with a smile as, "Sean, the son I never had." His radical acceptance of the child made the year a successful learning year.

Another traumatized child was assigned the same parent driver on every school field trip for three years. The parent always volunteered, so the child was intentionally paired with this adult on trips. The parent was careful with details, consistent in manner, and provided safety and predictability. An educator discerned the natural good pairing, finding out later that the parent was a children's mental health specialist.

Educational Testing

Neurological differences are common in children with attachment issues. Lack of stimulation, poor nutrition, trauma, and exposure to toxins can all compromise the ability to learn. Testing that is broader in scope and quickly administered masks difficult perceptual challenges. A thorough educational assessment, consisting of about four hours of direct testing, can yield answers to mysteries about why school is not working well for some children, along with recommendations for approaches that match better. Neuropsychologists do this type of testing, giving specific recommendations for the classroom. Dr. Ronald Federici has described some testing for complicated children in his book, which is listed in the Resource Guide.

One more important member of the support team for many families whose children have attachment challenges is a qualified mental health professional. So specialized is this team member that the entire next chapter will be devoted to how to select that professional.

 Getting Professional Help

Parents often entertain the notion of seeking mental health help for members of the family with trepidation, observing the adage, "Beware the helping hand!" When one is in the midst of complex and challenging situation, it is often difficult to see that it is time to reach out for help. For those who do reach out, it is difficult to find therapists who know adoption and attachment issues. This chapter describes how and when to get the right kind of mental health help. A sample interview guides in finding a good match with a therapist.

When to Seek Help for Children

I believe that all children who have been adopted after three months of age benefit by having an assessment by a therapist experienced in attachment and adoption issues. Nothing is more pleasant for a family than having a professional give tips about stages and then say that there are no treatment issues. However, if there are issues, the family can make a plan for treatment after the assessment. The following are items that indicate that children need assessment and treatment:

- Your child describes adoption as the most significant factor about himself. She may say something like, "I cannot get friends because I am adopted." Instead of *having been adopted*, this child's identity is that she *is adopted*.

- He shows any of the classic signs of childhood distress: hoarding food, wetting or soiling after toilet training has been established, insomnia or oversleeping lasting two weeks or longer, a fascination with horror, persistent fear of being alone, or (past toddler age) cruelty to animals or people.

- Your child over age nine cannot talk about her adoption story using both sad and happy emotions.

- Your child has learning disabilities or attention deficit disorder.

- Your son or daughter over age seven doubts the stability of the adoptive family, even after the facts are clearly presented.

- Your teen cannot seem to figure out how she will eventually leave home in an appropriate way. She seems to be foggy about her own identity and how to establish independence.

- Your child does not seem close to you, does not attempt to please you, and shows poor conscience development.

- Your child has rage that seems to come out of nowhere, and rage that seems out of proportion to the circumstances.

- Your child has a history of physical abuse, sexual abuse, or extreme deprivation. Even if the child cannot remember the abuse, get the help anyway. There tend to be distortions in beliefs that are a result of early damage.

- If the child witnessed violence, especially lethal violence, get help. Often there will be bizarre symptoms and distortions of reality that are related to the terror the child experienced.

- Your child has a family history of bipolar disorder, particularly if one of the birthparents was, or has become, impaired by this mental illness.

- Your child was prenatally exposed to alcohol and drugs.

When to Seek Help for Parents

Stresses on Relationships

When children have been exposed to unhealthy behaviors, it is not their fault that they learn them and then bring these behaviors into the new home. It is a pressure on all family members to continue to be healthy while living with unhealthy behaviors that may not change for years. People find that under this type of pressure their own strength is not bottomless. They are more vulnerable to stress than they thought. Or, they find that their child's neediness brings out some of their own unhealthy behaviors or those of the other children.

> For example, parents ignored that their oldest boy was both overindulged and a bully. School reports were dismissed. This unpleasant reality became unavoidable when a younger, easily victimized daughter joined the family. As the father put limits on his son, the mother indulged him further. The children were being split into Mom's favorite and Dad's favorite.

Parents in situations like these need to find help.

Parents' reactions to trauma, as described in Chapter 5, often require that parents obtain steady counseling. Especially when parents have adopted or fostered very traumatized children, parents may need assistance with processing toxic material from their child's trauma. Or, if a child behaves violently towards another family member, particularly if a family member either minimizes or overreacts to the violence, professional help is needed to process the meaning and emotions from the event.

Parents with the most challenging children are finding that the performance demands on them as compared to demands placed on parents of average children are comparable to the demands placed on racecars, as opposed to vans. Families with challenging children need a pit crew just to keep them in the best possible running condition. Parents of children in individual therapy frequently request therapy time for themselves or other family members in order to keep their family functioning high.

Individual and Family Therapy

Issues that may come up for parents are explored in Chapters 4 and 5. However, this short list describes when families know that it is time to make an appointment:

- They do not like their child. (If the parents love their child, but do not like their child, this qualifies.)
- Parents find themselves fantasizing about developing diseases that require them to go to bed and have others wait upon them.
- Parents find that their need to control life is escalating in other areas. (For example, yelling at people in the community who perform services would be a symptom of a problem here.)
- Parents begin to hit, push, or scream at their children.
- Parents or other family members develop a point of view that one is the winner, and the other is the loser.
- The challenging child's issues dominate all of the energy of the family.
- A family member has been depressed for over two weeks, i.e. irritable; over or under sleeping; lacking pleasure in activities that normally seem pleasurable; thinking that the world would be better off without them; feeling hopeless; feeling guilty; having difficulty making decisions; and having difficulty concentrating.
- Any member of the family feels constantly under barrage by another family member.
- Parents begin to feel traumatized by exposure to the child's trauma or their child's reaction to trauma.
- Parents find that unresolved childhood issues begin coming up, interfering with their emotional wellbeing and judgement. Or, they find that formerly resolved issues from trauma and childhood are being reactivated.

The first goal of individual therapy is to stabilize an individual. After that, the therapist and the person in therapy work on goals together and determine how to achieve those goals. Typically, the goals are pragmatic: how to face criticism of a child that is experienced in the community, or how to cope with the grief over a child's abuse, or how to cope with control battles in a child, or how to discipline instead of screaming, or how to stop a traumatic response in the parent when the child screams.

Family therapy helps with factors such as defining roles in the family, supporting each other, ensuring fairness for all family members, having fun, and helping parents and children to get needs met in a healthy way. It gives the entire family support, so that in a high-stress situation the family does not fall into dysfunctional patterns. Some family work should be included in the counseling plan for a child who has challenges and who is entering a family.

When parents adopt a child who is much more impacted than they anticipated, counseling helps them to grieve, as well as to adjust to a new family image. It can be preventative. Parents describe that it helps that they do not have to find the energy to think through all of the issues by themselves.

Marital Counseling

Couples often find that they let their own marriage slide for a period of time as they attend to the initial adjustment of a child who arrives with his own set of challenges. The adjustment period can turn into years. Parents can end up with major marital problems resulting from neglected marriage tune-ups. They owe it to themselves to take the time and energy necessary to overhaul their marriage. Even if it means deferring something for the child for a time, putting their marriage at the top of the priority list is healthy.

One can observe pragmatically that married couples are unlikely to be cheery and nurturing when their marriages are on the rocks. Parents need all the happiness and fulfillment possible when trying to care for a challenging child. Sadly, parents do let their marriages slip, save back nothing for each other, and then have to supply the needs of their children throughout a separation and divorce. It is unbelievably taxing.

There are instances in which one parent finds that the stresses in the family are overwhelming. That parent begins to pull back; the other parent gets overloaded. Particularly when the desire to have another child was more the desire of one parent, the other parent may feel entitled to pull back. This is an issue that tears relationships apart. It is not an unusual issue. Marriage counseling, conducted from a family perspective, can help couples renegotiate their commitments to the child and to each other.

At times, a withdrawn parent whose behavior toward their child seems callous is simply feeling so hopeless about their child's future that they cannot bear to get any closer. All this parent can feel is grief. Their partner finds compassion easier if this is revealed, with a therapy plan made to assist the partner through grief. Therapists can help with the emotional support of the family, in cases like this, so that the parent who is shouldering the responsibility for the child does not shoulder all of the responsibility for supporting the partner's grief.

Self-Help and Support Groups

Support groups that match the level and type of family needs tend to be most helpful. But since support groups vary by type, it is important that parents decide in which areas they need the most support. On one end of the spectrum are professionally facilitated therapy groups for parents. Parents work on issues common in their situations, i.e. facing serious ADHD or attachment issues. These groups offer a combination of education, emotional support, behavioral goal-setting, and insight work. These sessions help parents who want to grow, and who need help growing. These groups are started by therapists who note that several families are facing the same issues and would be well-served to make changes together.

Some groups are focused around the support of adoption in general, or around a particular type of adoption experience. These are peer-led rather than professionally-led. These groups tend to set their objectives clearly. Parents should inquire about the goals and the level of sharing. Parents may find that they enjoy a support group that focuses on supporting their child's cultural or ethnic identity, without requiring the group to support attachment issues. However, it can feel strained for a parent to sit in a group, wondering whether only their child has an issue. Think through whether the group has as its agenda the support of special issues. Some support groups welcome diverse issues, some do not.

Groups that focus on a particular problem area, such as supporting families with a member who has FAS, Attachment Disorder, or ADHD, can be invaluable in giving specific, locally-oriented guidance, as well as emotional support. Groups have life spans and tones. Some parents have gone into established groups and have found a wealth of information, caring, and experience. Other parents have gone into established groups and have found that the group's members consist of those whose children had the worst outcomes—the group supported those whose children did not respond to treatment. One parent had to pull off the highway to weep on the way home from a "support" group like the latter. In fact, her son was improving. The group disbelieved her report of progress. Parents should ask questions about the composition of the group, and how well their children are progressing. That way they can match the group to their needs.

Parents frequently start groups rather than wait around for someone else to decide to meet their needs. Some people find that affiliating with a chapter of an existent organization is a good choice. Other parents want a specific focus and age range, preferring to include new members by invitation only. Often they will ask for suggestions from their agency or from a therapist.

Parents who start or join groups find that they make close friends in the group. They can begin a group that meets their specific need for support. But in terms of boundaries, especially if members are meeting in a person's home, they find it helpful to have limits on membership and number of meetings. That way, if they have a person with more needs than the group can accommodate or more words than the members can hear, they have a natural end to the commitment. If the group is going well, they can always extend for another set length of time. Parents who begin a group also report that it helps to pass the hat for the phone bill, if they are expected to make or return a number of calls. The total adds up!

Parents have described their groups as lifelines for them. Sometimes parents can support each other with ideas and techniques, which helps them to get past a rough spot. They can always care for each other. One woman said, "When I hear about what someone else is going through, my problem does not seem so bad. I know that they say the same thing back, but I still feel better. I like to hear when some of the children are getting better. It gives me hope."

What to Look for in a Therapist

A successful counselor for families with challenging children should have several areas of expertise:

1. She should have hands-on experience with children, and early child development knowledge, with excellent abilities in helping assess and facilitate attachments.
2. Degrees to look for are: Clinical Social Worker (M.S.W., A.C.S.W, or C.S.W.), Psychologist or Child Psychologist (Ph.D. or PsyD.), Marriage and Family Therapist (M.F.T.), Psychiatrist or Child Psychiatrist (M.D.), Counselor (M.A., M.Ed.) Ask if they maintain a license, and from whom. There should be accountability to some organized State or professional body.
3. Effective counselors need good family therapy expertise. Other members of the family should be able to get help in building attachments to the new member. It can be taxing to begin to implement specialized parenting techniques. It is critical to have a therapist who can appreciate the effort that it takes to use specialized parenting, and the transition for the whole family in adjusting to specialized parenting. A good family therapy background helps a therapist to keep the whole family balanced. Me becomes an essential part of the family's team.
4. The therapist must value the parent's roles. Effective therapists see themselves and the parents as on the same team. Therapists who use this approach frequently see the child with the parent in the room. The parent should be able to detect that the therapist is playing up parental strengths to the child. The therapist should be much more interested about how the child is relating to the parents, than how the child is relating to the therapist.
5. The therapist should be energetic and active in treatment planning and execution. He should be requesting and reading historical information, and collaborating with other professionals, as needed.
6. The therapist should be skilled in treating a variety of presenting problems with a variety of techniques. For example, commonly he would be comfortable aiding in attachment building, working on behavior

management strategies, working with ADHD and/or learning disabilities, helping with grief work, treating PTSD, treating sexual abuse issues and helping with adoption-related issues..

Interviewing Mental Health Providers

A sample phone call to a prospective counselor might sound like this:

> "Good morning. Two years ago our family adopted a five-year-old child. He has made progress in attaching to us, but still has a ways to go. We are also looking for help for him with physical and sexual abuse that occurred in a relative's home, prior to his adoption. Additionally, our son is beginning to process loss over his birthparents. Another important feature is that he is quite controlling. You have been highly recommended by our adoption agency. Does it sound like our needs fit into your specialty area?"

At this point, the mental health person may move smoothly into a description of how this is a good fit. She will show an interest in your child, asking questions. She may well answer the following questions in their response to your brief description. However, if she do not answer the questions, you should ask her:

What is your degree? (It should be at least a Master's degree in one of the areas listed above.)

How long have you been practicing in this field? (Five years is a minimum. Ten years or longer is a better answer.)

To what extent will we interact in my child's therapy? How does this interaction take place? Will I be included in sessions? Will I have time to speak with you every week? Acceptable answers include ample time with the therapist, preferably in the sessions with the younger child. The therapist needs the parent with the child to work on attachment. The work on abuse can be done without the parent, but often proceeds more smoothly with the parent present.

What do you consider your specialty area? The key words of children, adoption, foster care, attachment, trauma, loss, and families should be present.

What issues do you not treat? Certainly it is not a match if your family's issues show up here. If nothing is excluded, it does give pause for thought, as how can any person could stay abreast of all areas? The safety of the waiting room is an issue for children's specialists, with certain problems avoided for that reason.

What is your fee? Check their willingness to bill your insurance if you have insurance coverage.

How long has the treatment process lasted for your cases that have similar components to ours? In the example given, 9-24 months would be a typical range.

Do you foresee circumstances that would cause you to leave your position without the ability to complete our treatment? Unless the answer is that they can complete the treatment, do not start it. Hopefully, the person will be available for years after the initial treatment is completed. Often children need to be seen for sessions on anniversaries of losses, or during periods of regression, or when entering adolescence.

Are you familiar with the attachment literature? Are you familiar with the adoption literature? Are you familiar with the trauma and grief literatures? In the case example, the mental health professional would need to be conversant with all of these areas. If your child has not been adopted, or traumatized, those qualifications could be deleted.

How many children and families have you treated in the last five years who have had issues quite similar to ours? A minimum number would be about fifteen cases.

Hang up the phone without making an appointment if the mental health professional's responses include any of the following

1. She indicates that anything that the pre-adolescent child says to the therapist is private, and the time between the child and therapist is private.
2. He indicates to you his belief that the child's issues are primarily due to genetics or to past lives.
3. She likes to make up her own mind about your child. She neither wants to meet with you first, nor does she want any historical information.

4. He does not seem interested in the progress that you have made prior to counseling. He is not interested in your successes.
5. She seems depressed when hearing about your child. She sighs a lot into the receiver, as if regretting a commitment to your child.
6. He minimizes the complexities of your situation. Alternately, if he acts as if there is no hope.
7. This person is an intern, and will not be able to finish the treatment plan. (This child needs no more losses.)
8. She does not want to know any approaches used by the former therapists and the effectiveness of the past treatment.

Finding a Good Match

Sometimes a mental health professional is not available for a phone conversation like the one in the example above. By asking them to send a copy of their resume or curriculum vitae, or a description of their practice, parents can often determine some of the answers to the questions. However, parents may need to schedule and be prepared to pay for an appointment simply to find out if there is a good fit. Request a short visit of about thirty minutes rather than a typical intake visit, which is about an hour. Paying for such a visit is less expensive both financially and emotionally than is selecting a poor fit.

Some families will attend adoption and attachment conferences to hear the professionals who are presenting, so that they can select a counselor for their child. If the presenters are not located within commuting distance, they ask to be introduced to therapists from their area who are attending the conference. Many of the families with whom I have worked have listened to me present at conferences, and have spoken to me for a few minutes during the breaks. They have an informed look at the therapist's fit for their family that way.

Sometimes families find themselves in a remote location, after having adopted children with several severe problems. It is not good professional practice for agencies to encourage adoption of complicated children to locations that lack resources necessary for children's emotional, physical, and educational success. For families who find themselves in this untenable situation, there is sound advice. Move.

Sometimes moving could create an even greater calamity (poverty) than having no resources for a child's overwhelming needs. One alternative is that some families can arrange consultations with specialists in an urban area. They pay for consultation from professionals so that they can take the assessments and treatment plans back to their areas, where the treatment people in their community, who are likely to be generalists, can carry through the treatment plan, with regular access to consultation with the specialist. The most remote locations do not even have school psychologists who can implement treatment plans that come back with the child. There is not a good answer to help children in these locations.

The bottom line is that the therapist's job is to help enhance the entire family's adjustment. An effective therapist can help a child's health immensely. Parents will need to look for specialized help. The key is to find the right person to help with treatment.

Epilogue

Having finished this book, readers might say, "My brain is full," as well as, "But I have a number of unanswered questions!"

I do, too.

Often I am certain that I am missing some important "something" in working with children who share some similarities, and in understanding what makes them behave in the ways that they do. At times I stumble onto a strategy that works—without knowing why. While I am relieved by the success, I am annoyed and frustrated at my inability to decipher why it worked, or how it could be applied with better success. A theologian friend of mine sympathizes with my mixed reaction, quoting, "Even a blind pig finds an acorn once in a while!"

This is an exciting time in children's therapies, since brain research is just beginning to answer some of the baffling questions about what techniques work with which children and why. But as our explanations become biological and technological, it is humbling to note that our technological explanations are describing impacts on brains that either are deprived of, or favored by, early caring and protective relationships between parents and children.

The more we learn, the more we come back to the basics. For example, simple protection and nurturing of a child would have prevented damage from deprivation or alcohol exposure displayed by a sophisticated brain image. The technology helps us to work preventatively, articulating the necessity of protecting young children. When we have missed windows of prevention, we take advantage of early opportunities for treatment, helping children whose brains need more soothing, more nurture, and different interventions. This book proposes to give parents early, in-home techniques, which take advantage of the plasticity of the developing brain.

Parents may conclude that this book describes a type of family experience that they just were not expecting. Certainly grieving is a natural response to such an ambiguous loss. But after grief they move on with courage, living fully and enjoying the experience that is to be lived out. A friend with multiple sclerosis describes maneuvering her scooter in the bathroom, only to have the book that she was reading take a dive from her scooter basket into the toilet—the book: *Great Expectations* by Charles Dickens. As she says, "Sometimes that image says it all. Much of our life isn't what we expect, but it's life and we are so blessed to have it! Make the best of yours!"

As people tell their stories to me, they show dignity as they move beyond losses with courage, to enjoy the good times. A child with malnutrition and severe abuse in her background attempted to injure me several times. As she improved, she was invited to her first-ever birthday party. She brought me a chocolate covered peanut from the party—carefully saved in a plastic bag. "I saved two, one for my mom and one for you. Eat it," she said. "It's good. It's got a nut inside."

She shared her hurts with me; she shared her party. When living in that moment, watching her face and her mother's, life was sweet—and I have never savored a better nut.

Appendix

Diagnostic and Statistical Manual (DSM-IV) Definition of 313.89 Reactive Attachment Disorder

Diagnostic criteria for 313.89 Reactive Attachment Disorder of Infancy or Early Childhood

A. Markedly disturbed and developmentally inappropriate social relatedness in most contexts, beginning before age 5 years, as evidenced by either (1) or (2):

    (1) persistent failure to initiate or respond in a developmentally appropriate fashion to most social interactions, as manifest by excessively inhabited, hypervigilant, or highly ambivalent and contradictory responses (e.g., the child may respond to caregivers with a mixture of approach, avoidance, and resistance to comforting, or may exhibit frozen watchfulness)

    (2) diffuse attachments as manifest by indiscriminate sociability with marked inability to exhibit appropriate selective attachments (e.g., excessive familiarity with relative strangers or lack of selectivity in choice of attachment figures)

B. The disturbance in Criterion A is not accounted for solely by developmental delay (as in Mental Retardation) and does not meet criteria for a Pervasive Developmental Disorder.

C. Pathogenic care as evidenced by at least one of the following:

(1) persistent disregard of the child's basic emotional needs for comfort, stimulation, and affection

(2) persistent disregard of the child's basic physical needs

(3) repeated changes of primary caregiver that prevent formation of stable attachments (e.g., frequent changes in foster care)

D. There is a presumption that the care in Criterion C is responsible for the disturbed behavior in Criterion A (e.g., the disturbances in Criterion A began following the pathogenic care in Criterion C).

Specify type:

Inhibited Type: if criterion A1 predominates in the clinical presentation

Disinhibited Type: if Criterion A2 predominates in the clinical presentation

(American Psychological Association, 2000, p.130.)

Diagnostic criteria for 309.81 Posttraumatic Stress Disorder

A. The person has been exposed to a traumatic event in which both of the following were present:

(1) the person experienced, witnessed, or was confronted with an event or events that involved actual or threatened death or serious injury, or a threat to the physical integrity of self or others

(2) the person's response involved intense fear, helplessness, or horror. **Note**: In children, this may be expressed instead by disorganized or agitated behavior

B. The traumatic event is persistently reexperienced in one (or more) of the following ways:

(1) recurrent and intrusive distressing recollections of the event, including images, thoughts, or perceptions. **Note**: In young children, repetitive play may occur in which themes or aspects of the trauma are expressed.

(2) recurrent distressing dreams of the event. Note: In children, there may be frightening dreams without recognizable content.

(3) acting or feeling as if the traumatic event were recurring (includes a sense or reliving the experience, illusions, hallucinations, and dissociative flashback episodes, including those that occur on awakening or when intoxicated). **Note:** In young children, trauma-specific reenactment may occur.

(4) intense psychological distress at exposure to internal or external cues that symbolize or resemble an aspect of the traumatic stress

(5) physiological reactivity on exposure to internal or external cues that symbolize or resemble an aspect of the traumatic event

C. Persistent avoidance of stimuli associated with the trauma and numbing of general responsiveness (not present before the trauma), as indicated by three (or more) of the following:

(1) efforts to avoid thoughts, feelings, or conversations associated with the trauma

(2) efforts to avoid activities, places, or people that arouse recollections of the trauma

(3) inability to recall an important aspect of the trauma

(4) markedly diminished interest or participation in significant activities

(5) feeling of detachment or estrangements from others

(6) restricted range of affect (e.g. unable to have loving feelings)

(7) sense of a foreshortened future (e.g. does not expect to have a career, marriage, children, or a normal life span)

D. Persistent symptoms of increased arousal (not present before the trauma), as indicated by two (or more) of the following:

(1) difficulty falling or staying asleep

(2) irritability or outbursts of anger

(3) difficulty concentrating

(4) hypervigilance

(5) exaggerated startle response

E. Duration of the disturbance (symptoms in Criteria B, C, and D) is more than 1 month.

F. The disturbance causes clinically significant distress or impairment in social, occupational, or other important areas of functioning.

Specify if:

Acute: if duration of symptoms is less than 3 months

Chronic: if duration of symptoms is 3 months or more
Specify if:
With Delayed Onset: if onset of symptoms is at least 6 months after the stressor (APA, p. 468-469).

Diagnostic Criteria for Fetal Alcohol Syndrome (FAS) and Alcohol-Related Effects

I. Diagnostic Criteria for Fetal Alcohol Syndrome (FAS)

1. **FAS with confirmed maternal alcohol exposure**[1]
    A. Confirmed maternal alcohol exposure
    B. Evidence of a characteristic pattern of facial anomalies that includes features such a short palpebral fissures and abnormalities in the premaxillary zone (e.g. flat upper lip, flattened philtrum, and flat midface)
    C. Evidence of growth retardation, as in at least one of the following:
        —low birth weight for gestational age
        —decelerating weight over time not due to nutrition
        —disproportional low weight to height
    D. Evidence of CNS neurodevelopmental abnormalities, as in at least one of the following:
        —decreased cranial size at birth
        —structural brain abnormalities (e.g., microencephaly, partial, or complete agenesis of the corpus callosum, cerebellar hypoplasia)
        —neurological hard or soft signs (as age appropriate), such as impaired fine motor skills, neurosensory hearing loss, poor tandem gait, poor eye-hand coordination
2. **FAS without confirmed maternal alcohol exposure**
    B,C, and D as above

[1,2,3,4] A pattern of excessive intake characterized by substantial, regular intake or heavy episodic drinking. Evidence of this pattern may include frequent episodes of intoxication, development of tolerance or withdrawal, social problems related to drinking, legal problems related to drinking, engaging in physical hazardous behavior while drinking, or alcohol-related medical problems such as hepatic disease.

3. **Partial FAS with confirmed maternal alcohol exposure**[2]
   A. Confirmed maternal alcohol exposure
   B. Evidence of some components of the pattern of characteristic facial anomalies Either C or D or E
   C. Evidence of growth retardation, as in at least one of the following:
      —low birth weight for gestational age
      —decelerating weight over time not due to nutrition
      —disproportianl low weight to height
   D. Evidence of CNS neurodevelopmental abnormalities, as in at least one of the following:
      —Decreased cranial size at birth
      —structural brain abnormalities (e.g., microencephaly, partial, or complete agenesis of the corpus collosum, cerebellar hypoplasia)
      —Neurological hard or soft signs (as age appropriate), such as impaired fine motor skills, neurosensory hearing loss, poor tandem gait, poor eye-hand coordination
   E. Evidence of a complex pattern of behavior or cognitive abnormalities that are inconsistent with development level and cannot be explained by familial background or environment alone, such as learning difficulties, deficits in school performance, poor impulse control, problems in social perception, deficits in high level receptive and expressive language, poor capacity for abstraction or metacognition, specific deficits in mathematical skills, or problems in memory, attention, or judgement

II. Alcohol-related Effects

Clinical conditions in which there is a history of maternal alcohol exposure,[3] and where clinical or animal research has linked maternal alcohol ingestion to an observed outcome. There are two categories that may co-occur. If both diagnoses are present, then both diagnoses should be rendered.

4. Alcohol-related birth defects (ARBD)
   List of Congenital anomalies, including malformation and dysplasias:
   Cardiac
   Atrial septal defect— Aberrant great vessels
   Ventricular septal defects—Tetralogy of Fallor

Skeletal

Hypoplastic nails—clinodactyly

Shortened fifth digits—Pectus excavatum and carinatum

Radiooculnar synostosis—Klippel-Feil Syndrome

Flexion contractures—Hemivertebrae

Camptodactyly—scoliosis

Renal

Aplastic, dysplact, hypoplastic kidneys—Ureteral duplications, Hydronephrosis

Horseshoe kidneys

Ocular

Strabismus—Refractive problems secondary to small globes

Retinal vascular anomalies

Auditory

Conductive hearing loss—Neurosensory hearing loss

Other

Virtually every malformation has been described in some patient with FAS. The etiologic specificity of most of these anomalies to alcohol teratogenesis remains uncertain.

5. Alcohol-related neurodevelopmental disorder (ARND)

Presence of:

A. Evidence of CNS neurodevelopmental abnormalities in any one of the following: decreased cranial size at birth

structural brain abnormalities (e.g. mcrocephaly, partial or complete agenesis of the corpus callosum, cellebellar hypophasis)

neurological hard or soft signs (as age appropriate), such as impaired fine motor skills, neurosensory hearing loss, poor tandem and/or:

B. Evidence of a complex pattern of behavior or cognitive abnormalities that are inconsistent with developmental level and cannot be explained by familial background or environment alone, such as learning difficulties, deficits in school performance, poor impulse control, problems in social perception, deficits in higher level receptive and expressive language, poor capacity for abstraction or metacognition, specific deficits in mathematical skills, or problems in memory, attention, or judgement.

[a] A pattern of excessive intake characterized by substantial, regular intake or heavy episodic drinking. Evidence of this pattern may include frequent episodes of intoxication, development of tolerance or withdrawal, social problems related to drinking, legal problems related to drinking, engaging in physically hazardous behavior while drinking, or alcohol-related medical problems such as hepatic disease.

[b] As further research is completed and as, or if, lower quantities or variable patterns of alcohol use are associated with ARBD or ARND, these patterns of alcohol use should be incorporated into the diagnostic criteria.

All diagnoses by category 2, FAS without confirmed history of maternal alcohol exposure, require a history of maternal alcohol exposure. The committee defined the relevant history of maternal exposure as a pattern of excessive intake characterized by substantial, regular intake or heavy episodic drinking. As further research is completed and as, or if, lower quantities or variable patterns of alcohol use are associated with ARBD or ARND, these patterns of alcohol use should be incorporated into the diagnostic criteria.

 # Resources

Organizations, Newsletters, and Information Sites

This list gives resources that lead to other, more specific resources. For example, ATTACh gives locations to the attachment centers around the country.

Adoption Today
246 S. Cleveland Ave.
Loveland, CO 80537
970-663-1185, 970-663-1186 FAX
www.adoptinfo.net/AdoptionTODAY/adoptinfo.html

This magazine published by the adoptive-parent-owned Louis & Co supports adoptive families. It is readable, enjoyable, and informative. In 2001, the venerable *Roots & Wings* adoption magazine was folded into this publication. The website above has great links to support groups, news, and information.

Adoptive Families
2472 Broadway, Suite 377
New York, NY 10025

800-372-3300
www.adoptivefamilies.com
This excellent magazine, published by adoptive-parent-owned New Hope Communications, is a free-standing magazine carrying the same name as the magazine of the now defunct non-profit AFA. In 2001 Lois Melina's newsletter *Adopted Child* became a part of this magazine.

Adoptive Families Association of British Columbia, AFABC
104th Avenue
Surrey, BC V3K1N9
604 588-7300
info@bcadoption.com.
Publishes parent-friendly resources for families, and sponsors ongoing training for families and professionals. Includes a helpful representation by birthparents.

Adoption Medical News
Pierce Group International
2001 S Street NW Ste 302
Washington DC 20009
202-299-0053, 202299-0058 Fax
www.adoptionmedical news.com
An online subscription-only newsletter which publishes information on specific medical needs of internationally adopted children.

ATTACh, Association for Treatment and Training in the Attachment of Children
P.O. Box 533
Lake Villa, IL 60046
www.attach.org
This national organization publishes a newsletter, has a code of conduct for its members who are mental health providers, has listings of attachment centers and therapists, and has a superb yearly national conference. They post training events on their web site at info@attach.org

Attachment Disorder Network
14621 W 84th St
Shawnee Mission, KS 66215
913 888-5844

www.radzebra.org

A parent support group for families of children with Reactive Attach-ment Disorder (the most severe attachment challenge), ADN publishes the bimonthly newsletter *Hoofbeats.*

Center for Adoption Medicine
University of Washington Pediatric Care Center
4245 Roosevelt Way, NE
Seattle, WA 98105
adoption@u.washington.edu
www.adoptmed.org

This group has a splendid website for adoptive parents or profession-als. Julie Bledsoe, M.D. and Julian Davies, M.D. the Clinic Co-Directors, are also the FAS Clinic pediatricians.

Child Trauma Academy
Feigin Center, Suite 715
Texas Children's Hospital
6621 Fannin
Houston, TX 77030
www.childtrauma.org

This is an educational series for parents and caregivers. Bruce Perry, MD, Ph.D. composes or edits materials. Material is practical and ac-curate. It gives parents access to work from some of the finest caliber professionals.

CHADD-Children and Adults with Attention Deficit Disorder
8181 Professional Place, Suite 201
Landover, MD 20785
800-233-4050, 301-306-7070, 301-306-7090 FAX
www.chadd.org.

This organization is a *powerhouse* with information about educa-tion, medication, home routines, counseling, and local support groups. Invaluable in giving information to advocate for school planning.

Families by Design
PO Box 2812
Glenwood Springs, CO 81602

970-984-2222, 970-984-0422 FAX
www.attachment.org

Nancy Thomas, a skilled therapeutic parenting specialist for attachment-disordered children, has a web site supporting therapeutic parenting. It includes a list of attachment therapists whom *parents* have recommended.

Fostering Families Today
246 S. Cleveland Avenue
Loveland, CO 80537
1-888-924-6736, 970-663-11185
www.fosteringfamiliestoday.com

The magazine published by Louis & Co, publishers, as well, of Adoption Today, is packed with sound and well-written articles and graphically attractive as well. It is also helpful for later-placed adopted children.

FRUA (Friends of Russian and Ukrainian Adoption and Neighboring Countries)
P.O. Box 2944
Merrifield, VA 22116
www.frau.org

This powerful organization has a Family Focus newsletter, on-line discussion group, and yearly conference. Their resources are sophisticated, addressing ADHD, learning, auditory processing, attachment, cultural heritage, and trauma.

International Adoption Clinic
Box 211 UMHC
420 Delaware Street SE.
Minneapolis, MN 55455

This organization is on the cutting edge of medical, psychological, and social issues facing adopted children and their families.

Kinship Center
www.kinshipcenter.org

This is a great source for adoption-related information. Sharon Kaplan Rosia and her colleagues are the inspiration behind these materials. They cover important aspects of parenting and professional support.

National Foster Care and Adoption Directory
P.O. Box 1182
Washington, DC 20013-1182
703-352-3488, 888-251-00750
www.childwelfare.gov/nfcad/

Its name explains it! This section of the federal Children's Bureau, Administration for Children and Families, U.S. Department of Health and Human Services Child Welfare Information Gateway provides information about all aspects of adoption and foster care, including adoption publications, referrals to adoption-related services, searches of its computerized information databases.

National Council on Adoptable Children (NACAC)
970 Raymond Avenue, Suite 106
St. Paul, MN 55114-1149
1-800-470-6665
www.nacac.org

This organization has legal, ethical, and practice influences on children's adoption issues. It is a powerful advocacy organization and leads in improving adoption practices.

National Organization on Fetal Alcohol Syndrome
1815 H Street NW, Suite 750
Washington DC 200006
800-66 NOFAS   (800-666-6327)

Pact, An Adoption Alliance
3450 Sacramento Street, Suite 239
San Francisco, CA 94118
Voice: 425-221-6957, Fax: 510.482.2089
www.pactadopt.org

TAPS (Transracial Adoptive Parent Support) 888-448-8277
Birthparent Line 800-750-7590

This service organization specializes in adoption services to children of color. Its programs are excellent and its website outstanding.

Raising Black and Biracial Children (RBC)
1336 Meadow View Lane, #1
Lancaster, CA 93534
RBCeditor@aol.com
This magazine supports the parenting of African American, interracial, transracial adoptive, and foster families.

Sibshops
www.siblingsupport.org
This website has a national directory of these workshops for the siblings of children with special needs, whether physical or emotional.

Tapestry Books
PO Box 359
Ringoes, NJ 08551
www.tapestrybooks.com
This is a catalog of foster care and adoption related books and materials.

Resource Books

Adopting the Hurt Child: Hope for Families With Special Need Kids by Gregory Keck and Regina Kupecky, (Colorado Springs: Pinon Press, 1995). Good book for those adopting older (school age and up) or seriously troubled children.

Adopting: Sound Choices, Strong Families by Patricia Irwin Johnston, (Indianapolis, Perspectives Press, 2008). This is the go-to book for a thorough and up-to-date look at all aspects of today's adoptions.

Asperger's Syndrome by Tony Attwood (London: Jessica Kingsley Publishers, 1997). This is a great sourcebook for parents of children with Asperger's Syndrome. It describes people with Asperger's as they move through the life cycle, giving a much-needed optimism about ways to work with this form of autism.

Becoming Attached by Robert Karen. (New York: Warner Books, 1994). This is a book on for people interested in theory, attachment, and implications along the life cycle.

Brothers and Sisters in Adoption, Helping Children Navigate Relationships When New Kids Join the Family by Arleta M. James, (Indianapolis: Perspectives Press, 2009). This much-needed addition is filled with healthy insights, assessment ideas, and practical tips.

The Challenge of Fetal Alcohol Syndrome: Overcoming Secondary Disabilities. Ed. Ann Streissguth and Jonathan Kanter. (Seattle: University of Washington Press. 1997).

A Child's Journey Through Placement by Vera Fahlberg, M.D. (Indianapolis: Perspectives Press, Inc.1991). This is a well-written and lovely book for parents for further reading about ways to develop attachment.

Cline/Helding Adopted and Foster Child Assessment by Foster Cline and Cathy Helding. (Wisconsin: World Enterprises. 1999). This manual permits parents and professionals to score and consider simultaneous diagnoses or issues that can be affecting children.

The Development of Romanian Orphanage Children Adopted to Canada: Final Report (Romanian Adoption Project, Simon Fraser University, Burnaby, B.C. V5A 1s6 Canada, 1999). Report available at above address by sending $10. This gives an in-depth study of children's attachment and social adjustment post-adoption, and is relevant to other children previously institutionalized.

Facilitating Developmental Attachment by Daniel A. Hughes. (Dunmore, Pennsylvania: Jason Aronson/Inghram Book Company, 2000). Parents who are more sophisticated readers will enjoy this well-written book. Hughes describes not only the foundations of emotional relationships with parents and children, but sensitive ways in which to build on those relationships.

Fetal Alcohol Syndrome and Fetal Alcohol Effects by Diane Malbin. (Minneapolis: Hazeldon Books, 1993). Available: 1-800-328-9000.This is a booklet that is written for professionals, but quite useful to parents. It explains the variations in children's processing in a clear, succinct manner.

Filling in the Blanks: A Guided Look at Growing Up Adopted by Susan Gabel. (Indianapolis: Perspectives Press, Inc., 1988). This book helps pre-teen children and early teens with work on identity formation. It helps them to phrase questions and discusses the meaning of their life story. Parents can use this themselves or bring it to counseling for discussion.

Fostering Changes: Treating Attachment-Disordered Foster Children by Richard Delaney. (Fort Collins, CO: Walter Corbett Publishing, 1991). This book describes good techniques for severely disturbed older children in foster homes. The book is practical and respectful.

Ghosts From the Nursery: Tracing the Roots of Violence by Robin Karr-Morse and Meredith S. Wiley. (New York: Atlantic Monthly Press. 1997). This resource helps demystify the brain development and resultant behavior in children who have been deprived, neglected, and abused.

Growing Up Again, Parenting Ourselves, Parenting Our Children by Jean Illsley Clarke and Connie Dawson. (New York: Hazeldon Books/Harper Collins. 1989, Revised 1998). This book helps parents who lacked a good start themselves, to give a good start to their children and enjoy parenting. Connie Dawson brings an adoption perspective to the book.

Help for the Hopeless Child: A Guide to Families by Ronald Federici. (Ronald S. Federici and Associates, 1998. Available: 1-703-548-0721). This volume is written from a neuropsychological perspective, this book contains neurological information pertaining to older, post-institutionalized children.

I Can't Get Over It: A handbook for Trauma Survivors by Aphrodite Matsakis. (Oakland, California, New Harbinger Publications, Inc.1996). When parents have been traumatized, needing help while they are simultaneously parenting, they can get practical advice here, helping them to stabilize.

Inside Transracial Adoption by Gail Steinberg and Beth Hall. (Indianapolis: Perspectives Press, Inc., 2000). This book explores the complexities of transracial adoption while equipping parents with practical and compassionate advise. To top it off, it is a good read!

International Adoption, New Kids, New Challenges by Dana Johnson, M.D. Ph.D. Available from the International Adoption Clinic, This pamphlet describes common challenges and sensible plans for parents.

Launching a Baby's Adoption by Patricia Irwin Johnston. (Indianapolis: Perspective Press, Inc. 1997). This book guides the process up to and through placement so that babies get off to an optimal start. Parent's inner work is sensitively described through case examples. Attention is given to some of the early problems of attachment that infants may have, and ways to help infants adjust. Sound adoption practice standards that emphasize honesty among all members of the triad make this a helpful addition to placement professionals, as well as parents.

The Mulberry Bird by Anne Braff Brodzinsky. (Indianapolis: Perspectives Press, Inc., 1986, revised 1996). Children who are in elementary school like this book. It is particularly helpful to children who have a history of poor care. The children use the metaphors to talk to parents.

Night Falls Fast by Kay Redfield Jamison. (New York: Alfred A. Knoff, 1999). This brilliant psychiatrist writes about her client's and her own experiences with mood disorders. Hers is a moving account that gives hard-headed but necessary information about medication. Her previous book, *An Unquiet Mind*, (New York: Vintage Books, 1995) is also excellent in describing mood disorders.

Taking Charge of ADHD by Russell A Barkley, New York: Guilford Press, 1995, Revised 2000). This author explains simply, but not superficially, what is going on with children with ADHD and what to do about it. Russell Barkley is not only a prolific writer and researcher, but he is a caring advocate for children and their families.

Teaching Your Child the Language of Social Success by Marshall Duke, Stephen Nowicki and Elisabeth Martin. (Atlanta: Peachtree Press. 1996). Just as the title suggests, it puts the learning of emotional intelligence into concrete exercises that school or parents can use.

Tell Me A Real Adoption Story by Betty Lifton and Claire Nivola. (New York: Alfred Knopf Publishing. 1993). Good book about identity formation and loss issues for ages 6-12.

Toddler Adoption: The Weaver's Craft – Revised Edition by Mary Hopkins-Best. (London: Jessica Kingsley Publishers, 2012). A guide to adjustment, attachment, learning issues and parenting for parents whose children arrive between ages one year and four years.

Troubled Transplants by Richard Delaney and F.R. Kunstal. (Ft. Collins, CO: Horsetooth Press. 1993.) This is another solid book by Richard Delaney, especially helpful for older children.

When Love is Not Enough by Nancy Thomas. 1997. Obtained through Nancy Thomas, P O Box 2812, Glenwood Springs, CO 81602. Cost: $12. This is the favorite book of parents with more difficult and/older children. Nancy Thomas is a therapeutic parent and parent trainer.

Zachery's New Home by Geraldine Blomquist and Paul Blomquist. (Hyattsville, Maryland: American Psychological Association, Revised, 2001).This has been the children's all-time favorite about beginning to trust after abuse.

Works Cited

American Psychiatric Association: *Diagnostic and Statistical Manual of Mental Disorders*, Fourth Edition, Text Revision. (2000). 1400 K Street, N.W. Washington DC, American Psychiatric Association.

Ames, Elinor, (1996), Workshop presented at 4th Annual Canadian Conference on Adoption, Vancouver, BC. Information available in article, "Child Behavior Problems and Parent Stress in Romanian Adoptees," Sara Morrison, Elinor W. Ames, Kim Chisholm, and Lianne Fisher, Simon Frazer University, Burnaby, B.C. V5A 1S6.

Bowlby, J. (1969/1982). *Attachment and Loss: Vol. 1*, Attachment. New York: Basic Books, p. 372.

Brazelton, T. Berry. (1980). Workshop Presented at the 1980 Conference on Perinatology, Boston, MA.

Bridges, L., and Grolnick, W. (1995). "The Development of Emotional Self-regulation in Infancy and Early Childhood," *Social Development: Review of Child Development Research,* Vol.15, pp. 185-211, Thousand Oaks, Sage Publications.

Briere, John, (1992). *Child Abuse Trauma,* Sage Publications, pp.3-15.

Brodzinsky, David and Marshall Schechter. (1990). *The Psychology of Adoption,* Oxford University Press.

Brown, Daniel and Alan Scheflin and D. Corydon Hammond. (1998). *Memory, Trauma Treatment, and the Law,* W.W. Norton and Co.

Call, Justin D. and Eleanor Galenson and Robert Tyson,Eds.(1983). *Frontiers of Infant Psychiatry.* Basic Books, p. 23-25.

Cassidy, Jude and Phillip Shaver.(1999). *Handbook of Attachment,* Guilford Press.

Chishom, Kim and Margaret Carter and Elinor Ames and Sara Morison. (1995). "Attachment security and indiscriminately friendly behavior in children adopted from Romanian orphanages," *Development and Psychopathology,* 7, pp. 283-294.

Cook, A., M. Blaustein, J. Spinazzola, and B. van der Kolk, (Eds.) (2003). "Complex Trauma in children and adolescents." National Child Traumatic Stress Network, http://htsn.org

Dalenberg, Constance. (2000). "Countertransference and the Management of Anger in Trauma Therapy," *National Center for Post-Traumatic Stress Disorder Clinical Quarterly,* Vol 9, Issue 3, p.39.

Duke, Marshall and Stephen Nowicki and Elisabeth Martin. (1996). *Teaching Your Child the Language of Social Success.* Peachtree Publishers.

Erikson, Eric.(1968). *Identity, Youth and Crises,* W.W.Norton.

Fahlberg, Vera, (1989). "Re-educating the Sexually Abused Child," Workshop through University of Washington Continuing Education, Seattle, WA.

Fahlberg, Vera, (1998). "Attachment Theory, Brain Development and Trauma: The Interface," Workshop presented in Bllingham, WA.

Fahlberg, Vera, (2012). *A Child's Journey through Placement.* Jessica Kingsley Publishers, p.8.

FAS Diagnosis and Prevention Network, (2009). http://depts.washington.edu/fasdpn/htmls/fasd-fas.htm

Foa, Edna and Terence Keane and Matthew Friedman. (2000). *Effective Treatments for PTSD—Practice Guidelines from the International Society for Traumatic Stress Studies*, Guilford Press.

Galler, Janina; Ross, Robert; "Malnutrition and Mental Development," *THE POST*, Issue #20, 1998, pp.1-8. Available from The Parent Network for the Post-Institutionalized Child, P.O. Box 613, Meadow Lands, PA 15347, PNPIC @aol.com.

Friedman, Matthew. (1997). "Coping with Loss During Adulthood," Workshop presented at Conference "Victims of Traumatic Loss," Whitefish, MT.

Goleman, Daniel.(1998). *Working With Emotional Intelligence.*(New York: Bantam Books.)

Hermann, Judith. (1992, Revised1997). *Trauma and Recovery*. Basic Books.

Horowitz, Mardi and George Bonanno and Are Holen. (1993). "Pathological Grief: Diagnosis and Explanation," *Psychosomatic Medicine*, Vol. 55, N.3, pp.260-273.

Human Rights Watch. (1998). *Abandoned to the State, Cruelty and Neglect in Russian Orphanages*, Human Rights Watch.

IOM—Institute of Medicine (U.S.), Division of Biobehavioral Sciences and Mental Disorders, Committee to Study Fetal Alcohol Syndrome (1996) *Fetal Alcohol Syndrome: Diagnosis, Epidemiology, Prevention, and Treatment*; Stratton, K.; Howe, C.; Battaglia, F., eds. National Academy Press. Washington, DC

Jamison, Kay. (1999). *Night Falls Fast: Understanding Suicide*. Alfred A. Knoff. New York.

Johnson, Dana E. (1997). "International Adoption: New Kids, New Challenges," p. 12. Available through National Adoption Information Clearinghouse, (703-352-3488)

Karen, Robert. (1994). *Becoming Attached*. Warner Books.

Karr-Morse, Robin and Meredith Wiley. (1997), *Ghosts From the Nursery, Tracing the Roots of Violence*, Atlantic Monthly Press.

Lobel, Arnold, (1979), *Days With Frog and Toad*, Harper and Row and Scholastic Inc.

Mash, Eric and Russell Barkley. (1998). *Treatment of Childhood Disorders*, Guilford Press, pp. 558-578.

Nathan, Peter and Gorman, Jack. (1998), *Treatments that Work,* Oxford University Press, New York, 1998.

Perry, Bruce, (1993), "Neurodevelopment and the Neurophysiology of Trauma," *APSAC Advisor* Vol. 6: Nos. 1 and 2.

Perry, Bruce, (1999), *Helping Traumatized Children*, ChildTrauma Academy, Vol. 1, Number 3. Available through www.ChildTrauma.org, or ChildTrauma Academy, Feigin Center, Suite 715, Texas Children's Hospital, 6621 Fannin, Houston, TX 77030.

Putnam, Frank, (1997), *Dissociation in Children and Adolescents*, Guilford Press. pp. 59-75.

Putnam, Frank, (1999). "Dissociative and Altered States of Consciousness," Workshop presented at 4th Annual NW Regional Conference on Trauma Stress Disorder, April, 1999 in Chelan, WA.

Pynoos, Robert. (1997). "Traumatic Bereavement in Children and Adolescents," Workshop presented at Conference, "Victims of Traumatic Loss," Whitefish, MT.

Sampson, Paul and Ann Streissguth and Fred Bookstein et.al.(1997). *"Incidence of Fetal Alcohol Syndrome and Prevalence of Alcohol-Related Neurolodevelopmental Disorder,"* *Teratology* 56, pp. 317-326.

Siegel, Karolynn. (1997). "Children's Psychosocial Adjustment to a Parent's Serious Illness and Death," Workshop presented at Conference "Victims of Traumatic Loss", Whitefish, MT

Siegel, Karolynn and Frances Palamara Mesagno, and Daniel Karus et. al. (1992). "Psychosocial Adjustment of Children with a Terminally Ill Parent," *Journal of Child and Adolescent Psychiatry*, 31:2, pp. 327-333.

Solomon, Judith and Carol George eds. (1999).*Attachment Disorganization.* Guilford Press. pp. 132-181.

Southwick, Steve, and Rachel Yehuda. (1997). "Situations of Threat," *Clinical Quarterly, National Center for Post-Traumatic Stress Disorder,* Volume7, Issue 4, pp.78-81.

Sroufe, L. Alan, (1995). *Emotional Development.* Cambridge University Press. pp.172-191.

Streissguth, Ann and Jonathan Kanter eds. (1997). *The Challenge of Fetal Alcohol Syndrome, Overcoming Secondary Disabilities.* University of Washington Press.

Swanson, Joyce and Nancy Thompson. (1997). "Building a Better Brain," Workshop presented at 9th Annual International Conference on Attachment and Bonding, Available through Resourceful Recordings (203) 235-2230, 23A-9722 Parts A and B.

Thomas, Nancy. (1997). *When Love is Not Enough, Families* by *Design,* Glenwood Springs, Colorado, p. 27.

van der Kolk, Bessel A. (1994). *The Body Keeps the Score, Memory and the evolving psychobiology of post traumatic stress,* Harvard Review of Psychiatry, I. pp. 253-265.

White, E.B.(1970). *The Trumpet of the Swan,* Harper and Row.

Wright, Karen. (1997). "Babies, Bonds, and Brains," *Discover,* October.

Zeanah, Charles.(1996). "Beyond Insecurity: A Reconceptualization of Attachment Disorders in Infancy," *Journal of Consulting and Clinical Psychology,* Vol. 64, No 1, 42-52.

Zeanah, Charles. Ed. (2000). *Handbook of Infant Mental Health,* Guilford Press.

Index

Jessica Kingsley *Publishers*
London - Philadelphia - Sydney - Vancouver

Jessica Kingsley Publishers is a leading independent publisher with offices in London and Philadelphia, dedicated to publishing books that make a real difference to society and to individuals.

Visit our web site at www.jkp.com

If you have enjoyed reading Attaching in Adoption, *you may be interested in reading:*

Nurturing Adoptions
Creating Resilience after Neglect and Trauma
Deborah D. Gray
ISBN 978 1 84905 891 9

Toddler Adoption
The Weaver's Craft
Revised Edition
Mary Hopkins-Best
ISBN 978 1 84905 894 0

Adoption is a Family Affair!
What Relatives and Friends Must Know
Patricia Irwin Johnston
ISBN 978 1 84905 895 7

Creating Loving Attachments
Parenting with PACE to Nurture Confidence and Security in the Troubled Child
Kim S. Golding and Daniel A. Hughes
ISBN 978 1 84905 227 6

Connecting with Kids through Stories
Using Narratives to Facilitate Attachment in Adopted Children
2nd edition
Denise B. Lacher, Todd Nichols, Melissa Nichols and Joanne C. May
ISBN 978 1 84905 869 8

Photograph by Don Marshall

Deborah Gray is a clinical social worker specializing in attachment, grief, and trauma. She enjoys helping children and their parents in situations where deprivation or attachment losses make attachment formation challenging. In her private practice, parents are usually present in the therapy sessions to provide comfort and safety for their children's trauma work, or to work with their children on attachment-related issues. Her philosophy empowers parents with information, offering new skills and techniques to meet the needs of their children.

Deborah's professional interests and direction were piqued by having grown up in an extended family with many adopted members. Watching their unfolding stories, which showed successes in forming close relationships as well as how painful losses impeded them, she observed clear passages as well as barriers to forming confident identity. She saw, too, that sometimes problems come into focus at the same time that the window of opportunity for prevention or help is closing.

Since receiving her M.S.W. and M.P.A. from Syracuse University in a program involving internships and research emphasizing early bonding with high-risk infants and toddlers at the Regional Perinatal Center at Upstate New York's Medical Center, Deborah has worked 19 years in children's therapy, child placement, and foster and adoption counseling. She has also been a therapeutic foster parent. Over the last decade she has spent over 10,000 hours counseling children and their families. Because of her practical approaches to promoting attachment and reducing the effects of trauma and grief, she is a popular presenter at conference workshops for professionals and parents.

Attaching in Adoption is one more step in Deborah's personal and professional life journey with adoption. It represents her "next generation" attempt to equip today's adoptive parents with the tools necessary to form close relationships with their children. It gives avenues for parents to follow in getting early, effective help for their children's needs.

Deborah Gray lives in the Pacific Northwest with her husband and their three children.